A LIE in the TALE

A Lie in the Tale © 2023 John Alexander.
All Rights Reserved.

No part of this book may be reproduced in any form or by any electronic or mechanical means including information storage and retrieval systems, without permission in writing from the author. The only exception is by a reviewer, who may quote short excerpts in a review.

This is a work of non-fiction. The events and conversations in this book have been set down to the best of the author's ability, although some names and details may have been changed to protect the privacy of individuals. Every effort has been made to trace or contact all copyright holders. The publishers will be pleased to make good any omissions or rectify any mistakes brought to their attention at the earliest opportunity.

Printed in Australia
Cover and internal design by Shawline Publishing Group Pty Ltd

First Printing: June 2023

Shawline Publishing Group Pty Ltd/New Found Books
www.shawlinepublishing.com.au/new-found-books/

Paperback ISBN 978-1-9228-5185-7
Ebook ISBN 978-1-9228-5192-5

Distributed by Shawline Distribution and Lightningsource Global

A catalogue record for this work is available from the National Library of Australia

More great Shawline titles can be found by scanning the QR code below.
New titles also available through Books@Home Pty Ltd.
Subscribe today at www.booksathome.com.au or scan the QR code below.

A LIE in the TALE

JOHN (JACK) ALEXANDER

*To those who have a go no matter how tough it gets
and are successful in the end.*

To my wife Helen, the love of my life for 56 years.

C.1

The Beginning

High Heeled Boots, A Bike Ride, Lost, Heaven

He landed on his back and started to twitch. His face went purple. His eyes started to roll to the back of his head. Dennis yelled, "You've killed him! If he dies, you could be up for murder – and they hang people for murder." I thought about jail and hanging. In just one second my life had turned from a happy jackaroo to a potential murderer. But that's later. One must start at the beginning.

So, it was a cold, wet August evening with water trickling down the Pioneer bus window. I was on my way at last. An unknown adventure and the start of the rest of my life. The excitement and the unknown lay ahead, as we left the city and passed the neat little brick houses with their manicured gardens and lawns. Blue flickering of the black and white televisions reflecting out of the windows, street lights mirroring the steady drizzling rain on the wet shiny road. I knew I was doing the right thing, leaving behind the suburban life that felt so foreign to me.

I had spent the last four years at a textile importer office listening to the salesmen with their boring talk of families, football, the gardening that was planned for the weekend. But not as pathetic as my own. Being a small lad, 5 foot 5 inches in height and weighing 8 1/2 stone and just past my nineteenth birthday, I was not the most confident or educated, leaving school (which I hated), in grade eight. Everyone kept saying school days were the best of your life. If that was the case, what a miserable existence I was going to cop after leaving school.

As the bus travelled away from the city into the fresh countryside, I stopped looking out the window and noticed the boy sitting next to me. He was tall and lanky, about nineteen, with a ruddy complexion and pimples all over his face. Dressed in jeans and a checked shirt, he was wearing an old leather jacket, but what caught my eye about him were his shoes. No, not shoes, but boots. Not ordinary boots, but high heel riding boots. WOW. He had to be a jackaroo, 'cause that's what I wanted to be, and that's why I was on that bus.

I was leaving Melbourne for Brisbane, Queensland, and if it is called Queensland, there must be room for a king and I would be king of the jackaroos. Not that I knew anything about being a jackaroo, but what the hell, if yer going to be something, you might as well be the best.

Turning to my travelling companion, I asked, "Travelling to Queensland?" He smiled and in a rather ordinary voice told me he was going to work on his uncle's banana farm. Banana farm! Hey, what the...?!

"Oh, I thought you might be a jackaroo, you know with them high heeled riding boots and all."

He exclaimed, "Hell no! I just like wearing them and anyway they make me taller." First on my shopping list was a pair of riding boots, high heel ones.

The bus droned on. Our first major stop was Canberra. This

was to be my first time going out of state. Well, that's not quite right. You see, I was sent to this posh boarding boys grammar school, (how that came about you will hear later on), and all the kids kept skiting that during the holidays they went interstate to Sydney, Perth, Tasmania and all the exciting things they did. So at thirteen years of age, I decided interstate for the Christmas holidays was for me. With the blessing of my mum and grandmother and the skepticism of my sister, I headed off on my pushbike for New South Wales.

Leaving on a very hot December morning just two days before New Year, I started peddling and peddling. No hat, not much water, and a real stinking thirty-eight degrees with heat, flies, cars and trucks whooshing past. I had dust in my eyes going uphill, then downhill, getting tired of all the peddling. Look out New South Wales! I would have something to tell the kids back at school. I went interstate! Euroa was the first night, a heat exhausted, peddle exhausted, I booked in to the pub for the night.

"Yer not running away from home luv, are we? Such a dear little boy on his own. Where is home dear?" enquired the big-busted, big-bottomed aproned lady.

"Melbourne."

"Goodness gracious me, what's your phone number? I aim to ring yer mum." The information was relayed quickly as I was tired. So tired. Dragging my bike into the room without her noticing, I shut the door and immediately vomited. Moving the square of carpet over the vomit, I rinsed my mouth out and lay on the saggy bed and promptly fell asleep.

Next morning, I had breakfast in the dining room. Still feeling a bit crook, I managed some cornflakes and peaches, sausages, bacon and tomatoes. I paid the bill out of my savings from sweeping buses last holidays. Back on the Malvern Star bike in the summer heat, I headed for my destination: Yarrawonga. 150 kilometres to the Victorian-New South Wales border.

I am lost. The white marbled road blinding me. The heat is horrific, burning, burning my neck, face, arms and legs, nothing to eat or drink. Where am I? Where are the cars? Just open wheat fields, mile after mile after mile. I must have eaten or drunk somewhere, but where? Miles of nothing, burning, hot white marble road. Push the peddles around, around, so hot, burning. Why don't I have a hat? I need sunglasses as the tears are coming. My little body aches. Will I perish out here, peddling, peddling? What, a mirage? No, it's a sign saying 'Yarrawonga 7 km'. Oh God, I will make it. Can I make it? Hot, tired, slow, mile after mile.

The outskirts of the town appeared. What is this? Was I delirious? Crowds were lining the main street. Colourful streamers, balloons and all. Oh my God, my mum's told 'em I was coming on my bike from Melbourne and they were here to see me. ME! With a newfound energy, I rode past the cheering crowd on both sides of the street, waving like a true hero to them. With renewed strength, I peddled my way to the end of the throng, then my tiredness came back double fold.

Stopping at the first pub in sight, I asked for a room for the night, but there was no room at the inn. It was the annual speedboat carnival and I unwittingly and unknowingly had just ridden a minute ahead of the huge procession. It wasn't for me at all. My mum had not rung and there was nowhere to stay in town. I went back to the first pub and begged for somewhere to lie down. The kindly woman told me, "Sorry sonny, we are all booked out but I will tell you what, there is a tin shed down the back of the beer garden. You can have that. It's got an old bed in it. Hang on and I will get you some linen."

So exhausted after my marathon ride, I just wanted to collapse where I stood. She soon turned up with the bedding and pointed the way to the shed. Turning around as she went back inside, she yelled, "I will be notifying the police if you have run away," and then I heard her mouthing about kids these days. I chucked the sheets over the holey coconut fibre striped mattress, feeling sick and totally buggered. I pulled the sheet over my body to try and ward off the mosquitoes and soon fell asleep with the echo of celebrations and drink parties in the beer garden.

How long I was sleeping for would be anyone's guess, when I felt a terrific weight on top of me. It was slowly crushing me. Then I smelt and heard a horrible, stale, rasping breath. Something horrible was happening. Was it a nightmare? Being so delirious, why not? My right eye very slowly opened and started to focus, then my left. In the moonlight, only inches from my face, were the hairy features of a wild and ferocious animal. No - my God, it was a huge, ugly German Shepherd dog lying on top of me, a whole chicken carcass between its jaws, presumably pinched from the hotel kitchen.

I tried to move and shoosh it off me. "Go. Get off. Nick off you mongrel." But it growled, wrinkling his snout, laying back its ears with the hackles up. Mine were too, you can bet on that. His lips curled, showing me all his huge fangs illuminated in the night light. With heart thumping, hands sweating, my body throbbing, I somehow nodded off to sleep again, not being brave enough or having the energy to fight the beast. The cracking and crunching of chicken bones, the smell of bad dog breath and the terror of being the next meal were my thoughts as I slipped into oblivion.

Surviving the night, I checked myself to see if all was in place. The dog was gone, and it was going to be another hot day.

Everything was quiet around the town, everyone sleeping off their hangovers and New Year's partying. I got on my bike and rode the few hundred yards across the bridge over the Murray River and stepped on to New South Wales soil, then promptly rode back over the bridge. Happy New Year, we made it interstate for the holidays. The next day, I caught the train home. It was not the plan, but it's a wise fellow that can change his itinerary.

Canberra at last. The bus pulled up at a servo after the two hourly short stops and not much sleep. It was good to relax awhile, have a feed and a decent stretch of the legs. The city of Canberra did not impress; my interest was Queensland and becoming a jackaroo. Anything other than that was irrelevant.

Back on the droning bus and on the way to Sydney town. The Harbour Bridge was great. More impressive that I thought, but Sydney was just another city. People seemed to be rushing everywhere, like people do in all cities. Wish the bus driver would put his foot down. Been on the bus for twenty-four hours and about the same amount of time to go. My travelling companion, like myself, had run out of conversation and with half glazed eyes we watched the passing scenery that appeared not to have changed much since leaving Melbourne.

But hey, the Pacific Highway was changing. It seemed to be getting warmer and the countryside more lush. A new world of storks and pelicans swimming and nesting on the Clarence River. Barges of bananas and pineapples were being moved by tugs, little trains with sugar cane on nearby tracks. Oh, it was warm and the hills we were climbing, alive with produce and the sparkling sea in the distance. This was heaven.

A few hours later, a sign appeared. We were at the Queensland Border. Travelling down the hills towards the sea, the bus came alive with conversation and people were pointing out to strangers to look at this and look at that. We started to travel now near golden beaches, past little seaside towns that looked more like country towns. One town we went through had more of the new accommodation called motels than I had ever seen. There were lots of service stations and the place seemed very Americanised. They said the town was going to be the holiday capital of Australia. What a joke, it didn't impress me. After passing through Surfers Paradise, it was only a few hours to our destination of Brisbane. I booked into the YMCA in Edward Street. It was expensive at $35.00 for a week and that was only board and breakfast.

C.2

Brisbane

Harold & Gladys, Prim Secretaries, Rejection

Dear Brisbane, a hilly city with houses on stilts. Gee, the tide must come in a long way! Seriously though, I was told they kept houses cooler. Funny silver pointy trams rattling along their tracks as smart conductors wore Foreign Legion type caps, swinging on the running board collecting fares. There were trolley buses and steam trains running down suburban lines. We only saw them in Melbourne at the railway museum. Believe it or not, you could smoke at the pictures. Yep, lean back and me and Cary Grant would pull out a fag and have a good drag. Like all young people, if you wanted to be sophisticated, you had to smoke. I smoked Rothmans filter tip from Pall Mall in a flip-top box.

Brisbane people weren't scurrying or hurrying. Everything was done leisurely and everyone had the time of day. Only that morning, while getting myself orientated, I stopped an elderly couple and asked them where Queen Street was.

"With pleasure, just keep walking two blocks and you will be at Queen Street," said the grey-headed, slightly balding man.

"Are you a stranger to Brisbane?" asked his wife, a grandmotherly figure all done up in her Sunday best. Harold, that was the husband's name, wasn't too badly dressed himself. "Look, we are just going in to this café for a cup of tea. Would you like to join us?" Of course, I accepted and we settled ourselves in to the booth of the café two doors up.

After ordering a large pot of tea for three and pikelets, the man asked me, "Where you from son? And what are you doing in Brisbane?" I told them I had arrived by Pioneer Bus from Melbourne yesterday and I was looking for work as a jackeroo in Western Queensland on a big sheep or cattle station. "My," said the wife, "you have got plans. Do you know anyone in Queensland?"

"Only two people that have just shouted me a cup of tea, otherwise no one," I replied. The man straightened up and looked serious, as people do when they are about to give world-shattering advice. "Could be difficult, you not knowing anyone in Queensland."

Then, with them both giving me a good once over, the wife said, "I don't mean to offend, but it's very tough out there, very hard work and dear, you don't look that strong."

"It's alright Gladys, he has to start somewhere," the husband continued, "I suggest you go down to Creek Street, that's where all the stock and station agents are and ask for a position, and don't be afraid to take a couple of knock backs. Stick to you guns son and you will get what you want."

It did not seem like earth-shattering advice, but it was the best advice anyone could have given me at that time, I realised later. During this time, I gave them my best manners as they were really a nice couple and I did want to impress my first Queenslanders. The man getting out of the booth behind me didn't help, however, as he bumped the back of the booth I was in. Turning around to see what was up, I knocked my cup of tea, not over, but filled some of the saucer with tea. Still trying to be on my best behaviour, the bottom of the cup kept dripping on the plastic tablecloth, which I tried to wipe ever so elusively with my sleeve. Finding later, to my horror, some had dripped on my shirt as well. We parted company after Harold paid for our morning tea promising to keep in touch and "let's know how you get along boy." We then went our separate ways.

My financial and asset situation was tight. Leaving Melbourne with $113.00 from savings, the sale of my bike, and anything else I could flog, was my total cash supply.

The bus fare was paid for previously. Assets included one good, large hiking haversack, a couple of trousers and shirts, two pairs of khaki cotton trousers and shirts for work, underwear, and a jumper that I half knitted myself. Talking about that, one of the reasons to go west young man was to become a man. I had a gut full of women being brought up by three of them. Oh yes, I had the poetry readings, the violin lessons, the one act plays and Christ, even the bloody ballet lessons. What did I know about footy, cricket, pubs and beer? Or other men's things such as masturbating and rooting? "Can you shoot to the ceiling?" Whatever that meant. Most of the conversations at home were about what my sister was wearing to that party, or whose hair is done what way, fashion and women's magazines. Being brought up in a feminine household, unfortunately, it rubs off. I was not the maturest of nineteen-year-olds.

Other assets I had besides clothes were a handmade sleeping bag, (compliments of my Gran), a pair of desert boots and leather work boots, a good torch, a sheath knife, a compass, sewing and first aid kit, toiletries, pen and writing paper, the Victorian Weekly Times Farmers Hand book, Man Magazine, and a packet of frangers, also known as condoms. All my worldly possessions were on my back. I did spoil myself and brought from the disposals a pilot's flying jacket with a fur collar, and yes, a pair of fine black high heel riding boots Ever tried walking in high heel boots? Ya legs bend in the knees and you seem to walk on the outside of your feet and it's rather difficult to get around.

Creek Street was the key to the outback. Dalgetys, Winchcome & Carson, Primaries, Goldsbrough Mort and other stock and stations agents. They were all there, ruddy faced men in large hats, light checked woolen sports coats, shiny flat heeled tan riding boots, the key to my future.

First stop, the New Zealand Loan Co. I stepped onto the polished floor, practicing to walk properly in the new boots and up to the prim secretary, who looked up from her typewriter and over her glasses. "Yes?"

"Um, I am looking for a job as a jackeroo." Not my most confident of statements.

Miss Prim replied, "Can you ride, milk and kill?"

"Uh no."

"Well, we haven't any jobs here unless you can ride, milk and kill." Then she went back busily to her typewriter. Crestfallen, trying to make a dignified exit, my all-leather soled high-heeled riding boots slipped on the floor and, adding to my knock back, my exit wasn't the way I planned, banging into the entrance doors and tripping back out on to the street. All the wonderful images I had, the practice of going over my interview, the new boots were all a failure. Indeed, a quick one, less than a minute, from my bold entrance to a bumbling exit.

Back to my room at the Y. Boots off. What a relief. I need a better plan; she said I gotta be able to milk ride and kill! I thought, *that can't be too hard*. Cows have tits, you pull them and you get milk, everyone knows that. Ride? Well, you just sit on the back of a horse. They do it in the movies. That can't be difficult, but kill? That's a bit weird. I once killed my sister's cat with my air rifle, thinking it was a wild tomcat that kept me awake at night. Yea, I reckon I can kill. The front entrance secretary, she is the problem. Gotta get past her, but how?

Putting on my normal shoes, I attacked the next agent with real purpose. No one, especially certain little Miss Prims, was going to stop me. I walked into the next stock agents, fronting up to the next Miss Prim, confidently saying in my best deepest voice, "Can I see one of the men?"

"Which department, sir?" (That was getting better, not often have I been called sir). She rattled off, "Stock, merchandise, real-estate, wool sales, or studs. Whom do you wish to see?"

"Someone from the stock department, please."

"Would you care to take a seat? I will try and contact our Mr Pearson. Oh, what did you want to see him about?"

"Oh, it's personal," I stammered.

"Your name?"

"Jack Alexander."

Phew, looks like I was going to get an interview. A newspaper called *The Country Life* was on the coffee table. Picking it up, I noticed it was the paper that needed my thorough investigation. Miss Prim came back and I stood up, holding the paper. She answered my enquiring expression, which I didn't really know I had, as I hadn't experienced it in the mirror. However, I know I can't raise an eyebrow.

"I am sorry, but Mr Pearson is out and won't be back till Monday." I thanked her and walked out with the paper, feeling proud of myself for handling the situation better than my first stock agent, and leaving with a name and newspaper. I had achieved a small gain.

Walking down to Eagle Street, I went to a café, where I ordered a pie with sauce and a pot of tea for lunch. I excitedly flipped through the just acquired paper with pictures of sheep, cattle, horses, real men, graziers, farmers and stockmen. Oh, it was *The Country Life* newspaper. Near the back were the situations vacant. The job descriptions fascinated me, titles I had never heard of. Ringers, bore workers, windmill experts, roo shooters, station hands, fencers, jackaroos, jillaroos, head stockman, overseer, cowboys, governess, kitchen boy, cooks, shearers, board boys and experts, wool classers and pressers, gardeners, tractor drivers to name a few. Looking in the jackaroo column wanted, they all required a GPS education, be able to milk, ride and kill and be a Protestant or Catholic. I could be any religion to get a job. I could handle confessions and own a set of beads or be a Protestant and be on my knees for hours. A GPS education. What in the dickens was that? I found out years later it meant Greater Public Schools. But I reckoned a fib here and there should not get in the way of a dream and employment.

After my pie and sauce and new information, my resources were renewed and my battle instruments honed for the kill. I marched into my next stock agent and asked for the manager of the stock department please, and yes, it was a personal matter. That got their Miss Prim moving. Soon enough, down the stairs came a middle-aged chap dressed in the outback uniform of a fine checked shirt with two buttoned pockets on the chest, a fawn woollen tie, brown Fletcher Jones trousers and the inevitable shiny tan riding boots.

"The names Mike, Mike Chudley, what can I do for you?" Shaking my hand with a very firm grip. "Sorry to bother you sir, but I am looking for a job as a jackaroo in Western Queensland and I was told you could help me."

That was a smart move, I thought. *Thank God he didn't ask who.*

"What's your name son?"

"Jack Alexander sir."

"Well Jack, can you milk, kill and ride?"

Fib number one, a big confident, "Yes."

"And where did you learn this?"

Fib two, "Worked on me uncle's farm down Victoria way."

"There is this fellow looking for someone like you," Mike said. "He has a jackaroo position at his stud near Meandarra, but he wants to do his own interviews. He will be coming down for the Ekka, so if you call at the agent's office at the grounds, ask for me and I am sure you will get a position."

Thanking him so much for his help, I assured him I would be at the Ekka to see him. We shook hands and parted company.

What in the heck was the Ekka? I couldn't ask, it appeared everyone knew what the Ekka was, right? Everyone except me. I strolled back to the Y to congratulate myself on the activities of the day. I lay on my bed, lit a fag and started reading the Country Life from cover to cover, but no mention of the Ekka.

Brainwave. I went down to the reception desk of the Y and asked the man on duty, "Excuse me, but do you know what the Ekka is?"

"Why it's the Exhibition, you must be from down south?"

"Yes, I am from Melbourne."

"It's the big show, like the Sydney show, when the country comes to the city," said the reception man, expounding the knowledge like a true showman.

I asked, "Could you tell me where it's held and when?"

"I think it's about three weeks' time and it's held at the showgrounds near the general hospital and the museum."

I thanked him and slowly walked back up the stairs to my room thinking, "Three weeks?" My money would not last till then. *Three bloody weeks, hell what am I going to do?* I went to the pictures, sat back, and watched a good cowboy and Indian movie and smoked. Watching the smoke curl up to the projector lights to meld with all the other smoke and traveling the lengths of the light. After the movie, I strolled down Queen Street, working my way to Edward Street, then back to the Y, when I came to the conclusion, I couldn't wait the three weeks for the Ekka. I must go back to the agent Primaries on Monday and see the Mr Pearson that had been "away for the day" and try my luck there. If no luck, there were two more agents and the ads in *The Country Life*. No one was going to stop my ambition to become a jackaroo.

I must have always unconsciously wanted to work in the bush as a young fellow. All I wanted to do was swing an axe, crack a stock whip and ride a horse, but what chance would a bloke have, being brought up by women in the city? Perhaps that is why I was not much good at school. They didn't teach me the things I wanted to learn, like ride a horse, swing an axe, and crack a stock whip, so I became the class clown. I was always kept in after school, getting Saturday morning detentions and the occasional cane on the finger- tips that hurt.

One day, in desperation, the master sent me to the headmaster's office. This was a very rare and dangerous experience. Only the worst boys were sent to the chief of staff's office, never the headmaster's office. Quivering, getting diarrhoea, and feeling very sick, I knocked on the door of the headmaster's office. "Come," was the sound of dread. I opened the doors into a huge office where few had feared to tread. And there, sir sat behind a huge desk littered with papers. He seemed a rather grandfatherly type, bald except for the grey hair around the sides and back. He was rather a small man, with small piercing green eyes. There was an aura about him, as if to say, 'I am okay until you mess about with me, then I can murder.' Anyway, that was my impression.

"What brings you here, boy?"

I stammered, "I really don't know, sir, but it could be something to do with making the class laugh all the time, sir."

"Ah, Mr Knight has told me about you. You're the class clown, is that right?"

"That's what some say, sir."

"Sit down, boy. It's time we had a man to boy talk."

Sitting down in the huge chair, just keeping my head above the desk, he continued in a surprisingly gentle voice with a hint of a friendly smile.

"Listen son, school is a place of learning, a place to prepare yourself for the rest of your life. You could say life is a big theatre and school is the rehearsal for the big show. Do you understand?"

I nodded an affirmative. Even if I didn't understand, I still would have nodded an affirmative. He went on and on. The lecture must have lasted half an hour in a monotone, boring voice.

You know how old people go on and on when they are trying to tell you or change your ways, but they say the same things over and over again? They just change the words. He continued, "Yes boy, it's a rehearsal, school is a rehearsal for what you want to do after you leave school. By the way, what is your career choice for when you leave school?"

"Aha, a comedian, sir." My answer just came out of nowhere. The friendly face disappeared and went all red.

He stood up, pulled his master's gown around him and said in a low menacing voice, "Get out, just get out."

I was out of there like a shot, thanking my lucky stars for no cane, no detentions and just a lecture. I left school for good the following year when I was fourteen, not because I was expelled. More like someone had not paid the school fees for a couple of years. As mentioned before, I was glad to leave school and surprisingly never regretted it.

The next day being a Saturday, I got some washing done at the Y, cleaned my room up and decided to explore this city. Now, the receptionist said the Ekka was near the museum, so I asked him for directions.

"The museum is on the corner of Gregory Terrace and

Brunswick Street," he said. "Just follow Edward Street all the way to Water Street, then turn left in to Brunswick street. You will see the museum, one of our imposing buildings."

He then enquired, "Are you walking?" And answering himself he said, "It's not a long walk for a young fellow like you." Not a long walk?! Gee, it was nearly three kilometres It was a strange building. Rather gothic and to me, a bit out of place for Brisbane. I paid the entry fee and passed the postcard and souvenir displays to check out the exhibits. It was very disappointing, nothing interesting or educational for me. It's funny how museums are so quiet and everyone whispers. There are musty sorts of smells. I imagine funeral parlours would be the same.

Leaving the museum, I followed my tracks back to the Y. Looking for somewhere to buy a sandwich, I saw a man have a fit. He was walking a few yards in front of me and started to stagger, went to grab the street light pole, missed and fell down writhing on the ground, doing horrible things with his body and face. A crowd appeared from nowhere like flies to dogs' poop. One man said, "Grasp his tongue or he will choke on it."

Another said, "Do that and you will get a finger bitten off."

So, we all just stood and watched the poor bloke. A woman from the crowd had a brilliant idea. "Someone call the ambulance." By this time, the man had stopped writhing and started to sit up, not looking very well at all. The ambulance arrived soon after. Two ambulance men opened the back door, pulled out the stretcher and conversed with the victim, then put him on the stretcher into the back of the ambulance and drove away.

Ten minutes later, just as I was coming to Upper Edward Street, a car ran into an electric light pole. Bang! Glass shattering all over the road. Another crowd arrived, different from the last one. We all gathered around, discussing what had happened. Someone said the driver must have been drunk, he was the only person in the car. A patrol policeman on foot came just as the driver heaved himself out of the car. The policeman told us to move on, which no one did except me. I was getting hungry and thinking all the best excitement was over. I went in search of a café and ordered a vanilla milkshake and egg and lettuce sandwich as well as a sausage roll.

It was starting to get late; I worked my way back to the Y. A small crowd had gathered opposite the People's Palace. Pushing my way through, I saw a small elderly woman poorly dressed. Indeed, she looked as if she hadn't changed her clothes for a week. She had a bible in her hand and she was preaching the good word.

"The Lord is our saviour. To be saved, you must know your Jesus." She paused, savouring the importance of what she had said. A drunk pushed his way through the crowd of the assorted Saturday evening people and stopped to see what was going on. The old lady continued, "Yes ladies and gentlemen, to get to the kingdom of heaven you must know your Jesus. I say unto you, know your Jesus."

The man who pushed his way into the crowd earlier said, in a slurred, drunken voice, "Lady, lady, I say unto you, that the only Jesus I know is Kraft cheeses." Well, we all laughed as we dispersed, leaving the old lady to her own religious beliefs and the happy drunk to his.

I ended up having an interesting day; the walk back from the museum was much more entertaining than the museum itself. Settling back into my room with a packet of bought biscuits and a bottle of coke, I studied my farmer's handbook and called it a night.

A river and bay cruise to Stradbroke Island seemed an excellent suggestion from the breakfast lady, to fill in my Sunday. It was a rainy day and only a few were on the boat that left from Circular Quay. A couple of families with kids running about, two sets of lovers necking and giggling on the whole trip and a smattering of others. To be honest, I really wasn't interested in the other passengers, except for the kids interrupting my private thoughts and dreams. I wished they would slip overboard or shut up, but no, one had to crack their knee on one of the bench seats and started to howl. *Serve him right*, I thought with a cruel, hidden smile. That *should keep them quiet*. We arrived at Amity Point on the island for a short stop and walked around. I picked up a couple of shells on the deserted beach as it was really a miserable, wet day. The boat only gave us an hour there, and nowhere to buy anything to eat or drink. I think you were supposed to bring your own picnic. My main thoughts were, what did the following week have in store for me? Will I get a job? Where will it be? How am I going to manage? I must have been a picture of a very lonely soul, but who cared?

Back in Brisbane, I had a good feed at my now regular café; I was starving, not having anything since breakfast. Then back to the Y where I took stock of my finances that weren't too bad. I still had $62.00 left after paying my board, meals, island trip and purchases, but I had better take things a bit easy on the spending for a while. I wondered what tomorrow would bring.

C.3

A Jackaroo's Position

Crocodiles, A Big Fright, To Greener Pastures

It was a fine sunny Monday morning; I spruced up and felt very confident. I marched back to Creek Street to Primaries and asked for their Mr Pearson.

"Would you like to go up to the third floor to the Stock department and Mr Pearson will see you there?" I thanked Miss Prim, bolted up three flights of stairs in my enthusiasm, but wished I hadn't, as I arrived puffing, flushed and I felt a bit smelly from the exertion. I asked a passerby if I could see Mr Pearson. I was told to wait at the lounge in the corner of the room and they would fetch my man.

"Pearson's my name. What did you want?"

Looking up, I saw a short, fat, bald man with a very ruddy complexion wearing a brown suit and brown brogue shoes, white shirt with a dark green woolen tie. He seemed a no-nonsense sort of person.

"Sorry to disturb you sir, but I was told you could help me find a jackaroo position out west."

"I don't know who told you, but you're in luck. I have just got off the phone from Gerry Gold out at Blackall. He is looking for a first-year jackaroo straight away. Are you available immediately?"

"Oh yes, yes, I am available right now."

I was flat out containing myself. I was going to be a jackaroo, a bloody fair dinkum jackaroo.

"There is a train leaving this evening. Can you be on it?"

I nodded enthusiastically. He continued, "See the receptionist at the front counter, give her your details and then see her later this afternoon for your travel arrangements. We will pay your second-class train fare to Blackall." Then he dismissed me with, "G'day to you."

I turned towards the steps, my heart pounding. I did it. I am a Jackaroooo! Then, as I was about to disappear down the steps, the voice behind me said, "Oh son, you can milk, ride and kill? As Gerry Gold said, he would teach anything to a young fellow, but he won't teach them to milk, ride and kill. That is the condition of the employment." "No worries, I did all that at my uncle's place down south," I lied as I scooted down the steps on wings I didn't think I had. I skidded to a stop at Miss Prim's desk who took down my name, age, where I was staying and a contact number, then asked me to call and get my train ticket, information, and directions at three this afternoon. Wow!

Going back to the Y, I stopped at a souvenir and newsagency shop on the corner of Edward and Adelaide Streets that fascinated me. They had all sorts of souvenirs, but it was the stuffed fresh water crocodiles only about thirty centimetres long and kangaroo paw bottle openers, 'roo skins, pigs' tusks and all manner of things that kept my eyes glued to the window. Desperately wanting to buy something but conscious of my limited financial means, and anyway, now I will be able to see the real things. Where was

Blackall? A map would be essential, so I went into my special shop and bought a road map of Queensland, then rushed out again in case I weakened and bought me a stuffed crocodile.

I couldn't contain myself. All my dreams had come true. It seemed too easy, but who cares? I'm about to be a jackaroo. Back in my room, studying my new map, I looked for Blackall.

"There it is, right in the middle. It must be nearly the centre of Queensland. I wonder which way I'll go." I studied the map further and decided the train could go via Roma or Rockhampton. Suppose they will tell me all the details in the afternoon. Folding the map carefully away, I decided I better do some washing and packing and clean up ready to leave, as I just had to be ready NOW.

After packing and getting everything ready for tonight, I went down to the front office and told them I would be leaving that evening. "Oh, and by the way, I paid for seven days' accommodation and I found that I only needed five." The young man at reception accepted the request and handed me $2.30 as a refund and jokingly instructed me to bank it before I spent it on some sheila.

Actually, that in a real way was good advice, so I went and found the Commonwealth Bank in Queen Street and opened a savings account with a precious $20.00. This was going to be my emergency fund, not to be touched, unless in dire circumstances.

It was soon 2:30 P.M. I couldn't wait any longer. With my heart doing a mild gallop, I bolted back to Creek Street. Skidded into the agent's office, walked up to Miss Prim who didn't look up from her typewriter until a few ah-ums. She finally looked up with a have-I-seen-you-before look, saying, "Yes?"

"I saw you this morning and you were arranging my trip to Blackall this evening," I stammered.

"Oh yes, Mr Alexander, I have all your details here." Searching amongst papers on her desk, she found a brown envelope. "All the information is here. I have put it all together for you.

"You must catch the Sunlander at 9.30 this evening at Roma Street Station for Rockhampton. You will then disembark tomorrow lunch at 12.05 and catch the Midlander train at 5.25 that same afternoon, getting off at Jericho early Thursday morning. Now it's all in the envelope."

Handing me the envelope she continued, "After getting off at Jericho you will catch a goods train the rest of the way to Blackall. Mr Gold from Farlee Sheep and Cattle Station will meet you in the front of the Tattersalls Hotel at three."

I worked out later on my map that the train trip would take me over 1300 kilometres.

Miss Prim took a deep breath, picked up a sheaf of papers and picked out a pink slip. Reading from it, she continued, "Your conditions of employment are two weeks holiday a year, you work six days a week, you get full board and lodgings, and as a first-year jackaroo, your weekly remuneration paid monthly is $15.00, plus two-ounces of tobacco a week. That is all the information I have."

Then bless my soul, she gave me a crinkle of a smile and said, "Good luck, Jack." I thanked her for the information; she wasn't so bad after all. As I turned around with the brown envelope in my hot little hand and started to walk out the front door, she uttered those terrible words, "Oh Jack the terms of the position are that you must be able to milk, ride and kill, you can, can't you?"

I could tell by her voice she knew I couldn't, but as my hand touched the shiny brass front door handle, I turned around smiling, "I'll make it, and thanks again."

I skipped – yes skipped – down Creek Street. A skid around the corner into Adelaide Street and managed a bigger skid into Edward Street and into the Y. I jumped the steps three at a time and into my room, emptying the contents of the envelope on my bed. Triple checked the information, fingered the second-class train tickets and plotted my route on the map. Wow, what a journey. Into the interior of the Australian outback. Wow.

Because the train wasn't leaving till 9.30 P.M. I decided to celebrate with a good dinner as I had only been having bits and pieces for meals until this night. There was a good-looking café cum dining room in Queen Street called Christi's, that I thought was a bit up market. Suppose you thought I should have gone to the pub and celebrated and talked to a few men, alas you could smoke in the pictures, but you could not drink in a pub unless you were twenty-one. They were a bit strict on that. But they didn't shut the pub doors like they did in Melbourne at 6.00 P.M sharp. Looking at the menu, I decided on the barramundi with vegetables please and for dessert a banana-split, thank you. A pot of tea would be nice, too. The waitress took the order and I leaned back, pulled out a Rothmans and tried to blow smoke rings in to the air feeling very secure at being employed. The waitress soon came along with my order and what a meal. The large plate was covered. I couldn't see the colour of the plate, a huge fillet of fish, chips, lots of veggies and the works; it was the best meal since leaving home. I am usually a finicky eater, not liking lumps of fatty meat although mince was okay, veggies were okay, salads and quiche were okay, (you could tell what sex influenced me).

As I was eating and enjoying my meal, I noticed two youths constantly looking my way. They were about my age but looked much bigger and tougher, dressed in the green tinted stovepipe trousers with leather jackets, ripple-soled shoes and greasy hair brushed back in a ducktail with an Elvis Presley curl licking their foreheads. They were dressed in the style of a typical bodge -an unemployed youth, a larrikin or a layabout. I finished my meal, had the pot of tea, lit another Rothmans from Pall Mall and waited for my bill to arrive. The two youths were still glancing my way, so I nodded to them as a form of greeting. Then the waitress came back with the bill. Christ, a blooming $4.50! Ah well, it doesn't matter, I will be earning money soon.

As I got up and went to the counter to pay the bill, the two boys also got up and paid theirs just after me. As I stepped back into the street, the boys caught up to me. The shorter of the two said, "You a stranger here."

"Yes, I'm from Melbourne." The taller one said, "I like your jacket," as he fingered the fur collar of my new flying jacket.

"It must have cost a dollar," said his mate. I started to get an uneasy feeling about these two.

"No, me big brother bought it for my birthday," I lied.

"Well, we've had a birthday, have we? And we got some money too, did we?" Things were getting bad. I saw the lights change at the intersection and a couple of cars pulled up.

"There's my brother in his car picking me up," I said with a voice quivering. I took off for the stopped cars, shooting around the back of the first one and then off up Edward Street as if the whole Japanese army was after me. In to the Y, up the stairs into my room. Christ, I was nearly done over. Thank God my legs would not let my face get hurt.

It was getting late; a train had to be caught. Picking up my gear, I made my way to reception to give them my key and set off for greener pastures. It was quite a walk up to Roma Street Station.

As I passed the Salvation Army building, I noticed the poor down and outs. Alcoholics, homeless old men, a couple of Aborigines, all looking very depressed, most with a roll your own cigarette butt hanging from their bottom lip. I happened to notice they were all men. Weren't there any down and out women? Or was there some other place for them? I felt very sorry for the men and thinking how fortunate I was that a job was waiting for me. How could people end up like that? I was going to find out sooner than I imagined.

I made it just in time to board the Sunlander. Whether it was the heavy pack, the near attack at the café an hour ago, or just excitement, I suddenly didn't feel very well. I was aching and had a bit of a headache and, excuse me, that was a sneeze.

C.4

The Journey

Rocky, Shopping, Train Drover, Arrival

The Sunlander was a large train looking rather new and pulled by a 'bulldog nose' diesel engine. I found a seat near the window, put my pack up on the rack and pulled out my map and Weekly Times Farmers Handbook for some real study. Other passengers were a mix of all sorts; two older couples visiting married sons and daughters, others going to places of employment, some on holidays and the two old dears near me who were discussing their relations, divorces, miscarriages, operations, new grandkids and everything imaginable. But as the train started to move out of the station, the rocking motion, the previous twenty-four hours of excitement and the oncoming cold, all collectively sent me into a deep sleep.

Now and then, when disturbed, I would drowsily stir and look out my window to see the passing scenes. We went near roads and you could see car lights like big white eyes of some monster running through the bush. Then we came speeding through towns with an array of lights suddenly appearing and then gone as we raced toward the next town. Not being able to get back to sleep, I opened my Farmers Handbook and started to read the dairy cow section. It was difficult to concentrate, feeling miserable with my new horrible travelling companion – the cold. Never-the-less I found the part on 'good milking' and read about having the teat cups warm, then wiping and massaging the udders. What made my heart skip a beat was the bit that said, "Operate machines according to manufacturer's directions." No worries about milking cows, it's all done by machines. What a relief.

Those old biddies, their whole bodies must be filled with lungs. I am sure they haven't drawn breath since they got on the train.

"Mary, poor Mary, she had to have the forceps, dear. She had been trying to push the bub out for the last thirty-two hours. You know what forceps can do to a baby, poor girl. She was in a right, awful dilemma. Mmmm, they got the baby out, of course, and it seems alright. They called it Beatrice. Yes Beatrice, supposed it looked so red that it looked like beetroot," said the one with the bun wearing the black and white spotted dress. Then they both cackled like a couple of chooks laying eggs. It didn't stop there. They continued on and on till I fell asleep again or should I say dozed, because it was difficult sitting up trying to sleep in a rocking train. I even tried putting my sleeping bag against the window for a pillow and neck rest, but it wasn't too successful. The effects of my cold were worrying me. I didn't want to be sick the first day of my new life as a jackaroo.

At Rockhampton, the train ran down the main street! No fences, no guardrails, just like a car. Here we were chuffing down the middle of the road. Can you believe it? The train arrived at lunchtime, which gave me half a day to fill in before the Midlander left late that afternoon. Brisbane had some houses on stilts, but Rocky had just about every house on stilts. Some were painted, but a lot were just bare wood, darkened by the weather over the years. All had little verandas with corrugated iron roofs.

It seemed a small town with dusty streets, but to me it had the feel of a wild west town. After a short walk around the place and a bacon and two egg breakfast, the shops had opened.

Promising my mum that I would buy a large hat for sun protection, I went in search of a suitable shop. Down a side street I found just the thing, a sign with 'The Rocky Western Outfitters'. They had everything. The smell of old and new leather flared my nostrils as I entered. There were hats, boots, saddles, stock whips and all manner of leather strapping. Plus, stirrups and bits, feed bins and stockman's clothes, torches and knives, veterinary equipment, and medicines in glass cabinets. Hurricane lamps and books, swags and rugs, clocks, and watches. They just had everything that was of the greatest interest to me. It was just the best shop. I looked and fingered, I smelled and handled.

The shopkeeper in a man's cloth apron over a flannel checked shirt and gray moleskin trousers approached. "Can we help you at all, son?"

"Um, er, yes, I am going to be a jackaroo out at Blackall and need a good, large work hat."

"Well, me boy, you must buy an Akubra. Everybody out west wears one."

We walked over to the hats of all types, shapes, sizes and colors. Tans and whites, blacks, and greens. There was a fine-looking hat that caught my eye. It looked like the sort that Hopalong Cassidy wore. I pointed to it. "Oh, you like the ten-gallon hat with the twelve and half centimetre brim."

"Yep, that's the one, the tan with the cow hide fur hatband." He handed it to me and I tried it on. The only thing stopping it from falling over my face were my ears.

"It's a bit big. Have you a smaller size?" I said, handing the hat back.

"No son, it's just the right fit for you," he said. "You see, the hat will shrink a bit due to your sweat and the hot dry heat you will experience. I suggest you get some toilet paper and wind it round inside the inner band until it's a snug fit. After a while, you will find that the hat will fit perfectly, and anyway, the toilet paper is handy in an emergency."

I bought the hat and the salesman kindly put a good hat string on it so I wouldn't lose it, "At no extra charge". I also bought a two metre hide stock whip with a half-plaited cane handle, a rather large silver alarm clock, with two big bells on the top, and a pair of khaki stockman's cotton trousers, the ones with the patches on the inside legs and the bum. Boy, did that burn a hole in my finances. That lot cost me just over $24.00. But I will have a paid job. Hang on! Only $15.00 a week, Miss Prim said my wages would be as a first-year jackaroo. Cripes, I was getting twice that in Melbourne. Gee, I better take care or I could end up penniless.

I took my purchases back to the station and placed them in the allocated railway locker where the rest of my gear was. All except the new hat. I looked around and found a toilet. Hat in hand, I closed the door behind me. I sat on the dunny and started to peel toilet paper from the roll and wound it around inside my new hat and checked the fit every now and then. When I felt it was right, I left it on my head and decided to have a poo while I was there. Walking back on to the platform, I saw my reflection in the window and a slight feeling came over me that the hat might be too large for a person my size. It may have been made for big, tall men. But then I thought windows could give a distorted image, so I squashed the funny feeling. Time was getting on, but I dashed down the street and bought some Band-Aids for my blisters and Irish moss for my cold that was worrying me. Even my purchases didn't make me feel the hundred percent that I should have.

I boarded the Midlander at 5.15 P.M. I thought the Sunlander was a modern train. Boy, the Midlander was so much better and the conductor told me I could use the dining car as well.

Feeling like a millionaire (with a cold), I sat in the dining car with flowers in a vase on each table and the logo of the Queensland railways on every piece of crockery and cutlery. I ordered the Duck a l'orange as the train moved out of Rockhampton and well in to the countryside. The Greek couple sitting next to me were going on to Longreach to take over their uncle's café, as he apparently had a stroke and wasn't managing very well. That was all I managed to get from them. They appeared not to have been married long. She seemed very attracted to his neck and he had his mind under the table. He stroked my leg with his. I gave him a scowl and he excused himself and went back to doing what he was doing in between flurried bites of his meal. They both could not have been very hungry, as they didn't stay long at the table.

Sitting back on the padded bench seat in my section, I tried to make myself comfortable for another night's sleep on a train, as I knew I would have a very strenuous and exciting day tomorrow. I knew the next sleep would be at a western sheep and cattle station.

In the twilight there were a few kangaroos hopping along outside my window beside a river and I vaguely wondered as I fell asleep, how do female kangaroos swim without drowning their joeys in their pouches?

"Next station Jericho, son," the conductor said, in his smart navy-blue uniform with the wide blue stripe down the side of his trousers as he woke me. "You have thirty minutes to get yourself ready, and son, it's bloody cold outside."

It was warm in the train, but through the window the whole countryside was white with frost, except for the occasional water hole we passed with a fog swirling from it. Had the wash, shave and freshened up in the communal washroom down the passage. Peeled on the riding boots that were giving my blisters a hiding, got all my gear together, and did not forget the hat, as the train pulled in to Jericho.

Was it cold? It was freezing. It was hard to believe, here I was in western Queensland just near the Tropic of Capricorn, the tropics which I thought were hot and to my utter dismay it was, as the conductor said, "Bloody cold."

It was later, through experience, I found western Queensland could have the best winter weather in the world during the day, but like all deserts and semi-arid countries, the nights were freezing.

As the Midlander left me shivering on my own, on a tiny platform at 5.30 A.M. in a town that really wasn't there, with a sun that wasn't really there yet, either, I did not have to despair for long, as the goods train appeared. It had flat trucks with cars and tractors on them, empty stock wagons and wagons carrying feed and goods. I counted twenty-one in all, including the guard's van. As the train stopped, the guard stood leaning out the back door of his van, looking nowhere in particular shouting, "Anyone for Blackall?"

As I was the only one on the platform with not another living thing in sight and the train was heading for Blackall, it was bleeding obvious that I might be the "anyone for Blackall." But I made the right gestures and found myself sitting in a very old carriage, which was part of the guard's van.

There was another passenger sound asleep, covered in an old army blanket, lying down on the wooden seat bench opposite me. I was guessing it was an old man, as the hat was over his face. The hat was a battered old sweat-stained grey thing that no real woman would have in her house, let alone on her face. But what fascinated me was, the brim was level with his mouth and you could see a slight movement of his lid as he snored. And he did snore. How anyone could sleep so soundly with a goods train shunting and jolting, jerking, and working, stopping and starting all the time, beats me. Anyhow, I think he was drunk, as there was a slight odor of rum amongst other odors in the carriage which were beyond me to describe.

The sun started to come out and warm the countryside, but forgot about the carriage I was in, as it was still freezing. My fellow passenger began to stir, rolling around; I was amazed he did not roll right off the bench on to the floor. He sat up, pulled a pouch of tobacco, and rolled a cigarette, which I watched intently because I knew I would have to learn the art of rolling one. Then before putting it in his mouth, he wet the whole end by moistening it with the inside of his lips, cupped a box of matches in his hand and lit up, taking a deep draw of tobacco, and letting the smoke slowly curl out of his mouth.

He reached in to his great coat pocket and pulled out a half bottle of overproof Bundaberg rum. Unscrewing the cap, he took a swig of the dark liquid. He then noticed he had company and handing the bottle toward me, said in a gravelly voice, "Want some breakfast?"

Well, I did, but that wasn't what I had in mind. I politely told him thanks, but I already had some on the Midlander and couldn't fit another thing in. Which was ridiculous, because you can always fit a drink of something in! He took another swig, looked out the window enjoying his rolly and gave me up as a lost cause.

I had nothing to do, so I studied his features. They were like the countryside we were passing through. His face was well weathered, with a stubble of grey beard covering his cheeks and chin, like the frosted tinges of Mitchell grass. Skin like the brown burnt earth, the deep creases or wrinkles stretching from his eyes to the corners of his mouth were the dry creek beds. His battered, bumbling nose was like the termite mounds scattered amongst the scrub. His eyes were a deep, blue green colour like the occasional water hole we passed. The ears were large, appearing like the foliage of gidgee trees, and his mouth, when shut, looked like a scar on the earth's surface, and when opened, like a big dry dam. Yes, he was a man of the bush, an old man. How old, it was hard to tell.

Pulling out and lighting a Rothmans filter tip, the old bloke said, "You got tailor mades?" I took that as a hint and offered him one. Lighting it, he said, "You a new chum?"

"Yea, I am from Melbourne and going to Blackall as a jackaroo."

"Don't know where Melbourne is, but if ever I saw a raw prawn, it would be you," his gravelly voice said.

I was a bit humiliated as I thought I looked the part and being called a raw prawn was a bit rude. "Listen, I want to be a jackaroo. I gotta start somewhere," I answered rather more rudely than I meant.

"Don't get shirty with me, young 'man. I was just making an observation. I'm eighty-one years of age. I seen a lot in my time. I've been through flood, fire, drought and marriage. Survived the lot except the last one and I reckon I know a thing or two."

He stubbed out my tailor made. I thought he was old but eighty-one, cripes!

Wanting to soothe things over because I needed some urgent guidance, I enquired, "You going to Blackall?"

Undoing the cap on his bottle of rum, he again offered me a swig, saying, "If you want to be a man, you better get this into you."

I wasn't game to say no. Grabbing the bottle I felt nauseated, not because I had an empty stomach, but because I looked at the spit on the neck of the bottle and the unsavoury hole of his mouth with the broken tobacco-stained yellow fangs. I was sure it was the toughest thing my body had ever been subjected to.

I lifted the bottle to my youthful lips and took a rather tiny sip, trying not to shudder. I handed the bottle back as I felt the burning liquid run down the back of my throat. Refusing to take the rum back, he looked me straight in the eye, saying, "If you want to be a real man, then have a real swig." So I did.

Dying was high on the agenda, with the duck a l'orange being my last substance from the night before. Downing that op rum knocked me for six. The eyes watered, the throat slammed shut and the duck a l'orange came alive, swimming and flapping and pecking in my stomach. I took a deep breath and needed a good drink of water that was not available. I handed back the rum, saying in a choked voice, "Thanks." It was all I could manage.

His eyes seemed to twinkle as he took the rum back and had a good swig himself. And answering my question, "Yea, I got to pick up a couple of k, wagon of sheep."

Noticing a puzzled look on my face, he continued, "I'm a train drover. Been doing it for years." The hefty swig of rum was having a bit of effect on me. I was feeling warm inside and a bit lightheaded. A train drover? Wasn't a drover someone riding a horse, droving cattle or sheep along the stock routes, camping under the stars, boiling his billy on a campfire?

Guessing my line of thought, he told me, "I used to drove sheep and cattle on the road. Had a fine plant, including eight of the best horses, but the missus got tired of the droving and left me for some bugger in Winton. I was getting on, so I sold me plant. That broke my heart. Those horses deserved better. Bought me a cabin with the proceeds in Alpha, the town before Jericho. I now travel the railway tracks, engaged by stock agents to load the sheep and cattle in to the wagons, making sure they travel all right and don't go down and get trampled. I got my best mate, Rusty, me *dorg* in the dog box, in with the guard." He looked pointedly at my cigarette packet. "You got another one of them tailor mades?"

We both lit up and I hesitantly asked, "They use machines to milk cows, don't they?"

"Maybe in the big dairies down south, but out west you milk 'em by hand."

"Can I have another swig?" Handing me the bottle and having

O.P. courage in my gut, I took my third drink from the bottle. Wishing I hadn't, as my lightheadedness got worse and I was getting relaxed, oh so relaxed, that I was having trouble sitting up straight and trying to look intelligent. I got game. "How do you milk a cow?"

Smiling in a friendly way he said, "You really are raw prawn, aren't you? Look son, just grab the tit between thumb and first finger, squeeze and pull, nothing to it. You will get the hang of it."

"When they say can you kill, what's that mean?"

He nodded his head slowly, expounding, "Have you got some learning? Killing means butchering a sheep or beast and being able to cut one down."

I didn't really know what cutting down meant but thought I had shown too much ignorance already to further elaborate on the subject.

The train pulled in to a station that had Blackall written on the sign. The old feller gathered up his swag, opened the door and as he levered himself down to the ground, he looked up at me and said, "Good luck son." He turned and muttered, just loud enough for me to hear, "There's fuck all at Blackall," and disappeared around the back of the van supposedly to get his *dorg*.

C.5

Farlee Station

Blackall, Snake, The Family, Flossy

At Blackall, stacks of goats were hanging around the rail yard, picking up spilled grain from the trucks. Some were even standing on the backs of other goats, ripping open bags of feed that were on the rail trucks. I guessed they were a pest. I walked down the street from the railway to a busy little township; it had a main street with shops and hotels each side.

It wasn't hard to spy the Tattersalls Hotel, the place I was to meet Mr Gold at 3.00 P.M. It was now midday as I checked my watch and walked in to the hotel with the wide veranda. Looking for a receptionist or someone, I rang the small brass bell on the counter and waited. I was about to ring it again when a woman, who I guess was the maid, tall and skinny, wearing an apron with her hair done up in a scarf like my mother used to do on weekends.

"Excuse me, I was wondering if there was someplace I could leave my pack for a while," I asked.

"Just shove it behind the desk, love. It will be safe there."

As I proceeded to place the pack behind the counter, I enquired to the whereabouts of the toilet.

"I think you might need the bathroom love, go up the stairs, third door on the right. I don't think the boss would mind."

Thanking her profusely, wondering if I smelt or was so dishevelled from all the rail travel that a good shower and a change of clothes would do wonders for my cold and my body, still recovering from the swigs of op rum. Retrieving my toilet bag and towel, last set of clean undies and clothes from my pack, I took to the stairs and found the room marked 'Gentleman's bathroom.' It stunk; it stunk like rotten eggs. The shower cubicles were all stained a brown color and did not look at all the place one could clean one's self. However, I stripped off and turned the shower on. It was the water. It was vile smelling liquid. Hot and refreshing, but vile. You were flat out getting a lather from the soap. (I later learnt the water at Blackall was bore water and the smell of rotten eggs was sulfur).

But the shower refreshed me and the clean clothes did wonders for my well-being. Leaving off the riding boots and going back to my desert boots, I went back down the stairs, put my dirty gear in my pack with the wet towel and went in search of a café. *The Bellevue* seemed the place, with the booth-type benches, plastic tablecloths and fly spotted artificial flowers in each booth. Picking up the menu, I was starving, so ordered a mix grill and a vanilla milkshake to absorb the rum in my gut. My celebration meal back in Brisbane, I thought, was grand. But a western mixed grill beat anything ever that has been set before me in my life. Can you imagine a T-bone steak, two mutton chops, three pork sausages, some grilled ham, tomatoes, onions and two fried eggs with bacon, potato chips and salad, all for 75c? I made a pig of myself, enjoying the lot. It's amazing what a good shower and a good feed can do for a man. Ordering a black coffee from the Greek owner, I sat back, lighting a cigarette, feeling very comfortable.

Paying the Greek the check, I had an hour before my rendezvous with my new boss and started to feel apprehensive. A walk around the town might ease some of my building nervousness. There were agents' offices showing the latest animal husbandry equipment, stockman outfitters Wiggins' huge store, pubs and necessary shops. Walking around to a side street, there were modest little timber houses with unkempt front yards on a dusty dirt road lined up side by side. Now and then a dog would fly out, barking, hackles up, ready to tear my throat out at the slightest hint that I might walk into their front yard.

No way. Shit! I came to a sudden stop. My heart thudded, pumping through my chest and I went hot all over. Dead in front of me was the biggest, ugliest, deadest snake in the world. It must have been two metres long and at least twenty-two centimetres in diameter. A small voice in my head told me going to work in Western Queensland was a terrible mistake. Another voice said, you'll be right, but be bloody careful. Thank god the snake was dead, but it did give me quite a start.

I was brought up not to swear, or all hell would break loose. The acceptable swear words were crikey and damn and if by chance you severed your arm a loud 'blast!' might be accepted, but seeing that snake, well...

I worked my way round back to the Tattersalls hotel, ready to meet my new boss, Mr Gold. Stopping on the way to buy my first tin of Log Cabin tobacco and Tally-Ho papers as I was running short on smokes.

Three o'clock, 3.15 P.M., 3.30 P.M. Had I got my instructions right? 3.45 P.M. Was it all a mistake? I was getting worried.

"You Jack Alexander?" said an assertive voice behind me. I turned and saw a tall, slim, fit man, late thirties, with a permanent five o'clock shadow, wearing cotton khaki riding jodhpurs, the shiny tan riding boots, a light blue countryman's shirt with an open neck with black chest hairs fighting for sunlight. I answered in the affirmative.

"Sorry I'm late. Got held up at the agents. Where's your stuff?"

"Just here in the hotel," I replied.

"Then get your gear and wait for me here and I will bring the car round and pick you up. I won't be long."

Fifteen minutes later, a blue V8 Ford Fairlane pulled up. The passenger side window opened and Mr Gold leant across from the driver's side, telling me the boot was open, to put my gear in and make sure it was shut and hop in. It was a beaut car. He started the first bit of conversation.

"Shut the window." I soon learnt why, as the main street was the only bit of tarred road. We hit the dirt road just outside the main strip and it was rough. Potholes and old wheel tracks rutted the road from ages ago when it had rained. Mr Gold used the palm of his hand to turn the steering wheel. I thought, *A bit of a show off*, but he could drive.

He asked me where I came from, how many brothers and sisters did I have, what did my dad do for a living? My father was a salesman and had separated from my mother when I was three. All the usual questions one asked. I wanted to know how big the property was.

"Fifty thousand acres."

"How many workers?"

"None, just you and me, plus the wife and governess and my two young boys."

"How many sheep and cattle on the place?"

"Five thousand sheep, three hundred cattle and twelve horses."

"And where exactly was the property?"

"Seventy-three kilometres northwest on the Barcoo River."

We came to a sudden stop where there appeared a fence across the road. "Could you get the gate?" I started to open the door.

"Not yet," was the firm voice from my side, and the reason became quite clear. The dust the car was making caught up to us and if I had opened the door, we would have been covered in it. After it passed, I got out to get the gate, but all that was there was the fence across the road. Four strands of barbwire and two stout sticks dividing the wires about a metre apart.

From the car came, "Well, don't look at it, open it."

I did not have a clue. He got out of the car and unhooked a stick held horizontally to the top wire by a round loop of plain wire. He unwound the "handle" from around the upright support and opened it up. I had never seen anything like it in my life. It was called a 'cocky's gate'.

I lamely muttered something about having iron gates on hinges down south. He proceeded to get in the car and I followed.

"Will you wait here and shut the gate after I have driven through?" he said in a rather exasperated voice. He drove through and stopped the car about twenty metres on the other side. I managed to shut the cocky's gate, taking my time to make sure I did it properly and ran to the car. I am sure he drove further than need be to teach me a lesson. Then the important questions came.

"Can you drive?"

"Yes, of course, I've had my license for a year," I boasted.

What male didn't get his license in the late fifties as soon as he turned eighteen? I had to go through a driving school to get it as we didn't have a car, but between you and me, my driving experience was very limited.

"Can you ride a horse?" A little 'yes' came from my lips.

"And where did you learn to ride?"

"At a riding school," I replied. *Where else would you learn to ride?*

"Umm and what about milking?"

"At the family's friends' farm," was the meek reply.

"And what about killing?" His voice was getting more tense. I confessed I hadn't done any killing. He hit the roof, as we had just gone over a large pothole.

"I told that agent Pearson that under no circumstances would I employ a first-year jackaroo that couldn't milk, ride and kill. I don't mind teaching them anything, but I won't teach them those chores." He calmed down a bit and said, "It's probably not your fault, but you can be sure I will be having words with Pearson."

Things went silent as we were both deep in our thoughts. My thoughts were, *It's not like I thought.* I had imagined, or should I say dreamt, of lots of workers and stockmen (that might be able to teach me things), Aboriginal camps and station life that I had read about. And me riding up on my white charger that I had just tamed, cracking my stockwhip and fascinating all the females on the station. Instead, I was going to work on a dad and mum's place. Well, you got to start somewhere.

His thoughts would probably be, *I will kill that bloody agent sending me out a city kid who can't even open a bloody gate. What I have to put up with, that bloody big hat he has wouldn't be able to see one foot in front of him. And I doubt if he would be strong enough to do a decent day's work.*

We came to another cocky's gate. I waited till the dust went past, then hopped out and ran to open the gate, but it was fastened a different way. Studying the gate, I managed to work it out and after a short while, opened it to let the Ford through. The sun was starting to head towards the horizon as we continued over the rough dirt road to our destination.

Mr Gold asked, after a bit of thoughtful silence, "Jack, would you mind if we call you John? As our last jackaroo was with us for four years and his name was Jack and I think my two young boys could be confused. Do you mind being called John?"

"My grandfather was called John. No, I don't mind a bit," was my answer. "Glad to be of some help."

We turned a sharp corner and in front of us was, would you believe, an iron gate. After opening it, it was then a short trip to the homestead, which in the fading light seemed like a modern timber suburban house. Nothing like the homesteads I had seen in pictures.

Pulling up to the front of the house, he got out of the car, saying, "Wait here, John." I looked around and there was no one there, then realising it was me with my new name.

He came back shortly saying, "It's getting dark. Come with me. I want to show you where to find the cow in the morning and where the yard is." I dutifully followed him, passing a large, corrugated iron shed, then a hundred metres further on was a large timber bush rail and post yard. He showed me where to milk the cow in the bale and pointed to one of the gates in the yard. My new boss informed me that through the gate was the cow paddock and that's where I would find the house cow.

"Well, come along John, I will introduce you to the family, show you your room and you can shower and change for dinner. Dinner is at seven." Walking toward the house, my thoughts were slightly worrying. I had already had a shower about four hours ago and was wearing my last clean pair of clothes. What was I to do?

Walking into the house, which was very nice inside with comfortable furniture and a homely atmosphere, two young boys about seven and nine years, in striped pyjamas, appeared around the corner looking very inquisitive. Their father introduced me, "This is John, the new jackaroo who is going to work here to help me like Jack used to do. And John, this is Gary and Peter."

I stepped forward and said, "How do you do?"

They looked surprised at my greeting and said, "G'day" and ran off giggling. Their mother appeared from, what I guess was, the lounge room. A slim, pretty woman. Quite the opposite to what I imagined a station owner's wife to look like, which was large and masculine, wearing male clothes and with a horsy sort of face. I know it's not right, but that's what I thought.

She had a pleasing round face, a nice complexion with a hint of rosy cheeks, light brown hair brushed well off her face with a small fringe and hair tied back in a pretty clasp. She appeared to be going out, as she had a hint of makeup on. She wore a pastel yellow jumper and cardigan called a twin set, with a pretty skirt and stockings. She introduced herself as Nancy Gold and she went on to continue, but my new boss interrupted her and said, "You can call Mrs Gold the missus and me, if you like, boss. You will meet Nan, the governess, at teatime."

He escorted me down the passage to a lovely bedroom at the end, made up with two towels folded up on the bed, a desk, chair, wardrobe and dresser. It was one hundred per cent on the cold, flyscreened sleep-out that was my room back home. "Boss" showed me my own private bathroom with a shower and toilet, just two doors to the left of my room and said, "Once you're cleaned up, come on down to the lounge room as soon as you can for pre-dinner drinks." I undid my pack, pulled out my wet towel and gear, and sorted a few items out. Looking through some of my gear that was dirty, I hoped it might look clean. There was nothing, so grabbing my toilet bag and the nicely folded towel on my bed, I went to my private bathroom and had another shower, a shave, put on some old spice deodorant and aftershave, shook my clothes out and put them on again. I took special care and attention to combing my hair. I put my things back in my new room, then went to find the lounge for pre-dinner drinks.

Entering the lounge room I saw Nancy, Mrs Gold, (the missus) sitting in a large floral lounge chair sipping what I guessed to be sherry. She did not seem to be going anywhere. My new boss was standing with a darker drink that I took as a port at a small bar in the corner of the room.

"Will you have a drink John?" he cordially asked, "Sherry or port?"

"A port would be fine," I answered.

He reached for a crystal cut glass and with the port decanter, filled it to two-thirds.

Handing it to me, he said, "John, we change for dinner here."

I was about to apologise, saying I had nothing clean to wear, when his wife interrupted and spoke to her husband, "Dear, John's traveled a long way and perhaps he hasn't any clean clothes to change into." Bless her.

"Is that right, John?" *I keep waiting for another person to answer. I just can't get used to being a John.*

I did apologise that it would not happen again and was it possible to wash some clothes tomorrow.

"Don't worry about that. You will find a wicker basket in your bathroom. If you put all your washing in it, Nan will take care of it. I am sure Gerry–" *I had forgotten the boss's first name was Gerry* "–wants you to work with him instead of you bothering to do your washing." That was fine by me, but I wanted to check my underpants that there were no skid marks in them.

Mrs Gold was asking me lots of questions about Melbourne. I got the feeling she was rather lonely and desperate to get all the information about my life in the city. The boss, still standing at the bar fiddling with some obscure gadget, asked me, "Do you smoke at all John?" I answered, yes.

"Well, that's fine, but Mrs Gold has banned it in the house and that includes your room, so we would appreciate if you kept your smoking outside like I do."

I lied and informed him it was the same rule at our house in Melbourne. By this time, I had manoeuvred myself to a lounge. Sitting down, I wondered where the kids were. Probably in bed.

Soon we were called to dinner. I rose from the couch first, as I was always taught you must stand when a lady enters the room and do the same when she leaves. I waited till they both left the room and followed them to the dining room where a table was beautifully laid out with a bottle of red wine on the table, breathing; I was quite comfortable and knowledgeable about good manners and the correct way to do things. I waited till all were seated and took the place that was indicated to me.

A large, pleasant woman entered the room wheeling a mobile tray. Stopping at the head of the table and placing a roast leg of lamb in front of the boss and then moving on to the missus with a plate of roasted vegetables. A small dish with peas and two silver jugs, one with gravy, the other with mint sauce, followed. I decided rather quickly that I was going to like this place. I stood up as I was introduced to Nan, the governess, shook her hand, and wondered why she didn't join us for dinner. Placing my serviette on my lap, I watched the exhibition the boss was making steeling the carving knife before expertly carving the meat.

As each plate had carved meat put on it, it was then handed to the missus who asked, "Do you eat everything John?" I nodded.

"One or two potatoes?"

"Two, thank you."

After everyone was served their meal, silence reigned, except for the slight sound of knife and fork scraping a plate. When we finished, the missus asked me to take the used dishes to the kitchen.

As everyone handed their empty plate to me, I stacked them on top of each other, excused myself and found my way to the kitchen. Nan was placing a hot chocolate pudding into three pudding bowls and pouring cream on top. They looked delicious and I said so. Nan smiled and said thanks. She then advised me that after pudding with the Golds I was to clear the table, bringing everything into the kitchen on the mobile tray, then help her wash up. She also informed me the boss and his wife liked to have their pot of tea in the lounge and that it was their private time. If I wished, I could have a cup of tea or coffee in the kitchen, or for that matter any time I liked.

Taking the chocolate pudding out to the dining room, I managed to carry the three bowls at once without a mishap and placing them in front of my superiors. The missus started the conversation by asking me if I had been confirmed in a church. I told her I had. In fact, once I had thoughts of being a missionary in New Guinea, but taming a white charger and impressing the outback girls seemed a much better career move. She then went on to tell me she was doing correspondence by the church so she could be confirmed.

"John, what was it like being confirmed and what did you have to do?"

I started to elaborate on the whole communion thing, but I was noticing my new boss getting rather restless and bored by the conversation between his wife and myself. He interrupted and started to talk about mustering wild horses for the up-and-coming rodeo in Blackall. Here could be a bit of trouble; I was used to being around women. I seemed to be able to communicate better with them than men. I had better start learning to do the opposite if I wanted to get along.

"Well John, it's time for you to help Nan do the dishes. Ask her where you are to find the milking bucket and remember the house cow must be milked before breakfast, which is seven in the morning."

I said, "No worries, Boss."

I collected the empty bowls and other utensils and placed them on the tray and started to wheel it out to the kitchen. They both stood up and the missus said with a lovely smile, "Goodnight John," and the boss muttered the same.

I reciprocated with, "A very good night to both of you."

We scraped the dishes in to a bin that was for the pig and we did the dishes. I asked Nan, who was a big woman with a heart to match, why she didn't have dinner with the family. She told me she had tea with the two young boys an hour earlier than us in the main dining room, and that gave her time to clean up after the day, as the engine was always turned off at 9.00 P.M. sharp. I heard the low thump, thump of a diesel engine but until told, did not realise that it was a generator to charge a whole bank of batteries, giving us a 32-volt lighting system. When the engine went off, there was no power, hence no lights. So one had to do everything before nine unless you liked walking around in the dark. After we finished the dishes, Nan showed me where the milk bucket was kept and the netting vale with colorful glass beads all-round the edge to put over the milk when I brought it back to the kitchen to stop the flies having swimming lessons. We both said good night and retired to our respective rooms.

I unpacked my new silver alarm clock and set it for four in the morning. Because I had to learn to milk a cow, that gave me three hours before breakfast to have a full bucket of milk in the kitchen. I laid my clothes out ready and my new warm jacket as if it was going to be as cold as when I got out of the train at Jericho this morning, which seemed so long ago, then I would be prepared. Feeling very tired after my day's adventures, I hopped in to my new bed and thought about the morrow before falling asleep.

All hell broke loose. Where was I? It was an earthquake! No, the new alarm clock with both bells was ringing, enough to wake the dead six kilometres away. I bashed away at the thing, as it was pitch dark. I had forgotten to check the night before how to turn the darn thing off. I grabbed it and put it under the blankets to muffle the sound and pushed every knob, lever thing, that my fingers could find. At last I managed to quieten the monster. I quickly got dressed and crept out to the kitchen to find the milk bucket. Rattling around, I found it in the dark, and then I had to find my way out of the house. This, as you can imagine, was extremely difficult, as I had not familiarised myself with a floor plan. After more banging and finding walls instead of doors, I finally made it outside to a beautiful, starry night. The stars were so clear and everything smelled fresh in the cold night air. So cold it hurt my nostrils as I breathed in and watched the vapour as I breathed out.

The howling sounded extremely close. It must be dingoes on my first night. *It seemed like night, even though it was morning.* Yep, I was slightly scared. As I walked toward the large, corrugated shed, the howling seemed closer. So close I knew they were waiting for me behind the shed. With bucket upraised over my shoulder, I was ready to flatten any felon that attacked me. My step was caution, my body ready for action. My thoughts were of home.

I managed to pass the shed with body intact and relief, as the dingoes howling now seemed further away. I opened and shut the gate into the yard and found the cow bale. There was a strip of concrete with a log of wood, I guess, to sit on. I hung the bucket up on the bale and went out into the paddock to search for the cow. After a short while, she was spotted dozing under a small wattle.

"Well, old girl," I said, "it's early for you and it's early for me, but I have to learn how to extract some milk from you."

I drove her to the gate without much problem except for falling on a log and barking my shin. I have never been blessed with the best of night vision, but one has to manage.

The dear old cow, I learnt later, was called Flossy, walked directly to the bale and then pulled her head out looking at me, as if to say, "You gotta be joking." I realised the stainless-steel milk bucket I left hanging on the bale must have distracted her. I took the bucket down and tried to get her back in the bale. She nearly did, then pulled her head back, turned around quickly, placing her front foot into the bucket, which I had left on the ground. With much clanking and running around the yard, the bucket came free, slightly worse for wear and full of dirt and dust. I got out my hankie and tried to clean the bucket the best I could, as it was the only thing I could find to get the dust out. Wiping the bucket, I noticed Flossy nosing at a 44-gallon drum in the corner behind the bale.

Going over, I lifted the lid and found it was half full of grain. Then, seeing a little feed trough tied to the bottom of the bale with wire, I placed a dipper of feed into the trough. The cow put her head into the bale, which enabled me to close it behind her head. Now she was more interested in the grain than me. Spying a leg rope, I tied it around the cow's back leg and pulled it back as far as I could. I wasn't going to get kicked. Looking at my Smiths watch; I was horrified to realise it was nearly five o'clock. I pulled up the log to sit on, grabbed the dented bucket and, well, I never had tits in my fingers before and I felt a bit silly about my bashfulness, but gee, it was only a cow. With the dexterity of a virgin, I placed both hands on two teats and began to pull. Nothing came out, not a drop. I then remembered the old train drover saying to use thumb and forefinger and pull. This I did a bit hard as the cow kicked and did a nice sloppy shit. As it hit the concrete, it bounced straight up and out on to my leg, in the bucket and everywhere. Getting the hankie out again to wipe the bucket, the cow's legs slipped behind her in a sort of cow splits, back and not sideways, ending up on her tummy with her neck choking on the bottom of the bale and her tongue hanging out of her mouth. I stood up, lit a smoke and took stock of the situation. The leg rope was miles too tight and I had pulled her leg back too far. That and slipping on all the fresh sloppy dung, she didn't have a chance. Undoing the leg rope, getting my hands covered in muck and then unlatching the bale, I had to kick the poor thing to get her up.

Then I proceeded to place more grain in her feed tin, walked her round and put her in the bale again, this time pulling her leg back just past the udder. It was getting quite light now as I looked for a shovel to clean up the cow's mess. Again, I sat on the log and tried to milk. This time, the bitch peed. It splashed everywhere and it stunk. A bit went into the bucket. The time? My god, after six. I had about a litre of milk and a bit of pee in the bottom of the bucket. Then I heard the gate unlatch and my boss walked over and said, "How's it going?"

"Not too well," I answered. He looked at the dismal amount in the bucket. Telling me to get up, he sat down on the log and went whish, whish, whish and had the bucket full of milk and froth in no time. I hesitantly said she seemed to be holding the milk up. He replied, "I should have warned you; she doesn't like strangers and won't let her milk down." *Got out of that one.*

"Christ, what happened to the bucket?"

"Er, she put her foot in it."

All I got from my boss was a strange look and, "We will see how you get on a horse after breakfast."

Cleaning myself up before breakfast, I headed for the kitchen and couldn't help overhearing a conversation between the boss and Nan.

"Nan, did you hear all that noise early this morning? It woke Nancy, and the boys came running into our bedroom terrified."

Walking into the kitchen, Nan smiled at me.

"Good morning, John," and turning to the boss said, "I didn't hear a thing. It was probably one of those new jets flying over, and they do that occasionally." I hurriedly tucked in to my chops and eggs. I did not feel like the porridge as I knew what was in the milk. The boys and Mrs Gold were nowhere to be seen. The boss explained to me what was on for the day.

"Now John," *I'm starting to hate that name,* "after breakfast I will run the horses in, get yourself ready for a day's mustering, we won't be back till tonight. Nan has made your lunch. It's over there wrapped up in newspaper." He turned and pointed to a small parcel on the laminated kitchen bench. He continued, "Bring what you need with you for the day." Then tipped his tea in to the saucer and drank from it. "I better be going. See you at the yards in ten minutes."

Finishing my breakfast, I went to my room, quickly made my bed and put some Band-Aids on my blisters. Then placing my sheaf knife on my belt, compass and tobacco in my pocket and a clean handkerchief. My other was pretty dirty from its use earlier on. Picking up my lunch and thanking Nan, I proceeded toward the yards with the chops and eggs doing something funny inside me. I don't know but I had feelings the next hour may be one of the most exciting in my young life.

C.6

The Ride

Horses, Suicide, Sheep, Survival

Just as I got to the yards, a great swirl of dust came upon me and in the mists was my boss, mounted on a fiery sweating grey steed, cracking his stock whip, running what seemed to me, a mob of very wild horses into the yard. I was watching fascinated as the horses were wheeling around the yard kicking with all hoofs at other horses, some with ears flattened back against their neck, mouth open wide, teeth gnashing, trying to bite another's neck. Swirling, kicking, biting, dusty, screaming, they had to be the rodeo horses the boss was talking about last night.

Deeply entranced, observing the frightening melee taking place before my eyes, I failed to notice the boss had come beside me. He said, "Go catch the bay with the snip on the nose and the white socks."

I couldn't believe my ears. Does he expect me to go in to that wild ferocious mob and catch one? Let alone a bay with white socks and a snip, whatever that is. I would do anything, anything at all for my boss, but commit suicide? Not on yer Nellie. Looking up at Mr Gold, I said in a rather husky voice, "I have ridden horses, but they have been caught for me. I don't know how to catch them."

He swore under his breath.

"Watch and pay careful attention, as I will only show you once." His manner and voice, to put it nicely, was not in the friendliest tone.

He went to the small shed beside the yard carrying a bridle and just climbed over the fence amongst the horses. With a few 'woahs' and 'steady boys' and more 'woahs', he managed to put the reins around a brown one's neck and walked it to the gate. I opened the gate for him and shut it behind him and the horse. He slipped the bridle over its head, placing the bit in its mouth, then said, as he handed me the reins of my intended mount, "Your saddle is over there, let's see you put it on."

I diddled a bit, stroking the horse and brushing his back with my hand. The horse lowered his head and turned it towards me with a look in its eyes, "I will look after you, son."

The boss went and let the grey go and caught another fresh mount for himself. I watched and followed him, placing the saddle blanket on the horse and then the saddle, but hadn't a clue how to do the girth up.

The boss was just a bit friendlier, as after girthing his horse, he showed me that the girth on the saddles was a special type, called a bates girth. He showed me how to cinch it up properly. Putting my lunch into the saddlebag, the boss, standing beside his horse, said, *I felt rather sarcastically*, "Let's see how you mount." I stood on the left side of the horse, at it's flank, facing the same direction as the horse. I then proceeded to put my right foot in the stirrup and began to mount. The loud frustrating three words of, "For Christ's sake!" stopped me from completing the manoeuvre and ending up on the horse facing the rear. Then it all happened.

My new boss mounted in a flash and spurred his horse from a standing start to a full gallop. I don't know how I ended up in the saddle with my feet in the stirrups and my hands on the reins, but I did, and my horse was waiting for no one. He took off like a Ferrari in a grand prix. Grasping a full hand of mane as my head jerked backwards and my body thrust forward, we had caught up to the boss's horse in seconds. I could hardly see a thing, what with the dust and flying debris from the hoofs of the horse in front. My large hat came off at the start and the hat string that the salesman had kindly given me "at no extra charge" was choking me as the hat was ballooning behind me like a drag parachute. My thighs could feel the muscles of the animal surging under me, the smell of horse sweat and fear attacked my nostrils. My arms and hands on the mane and rein were being pulled out of their sockets. My whole body was being pummeled and we had just started.

Through the sandalwood brush twanging my ears, tearing at my new pilot's coat and pulling on my legs, could I hang on? The horse in front rose in the air as it jumped a log. Mine followed. We were sailing, the horse a metre off the ground. I was another metre out of the saddle. The horse landed safely; I landed heavily back in to the saddle, causing my testicles to join my Adam's apple.

Soon we were in a clump of Brigalow trees, trunks whizzing past. Will we hit a low branch? Duck! When to look up, no more brushing on my back must be clear of the Brigalow, swish as a low branch just missed decapitating me. The neck of the horse was going backwards and forwards, the mane in my face, as well as the wind and the dust. We were right up behind the boss's horse. How long can this go on for? How long can my body be pummelled? Back out in the open, a bore drain appeared in front of us. The horse in front leapt over it. Mine followed. I was thrown behind the saddle as the horse leapt forward and then slammed back into it as we touched mother earth again. I was glad my testicles were still in the upper part of my body. We galloped through the scrub, where a rabbit couldn't go. We jumped logs where kangaroos couldn't hop; we flew across the clay pans like an eagle on the wing.

The horse in front suddenly straightened both front legs out, as the back hunched underneath its belly. The boss looking behind and reined his mount to a screaming halt. So suddenly it happened, we cannoned straight in to the back of his horse. I knew immediately that my career prospects were in doubt, as I watched my employer forcefully ejected out of the saddle and over his horse's head on to the ground with a thud. I stayed on. How I managed that, only the Lord knows.

Mr Gold, sitting on the ground with his knees bent, both arms behind him for support, was not the happiest of men. I said lamely, "Sorry, I didn't know you were going to stop."

He said nothing. He didn't have to; his eyes and tight lips told me all the verbiage that was on his mind. He was a tough man. Dusting himself off, he caught his mount who was having a feed of grass, mounted and through clenched teeth, told me that seeing I was here we might as well drench the sheep.

The sheep were mustered the day before into a laneway, which we were now approaching. The boss indicated to me to dismount and open the gate. This I achieved without much trouble, the getting on was a bit more difficult, but I managed. My horse was called Bobby and he had proved to me that he could take care of my person, though he need not have been so enthusiastic in chasing after the boss's horse. The laneway, as suggested, was a narrow long paddock and we had entered at the top end so we just rode down the fence line, taking all the sheep before us until the sheep yards appeared at the bottom. This was where we manoeuvred the sheep. Closing the gate after the sheep entered the yard, we tethered the horses under some shady eucalyptus trees and loosened their girths.

I was sweltering in my pilot's jacket, but was glad I wore it to save my hide from all the scrub we had bolted through. I took it off and arranged myself for the next developments as we walked over to a small, corrugated iron shed beside the yard.

It was cool inside, with a dirt floor. A couple of wooden shelves were fixed on to the bush timber frame of the shed. The boss indicated to me to bring out two old tin kerosene buckets and all the gear that was on the old wooden table in the centre of the shed and bring them to the water tank that was just outside. He emptied packets of green powdery stuff into the buckets and mixed it with the water from the tank. I was informed this was Coopers Phenothiazine and was a drench to be given to the sheep for Round and Barbers Pole worms.

When the substance was mixed, I held up what appeared to be a large rubber hot-water bottle and, using a funnel, the boss poured the green mixture into the bag. Screwing a cork in to the top of it, he swung the bag on to his back with the attached straps. Leading from the bag was a small hose and at the end was a gun with a curved nozzle at the end. This, I was informed, was a drenching gun to deliver the drench to the back of the sheep's throat. I was told to push the sheep into a narrow race, as many as you can squeeze in. It was not as easy as it sounds. First, the sheep went in every direction except the one I wanted them to go. They pushed past me; they trod on my feet with their sharp cloven hoofs.

The boss was yelling, "Don't stand there, you're blocking the raceway. Move yourself to the right, move yourself to the left, go back, go back, oh you bloody fool. I knew I should have brought the dogs."

Eventually, I got the race full of the annoying stupid animals; the boss climbed over the rail and in to the race jammed packed with sheep. He started drenching by standing at the back of the sheep, grabbing them around the jaw, jamming the nozzle down their throat, squeezing the trigger, and going on to the next.

We had done about eleven racefuls, and then thankfully, a halt was called for lunch. What a relief. Ready to flop down and have a well-earned rest after the whole morning's episodes, as I was sore, very tired, and admittedly slightly exhausted. But no.

"John, could you find some wood and get the billy boiled?" was the order.

This I accomplished quite well using the matches I had been given, all the newspaper wrapping from my lunch and some from the toilet paper in my hat band as well as sticks and twigs lying on the ground. The boss came over just as the water was bubbling.

"Well, you can at least boil a billy," the boss said as he pulled a little calico bag out of his shirt pocket and emptying tea leaves in to the boiling water. He lifted the billy from the dying fire with a broad stick and produced two chipped white enameled mugs that had seen better days and had not seen a washing up sink or a tea towel for just as long.

We stretched out with our backs leaning on an old Ironbark tree eating our lunch and drinking tea. My lunch was a mess as the sandwiches were welded together. The fillings of meat and pickles had escaped from the centre of the sandwiches and being in the saddlebags all morning were quarter toasted. It was just another disappointment, like the mug of tea. It was so strong, as black as molasses and nearly as thick, and I did like sugar, but alas, there wasn't any. I went to the tank and hoyed the disgusting tea and had water instead.

It was all getting a bit much for me: the trip, the excitement, change of climate, water and food. My rotten cold that now was giving me the sniffles and a sore throat, or maybe it was the hat cord that half strangled me on that momentous first ride. The bumbling mistakes, the stupid sheep. My first day was the opposite of anything I had ever imagined.

I consoled myself by pulling out my new tin of tobacco and levering the lid off with my sheaf knife. All city kids seemed to have one of them.

"You better get yourself a good pocket knife before you stab yourself with that thing," was Mr Gold's thoughts on my precious knife. I placed some tobacco in the palm of my left hand and kneaded it with the side of my right, as I had watched the old train drover do. I pulled out the Tally-Ho paper and started to roll the cigarette. It was very fat and I was flat out rolling it. After ruining a few papers, I managed to get a smoke made about the thickness of a match as the tobacco kept coming out both ends as I kept rolling. I lit the thing, had two puffs and that was the finish of the smoke. I was about to make another, but no.

"Well John, we have another eight races to do, so let's get on with it."

We did about seven hundred odd sheep that day, letting them go back in to the lane-way after the last one was done. We girthed our horses up and started the long ride home. After unsaddling the horses and putting the gear away, I stumbled towards the homestead, taking my boots off my aching, blistered feet and headed for my beautiful bed.

On the bed was my washing, all clean and neatly folded. God bless Nan. I had a good long hot shower, changed in to some clean clothes and flopped on to my bed completely and utterly exhausted. I had been through more in that day than I can remember. I tried to go to sleep but couldn't; I lay there looking at the ceiling with glazed eyes, waiting for my call to dinner, which I really didn't want. All I wanted was to go into a peaceful sleep.

Gerry Gold called, wanted to know if I was interested in drinks before dinner. That was nice of him. I said my thanks but declined, because if I had one sip of anything alcoholic, I would not be able to finalise my duties for the night. Soon Nan called me for tea. I was starting to ache all over and my cold made me miserable. I tried to be a bright young thing at dinner answering Mrs Gold's questions about the theatres in Melbourne and restaurants and I thought I managed very well. But the boss said as I struggled through the pudding, "You better wake up John before your head hits the table."

Managing to clear away the dishes and just able to help Nan clean up, I said my goodnights. Before leaving the kitchen, Nan called me back and handed me an old tea towel saying with a hint of a smile, "John, you better wrap this around your alarm clock or stick it under your pillow so you don't disturb the family." I said thanks and practically crawled to my room and died.

C.7

Back to Go

Learning, The Bush, Success, Failure, Killing

Thank God I remembered to set the clock the night before. Its pillowed muffled ringing brought me back from the dead. But did it have to? Every muscle in my body ached, every tendon was stretched and ligaments were now hot knives, finishing the torture. My head was heavy with cold, my top eyelids had anvils on them, and I just wanted to have a very quiet permanent death. "Get off your arse, get the hell out of that bed and get that cow and show your body that you can hack it."

Well, that's what my really strong thoughts were, but my body had the upper hand. It just refused to budge. It could not move. I was paralysed. This was my career choice. I had made my bed now; I had to lie in it. Good one Jack. How I got out of bed, I don't know. There are miracles and this was one of them.

It took me some time to get dressed, bending my knees to put undies and pants on, bending elbows and shoulders to put shirts on. Socks, that was another miracle in itself. Creeping out to the kitchen like a hunchback crippled with rickets, I got the milk bucket and made it to the yards, not caring if a pack of dingoes jumped from behind the shed and devoured me. Flossy trembled when she saw me, but this time things worked out better. With grain put in her feed tin, she walked straight into the bale. When I put the leg rope on, she refused to let me pull it back any further than her rear teat, which was a nuisance. But we went all right and I managed to get a third of a bucket of milk with a slight garnish of poo that had accidentally splashed in. I was quite proud of my achievements as I walked back to the kitchen after spending just over an hour with the cow. I put the netting vale over the milk and cleaned myself up for breakfast.

It was Saturday and after breakfast me and the boss and one of his dogs called Ben, took the old army Willys jeep and drove to the laneway where we had left the drenched sheep the day before. The boss dropped me and the dog off at the bottom of the laneway. We had to gather all the sheep up and walk them to where the boss would be waiting two thirds of the way up at a gateway in to "Gidgee" paddock where the sheep belonged. As we walked up the lane way gathering up the sheep, Ben really knew his job, running backward and forward behind the sheep, blocking any trying to get behind us. In fact, I wasn't doing anything at all. As the dog ran backward and forward, he seemed to be brushing past me, even colliding with me. "Stupid dog, too busy pushing the sheep up and not seeing me."

But then, I noticed every time the dog brushed past me, he would turn his head and look at me. I started to wonder about the significance of his actions, but then just up ahead was the boss with the gate open and blocking the lane way with the jeep. He shooed the sheep, the dog helped. I was in the way, but all in all the sheep ended up in their paddock.

On the way home, a wild pig was spotted. The boss told the dog to 'stay' as he stopped the vehicle, picked up his rifle and shot the animal while it just looked at us. I felt a bit sorry for the pig, but the boss said, as he moved the gear stick into first, "Well, that's quite a few lambs that bastard won't be eating".

As we approached the homestead, the boss asked me if I would like to join the family and go to the pictures that night. To be honest, I didn't want to go, as I really was tired. But it was a nice gesture, and I wanted to do the right thing, so I accepted graciously.

I think I should explain a few things. A jackaroo, a female is called a jillaroo, is an apprentice to the manager or owner of a sheep and or cattle station. He is treated as one of the family, eats with the family, stays in the homestead or at special quarters adjacent to the main house. The apprenticeship is for four years and then, if successful, can graduate to a position as an overseer. After another three to four years, he might be lucky enough to be a station manager. There are a few interpretations of the word jackaroo. Mine is 'Jack' for jack of all trades, one that can lend his hand to anything, and 'Roo,' well hop and do this and hop and do that. I am sure the academics would have other meanings.

As a jackaroo, I had imagined myself as a tall strapping sort of bloke, suntanned with a square jaw, flashing white teeth, ropey veins on the inside of my arms and legs. A fantastic physique, a sparkle in my eye and some sort of aura that made all females swoon. Alas, on this Saturday, I was a disaster. I was about one metre sixty-five tall, a long body with short legs, hence the shirt- tail hanging out all the time, and trousers creased around my ankles. A very pale complexion from the Melbourne environment, a runny red nose with bleary eyes, compliments of the cold. Muscles that I am sure were there, but well hidden, a huge hat that made me look like a mushroom and to top it all off, limping in agony from the blisters caused by my new riding boots.

Looking at me from the outside, I appeared a weak, pathetic, miserable human. What could not be seen was the fire and determination to be a success, a driving ambition to succeed, a determination to shrug off the school boy's taunt of being a 'no hoper.' My God world, look out, Jack is on the tracks and he is going places.

At lunch with Mrs Gold and the two boys, I learnt that the kids were doing correspondence via the school of the air for their education, and they were doing a project on the first Olympic Games in Australia held in Melbourne in 1956. They asked a million questions about what it was like. Information about the city, the venues, and the crowds. I was very pleased to be able to answer most of their questions and found I was the last one to finish my lunch. After lunch, it was suggested I take a good look around and familiarise myself with the immediate surroundings of the homestead.

"The boys would just love to show you around John." But a warning from Mr Gold to be ready to leave for the pictures at four o'clock.

Peter and Garry, the boss's kids, were only too enthusiastic to show this strange city creature around the place. I get on well with kids but have difficulties getting along with ones that know more than me and aren't frightened of showing off their knowledge. City people reckon that country people are dumb but take a city person out of their environment and you get an imbecile. Well, I was shown the 'sucker' - the wild young pig caught and penned to be fattened up for a special time. It was fed kitchen scraps and milk left over from the day before. The thriving vegetable garden that Mrs Gold attended.

"You have to weed and dig it up as well as clean the pig pen out," my young host informed me, in not the most respectful manner. Then to the dog kennels. They were large hollow logs about a metre in length with a bit of tin nailed on to one end. There were four of them for the four working dogs. A collie called Reg and two tan kelpies. One I had met, Ben, the other Whisky and a black and tan kelpie called Sue. They were all chained up to their prospective logs, all contained in a large, fenced yard.

I was told by young Peter if I touched one of the dogs, "Dad will kill you." First bush law. Never touch another man's working dog.

Then we went over to the large shed that looked like a miniature engineering shop with welders, oxyacetylene sets, drill stands, a lathe and a huge assortment of tools and implements. Also, inside were a large tractor, the Willys jeep, an FJ ute and other engines and jetters and items that, at the time, I would not have had a clue about. I was not going to show my ignorance to the boys by asking what they were.

Garry, out of the blue, piped up and said, "Dad says you are useless on a horse and don't even know how to catch one."

He was only seven, I should have kept quiet, I should have known better, but with my dejected feelings, my misery, I just had to retaliate by saying, "Yea that maybe so, but I didn't fall off like your old man did."

That shut them up for a second, and I wondered later if that comment was one of the things that might make a change to my career prospects. We wandered about, checking this and that out. I was plied with a thousand questions like, can you crack a whip? Can you scruff a calf? Do you know how to rope? Have you ever shot a 'roo on the hop? All negatives for me and I was getting tired of the constant battering from them. Looking at my watch, I informed them we had better go back and get ready for the pictures, as we had to be ready by four.

After showering and getting ready, I was sitting outside waiting for the rest of the family while trying to perfect my cigarette rolling, which was still ending up with a very thin hot smoke that wasn't doing my tongue much good either. The family came out all dolled up as if they were going to the first night of a Dame Margot Fonteyn ballet. I realised later that in a rural environment people liked to really dress up when they go somewhere, as every outing is special for the hard-working people of the outback.

I had to open all the cocky gates, which I managed with some difficulty, and we arrived at Blackall just before six. I was dropped off at the Tattersalls Hotel.

"We have some things to do and we will see you at the pictures."

I walked the main street, checked out the windows in the closed shops and looked for the picture theatre that was only discovered by the picture posters on the side of a building. Thinking I had better have some dinner, I headed toward the Bellevue café. A thought struck me. I patted myself down and I put my hands in all my pockets. I patted them again, but all I could find was a tin of tobacco, a box of matches and a soggy handkerchief. But alas, no money. I forgot my wallet. I know I did not have much money left, but I had some. I walked past *The Bellevue*, glancing inside and there was the family getting stuck into mixed grills. There was no way I was going in there and asking for an advance or loan.

I went into the pub and into the lounge and found an empty table that happened to have a forgotten glass on it, about a quarter full of flat beer. This suited me fine, as I pretended it was mine, rolled my smoke slowly, lit it and held the glass, enjoying my hungry solitude. All I had to do was admire the architecture of the internal walls and the motifs on the carpet till seven thirty and then I made my way slowly to the picture theatre. There was a queue waiting to get their tickets from the booth. I was amazed to see so many people there. I spied the family in the middle of the queue, gave them a nod of recognition, then joined the end of the queue, pretending to purchase my ticket. When they had made their purchase, I left the queue as if I had remembered something, and walked the length of main street a few times, feeling like I was a thief checking which shops to break into. Then, a stroke of luck. I spied the boss's two tone Fairlane parked just opposite the theatre. I wondered if it was locked. No, it was open. Thankfully, I climbed in and lay on the back seat and if I wound the window down, I could hear the voices and sounds of the movie in progress. When I heard the first movie finish, I got out of the car and mingled with the interval crowd, met the family, and managed to comment how I enjoyed the first movie and the Joe McDokes short was funny. The family moved away and I rolled another smoke, waiting for the call back into the pictures so I could go back and crawl into my cramped position in the car. I listened to parts of the second movie so I could make some intelligent remarks about the show on the way home.

Going home, there was excited chatter about the movies until the boys fell asleep, Garry the youngest in the front, Peter in the back with me. He sprawled out with his head on my lap, which made it difficult for me to extract myself to open the gates without waking him up. Fancy driving 160 kilometres round trip just to see the pictures. I was a tired and hungry lad when I got to bed at midnight. I was pleased to hear the boss say before retiring that breakfast wasn't until 8.30 A.M. and I could sleep in. But the cow still had to be milked before breakfast, and then I could have the rest of the day off.

The cow and I were getting along much better. She was waiting for me at the yards and gave half a bucket of milk this morning. You have no idea how the muscles inside the front of your arms hurt while milking; I would hate to milk half a dozen. I was asked at breakfast what I was going to do that day. I said write a few letters.

"Oh, by the way, what do you do about mail?"

The missus informed me the mail truck came once a week on a Tuesday morning to pick up and deliver the mail. It also brought bread, newspapers, fuel and whatever else was needed.

"And what else have you planned, John?" I said I needed a good rest to try and get rid of my cold and be fit for work tomorrow. I got a look that seemed to say, me being fit by tomorrow would be an impossible task.

I did write to my mother, telling her where I was and my

address, as it had been nearly two weeks since I had left home. I had rung her when I got to Brisbane telling her I arrived safety but until now, had not bothered to contact her. Anyway, I didn't have the time. After the letter writing, I fell asleep on my bed only to be woken up by the eldest son. If I wanted any lunch, I had better get up.

In the afternoon, I found a bucket, *not the milk bucket*, and filled it half full of water, then with my tight, ill-fitting riding boots on my feet, I stood in it to soak the leather, to soften it. When both boots were saturated, I went off on a long walk, taking my new whip I'd bought in Rockhampton with me. I wanted to stretch the boots and mould them to my foot shape. It did a wonder for the boots, but my cold didn't appreciate it.

I walked along the bush track for two kilometres; I was well away from the homestead and into the bush proper. It was very quiet. It was a bit frightening but peaceful. I had a strange feeling of belonging, but knew I was still a stranger. I sat on a fallen log, rolled a smoke, and let the bush enfold me. I needed to feel and smell the environment. I wanted to belong. This was my belonging and my earth, my trees and waving grass, the blue sky, the fluffy white clouds, the soft breeze. This was my calling, a child calling back to his real mother – Mother Nature.

I thought about a few things, like the cow showing me where the feed bin was, the horse giving me a reassuring feeling and managing to keep me on his back. There was Ben, the dog, when we were working the sheep; he was knocking me and looking back at me as if to say, "Jack watch me, this is the way you do it." Was there, or is there, some communication between the animals and me, a communication that I was unaware of or unable to realise at this particular time.

It's stupid, fancy animals communicating with people. I bet as kids like me, we all wished we could talk to the animals like Dr Dolittle, have a chat with a bird, a yarn with a dog, a debate with a cat, but is there another way to communicate with animals? Maybe.

I stood up, shrugged off my strange thoughts and had a go at practicing with my whip. I was not very successful in getting it to crack like a rifle shot but was very successful at stinging my ears and hurting my face with the lash. So the practice did not last long. I decided it was time to make it back to the homestead as the gum trees were starting to throw long shadows.

The next three days, we mustered sheep and drenched them. In this time, I managed to catch Bobby, my horse, in the yards and mount correctly and we seemed to have formed a bond together. I by no means was a horse rider, but I did have a natural balance and Bobby was placid and an excellent first horse who looked after me. Flossy was doing well also; I was achieving a two-thirds bucket of milk with foam on the top and she wasn't crapping as much. Ben the dog was a good teacher and observing him the way he worked the sheep taught me so much more than a yelling boss. The soaking of my boots did wonders for my feet and blisters, and at last I was getting rid of my cold and feeling much better, thank you. Then there was that fateful Thursday.

We were mustering the woolly paddock and as usual, I went riding around the fence line, and if I saw any sheep, I was to drive them along in front of me until I came to a windmill and then I had to wait with the sheep, "I don't care how long," was the instruction, till the boss arrived. As it happened, he was there before me and had a couple of hundred sheep and lambs with him. I had none. Then the boss said, "Take this mob with you and drive them along the fence until you come to a gate. When you get there, hold the sheep and wait for me. I don't care if you have to wait a couple of hours, just wait at that gate."

Feeling really proud of myself driving that mob of ewes and lambs, using the technique that Ben the dog taught me, I managed to drive them all successfully down the fence line until I came to a gate. Riding around the sheep to stop them going further, they all settled down and a long wait ensued. The lambs were mothering up and having a drink. Some were grazing in the area; every now and then I had to turn them back to the main mob. Rolling a smoke and leaning against a log with the horse's reins in my hands, I was the picture of contentment. I waited and waited. It was over two hours since arriving at that gateway. The sheep were starting to get restless and I was getting worried, when suddenly, out of the peace and quiet came a crashing sound that scared the sheep, the horse and me.

It was the boss galloping his lathered covered horse straight for me and yelling, "You're at the wrong gate! You're supposed to wait at the proper one further along. You've got the sack!"

"Yea right- o," I said, willing to please any command from my boss.

We gathered the sheep up and drove them down the fence for about three k's, where there was a gate on a road. This evidently was the one I was supposed to be at. Why wasn't I told the gate on the road? Was it a setup just to get rid of this city slicker? We put the sheep through the gate into a laneway and then had a very tense and quiet ride back to the homestead.

I had never been sacked before, and when the realisation set in that I wasn't wanted, it was difficult for me to do or say anything. As we let the horses go, the boss said, "You have a week's notice," and walked to the house. Sheesh, I would sooner go now. I have got to stay and live with the family for a whole seven days in embarrassment and have them think I wasn't any good. Oh well, they thought that anyway. Well, I got the sack, nothing I can do about it except put my best foot forward, learn as much as I can, and be as pleasant as possible.

At the house, everything seemed normal. I had pre-dinner drinks with the family and general conversation over dinner. After doing the dishes and helping Nan clean up, I went outside, rolled a smoke and did some thinkin'. A week's notice, huh? Well, that's two weeks I will have been here and wasn't the Ekka in about three weeks. And wasn't I sort of promised a job from the stock agent Mr Chudley, if I saw him at the Ekka?

Things weren't that bad. I get a second chance and at least I will be able to be honest and say I can milk a cow and sort of ride a horse. I was sad about being sacked, but excited about the near future. I don't think I will write and tell Mum I got the sack; I'll tell her I got a better offer from another employer. Stubbing out my cigarette, I made my way to the bedroom to check on my financial situation. I had $20.00 in my Commonwealth Bank emergency fund, and I should get $30.00 for two weeks' wages from Mr Gold. Scrounging around in my gear, I came up with only $9.48 altogether, about $60.00 I should be able to survive on that till I got another job.

The next day, everything seemed normal. We drenched the sheep we'd put in the lane way the day before and put them back into their paddock. The lambs weren't big enough to mark, I was informed. Whatever that meant. We fixed a netting fence on the way home. 'Roos were the culprits in making holes big enough for sheep to get through. The boss stopped the Willys jeep after we entered a paddock near the house and told me to take the two dogs, Reg and Ben, that had helped us during the day and go and muster up the killers and bring them to the yard where I milked the cow.

The words "get the killers" worried me. Were they mad bulls or buckjumper horses? He did mention the rodeo coming soon to Blackall. The dogs, as usual, knew more than me and started to herd a small mob of about twenty sheep toward the direction of the yards. The boss was waiting for us with a wheelbarrow. Once the sheep and we were in the yards, I was told to catch one of them as the dogs held it in a corner.

I ran in and jumped on one, holding it around the neck; it took off, bucking me off and dragging me around as I still had hold of its head. The dogs thought it was great fun and chased the sheep and me around the yard. The boss was yelling about bruising, and I was impressed with his concern for me, but it was the sheep he was worried about, not me. After helping me bring the wether to a halt, I was informed that I was supposed to grab a hind leg. The boss showed me how to tie the two back legs and one front together and lifted the now hobbled sheep into the wheelbarrow, telling me to open the gate and let the remaining sheep go.

I was now about to witness a killing. Near the yard was a concrete block with a long wooden rail bolted in the middle to a post. This was the gallows. Beside it was a bucket of water, a white mattress cover and sharping steel and knife. Taking the sheep out of the wheelbarrow and putting it on the block, the boss straddled the animal and thrust the knife through its neck and pulled it forward as he pulled the head back. This all but severed the head except for its spine. Two jets of blood gushed from the neck as I watched the last kicking of the sheep and its eyes glass over. I was numb; it was so quick, alive then dead. I watched how the sheep was skinned and helped the boss lift the carcass on to the gallows. Grabbing the other end of the rail and tying it down on a small post there for the job, the sheep was now hanging upside down.

Removing the whole hide off the sheep with the head intact, what was left was quivering pink flesh. We opened the sheep and cleaned the guts out. Splitting the brisket was done expertly and quickly. It was the first time I had seen innards and thought I would be sick, but surprisingly I was more interested in the writhing mass than anything else. The boss slit open the large intestine and showed me worms with red stripes on them. I was informed they were barber's pole worms and that's why we were drenching the sheep.

The dogs were darting in and grabbing bits of guts. The boss put the sheep into the mattress cover, picked it up and swung it over his shoulder, then walked to a small gauzed out-building known as the butcher shop. My job was to slit the stomach open, spreading the contents on to the ground. Then pick up the guts, putting them into the wheelbarrow and take them to the incinerator, and wash the killing block down. These were my orders, which I managed to execute well, except it took a lot of my guts to handle the sheep's guts, putting them into the barrow. They kept sliding in my hand and slipping all over the place, but we managed. I even managed to eat the roast of mutton we had the next night.

On Sunday I went to my special bush spot, practiced with my whip, still not cracking it right, but my ears and head didn't cop too much of a lashing. Sitting on my log, I rolled a smoke. I thought to myself, *well Jack, you have another four days with this family. You probably will never see them again, and they don't know any of your relations.*

I decided I was going to ask and find out and learn as much as I could. I would be more knowledgeable at my next job. Even if I drive them mad with questions, they can't sack me. Didn't someone say, 'there's nothing wrong with being ignorant, it's staying ignorant that's the problem'?

The next few days went well, though I got some rotten jobs, like cleaning the dogs' kennels out. The same with the fowl yard and pig's pen and digging the vegetable garden over. But I was given the chance to muster a small paddock, put the sheep in the yard and drenched them myself, even though it was only forty-three sheep. I felt pretty proud of myself. I read my farmer's handbook and anything I didn't understand, I asked the boss. I asked, what sort of trees are they? *Leopard wood, Ironbark, Gidgee, Sandalwood*, the types of grasses *Mitchell, Flinders Wire and Buffel*, and burrs, *Galvanised, Bathurst and Noogoora*, and everything else I could think of.

Wednesday night at teatime, the boss told me Nan would drive me to town in the morning, so I should be packed up and ready by nine. I told them that would not be a problem and I would be ready. I was then asked by Mrs Gold, *I couldn't get used to calling her the missus*, would I be going back to Melbourne? I just said, "If you don't succeed the first time, try again."

Mrs Gold turned to her husband, saying, "I told you so." Whatever that was about.

The next morning, I milked Flossy for the last time, and she said goodbye, giving me a full bucket of milk with froth on the top in less than half an hour. I wanted to say 'see ya' to Bobby the horse, and thank him for not killing me, but he was in the horse paddock, so I left him my dearest thoughts. I stopped by the dogs' pen and tipped some warm milk into Ben's bowl and thanked him for showing me how to work sheep. I broke the number one rule and patted the boss's dog. Then after breakfast and helping Nan clean up, I went and did some final packing, had a shower and change, grabbed my pack and gear and waited for Nan, who soon drove round the corner of the house in her cream Holden FC.

I shook hands with Mr Gold and thanked him for giving me a go. He said, "Sorry it didn't work out and here's your paycheck."

Mrs Gold stood there with her arms folded and said, "It was nice having you, John."

She looked as if she really wanted to give me a hug. The two boys were told to say their goodbyes. I put my gear on the back seat and climbed in to the front beside Nan. I thanked them all and said a cheery goodbye.

To be honest, I felt quite sad to leave my three animal mates and disappointed that I wasn't given more of a chance to prove myself. I understand I lied to get the job about riding and milking, but I proved that I could manage after a while. If he could only see my burning ambition to learn and do well. All he saw was a sniffling cold-ridden city kid. Them's the breaks.

Nan dropped me off back at the Tattersalls Hotel in Blackall. We just talked about general things on the way in, such as why she became a governess. Her husband had been killed while felling a tree and she had no children of her own, so took up governessing. I asked her the quickest way to get to Brisbane and was told that the weekly Fokker flight from Longreach was scheduled that afternoon for Brisbane, "But if you can hitch a ride, it will be much cheaper."

I thanked Nan for all she had done for me, picked up my pack and headed for the Tattersalls and thought, *Goodbye John, welcome back, Jack.*

C.8

Returning to Brisbane

Devil-Devil, Ken, Roma, Drunk

The pub was busy that afternoon. I could not find anyone at reception, so I took it upon myself to go into the main bar where there were about a dozen men drinking. Some were leaning on the bar with one foot up on the foot rail, while others were sitting on stools. All were in their working clothes, from blue singlets with shorts and lace up boots, to the riding boot fraternity with the elastic sides worn and torn, saddle stains on the inside of their riding strides legs. Checked shirts, Jackie Howe singlets, striped Oshkosh flannel shirts. They were all there. Big, hairy, muscular men to small, thin, sinewy blokes and everything in between.

I sidled up to the end of the bar and waited for the Brylcreemed, slicked down haired barman to finish serving drinks.

"What'll you have?"

"Um, I am looking for a lift to Brisbane. Do you know anyone that could help me?" I said, answering his abrupt question.

He turned and faced the row of drinkers. "Anyone going to Brisbane? This here chap's lookin' for a lift."

Everyone looked up from their beers, took a quick look at me, all nodded a negative in unison and went back to their drinking.

"Sorry, I can't help you. Do you wanna beer?"

I said no thanks, but could I leave my pack somewhere?

"Oh, just leave it behind the counter at reception," and off he went to fill some more glasses.

Putting my pack behind the counter, I ventured back out into the main street, hoping to hitch a ride. I watched cars and utes and trucks pass by, but they didn't stop and most were only doing local business. As I watched the slow-paced passing parade, someone from somewhere yelled, "Look out! A devil-devil is coming."

People just vomited out of the pubs, shops and agent's offices. They all appeared from, I don't know, where. I looked west where everyone was looking; I couldn't believe my eyes. A wall, as high as the sky, was descending on top of us. It was made up of huge red clouds, rolling like a wild surf, one on top of the other, coming towards us at incredible speed. A western dust storm was about to envelop the whole town. Most of the town folk ran into buildings, shutting doors and windows. Sticking whatever rags or clothes they could find to jam into cracks and crevices.

All vehicles came to a stop, parked, and the occupants ran for shelter. A few, like me, just stayed and watched the force of nature before us. Litter and leaves and sticks and all sorts of debris swirled before us until we were covered in fine red dust blown with force into every facial and body crevices.

Doubled over and nearly blinded, I managed to get myself inside the hotel. I had to force the door open with all my body weight due to the wind and the packing behind it, but I did manage to get an opening to squeeze through, then someone behind me helped open the door further and we both tumbled in to the bar. Replacing the packing on the floor, the fella behind me said, "I need a beer, you havin' one on me?"

I said, "Why not," and blowing my nose and clearing my ears and mouth of all the fine grit, we joined the throng at the bar.

"The name's Tom, what will you have, a Bulimba or Four X"? I hadn't had a Queensland beer before and I really wasn't old enough to drink in this state. What the hell.

"The name's Jack and give us a Four X."

We shook hands and then my new companion held two fingers up to catch the barman's eyes for our orders. The beer was cold and bitter, but it was just what the doctor ordered and washed the gritty dust away from my tonsils.

"Gee, fancy having a storm like that in winter. We get them in the summer during a drought, but never in the winter."

Tom was a thin chap, not an ounce of fat on him. He didn't look as if he had much muscle either; I guess he was in his early twenties and had one of those prominent Adam's apples that went exploring up and down his throat all the time. A thin neck that seemed to be having difficulty holding his head, because when he leaned back slightly, his neck would bring his head forward and vice versa when he leaned forward. Tom had a nice open personality and humorous blue eyes, with dust in the corners and dust round the edges of his lips, all except where the beer had touched.

I pulled out my few dollars and put them on the counter in front of me. It appeared everyone had their money on the counter and you did not take it off until you left the bar for good. If you went to strain the spuds, *learnt that from Tom and thought it a good way of saying I'm going for a leak*, you still left your smokes and change on the counter to hold your place. I guess if anyone touched it, there would be a killing. Of course, women weren't allowed in the main bar except for barmaids. It was the place for men to escape the fairer sex and talk men stuff. No one wanted to know your business, just your first name, if you're staying or just passing through. If you wanted to say something, that was okay, but you never asked a man's past. As it was my turn for the shout, I followed Tom's queue and held up two fingers. We started on our second beers as the storm still howled outside.

Rolling a smoke, I asked Tom if he knew anyone going to Brisbane as I was looking for a lift. He said he didn't, and anyway, why would you want to go there? I said I had business at the Ekka. I was informed the Ekka did not start until the following Thursday, so why the panic?

Tom continued, "Look Jack, it's Friday tomorrow. A few sheds will be finishing their shearing and there are always a few going in that direction for the weekend. Even if you get to Charleville, it will be some of the way."

And then he stood up and addressed the whole bar.

"Me mate Jack here is looking for a lift to Brisbane. Anyone going?" There was a murmur from the bar, then a stocky bloke piped up from the centre of the throng. "If yer fair dinkum Jack, I will be leaving tomorrow at noon. If you're not here at the bar, then I won't be waiting," then he disappeared in to his drinking circle.

"Well, what about that?" said Tom. "You have your lift. That was Ken. He's a cattle buyer. He's okay, he drives a Ford Customline white ute with a big bull bar and spotties on it. You can't miss it."

Then he added, "Well mate, the storm looks if it has passed, so I better get back to the missus, 'cause if she catches me here drinking the housekeeping, I'm a goner."

We shook hands and said 'seeya' and he made his way to the entrance. I had consumed four beers and decided that was plenty. And anyway, I knew I better book a room for the night and get myself a feed.

"We will only charge you half price love, seeing as all the dust and mess that's about."

Which was okay by me, but everywhere in room six, and I guess in the others, the dust had settled itself. There was about a sixty millimetre layer of dust on the floor, furniture and windowsills. The dust even penetrated the sheets when I turned the cover down. It was incredible and it was everywhere. I decided to remake the bed, shaking the dust out of the bedclothes. It was a silly mistake, as I had now created my own mini dust storm. I made a hasty retreat from the room, coughing and spluttering, deciding it was time for a feed and I'd let the dust resettle itself.

I woke up the next morning with a clogged nose, dry mouth and enough grit in my eyes to feed a parrot; it was time for a shower. It was great, it stunk, but it was great. Changing into fresh clothes, I packed my pack, leaving it behind the receptionist counter and decided that after breakfast I would go and get a haircut and smarten myself up ready for the city.

I was early. Ken was late. After putting my gear into the back of the Customline, we were on our way to Brisbane via Charleville and Roma. Travelling down a mere strip of bitumen wide enough for just one car, which made one divert right off the road for oncoming trucks. Ken was a jovial kind of person, short and stocky, early thirties, clean shaven, with his hat brim turned down at the front and up at the back, which he wore all the time. He inquired if I was in a hurry to get to Brisbane as he had to meet some blokes at Roma and would be staying the night. We talked about everything and nothing; the countryside seemed to me to be changing from semi open to a lot of scrubby country. Mile after mile of this dense galvanized green leafy shrub and trees. Ken said it was mulga, great feed for sheep and good hard wood for wood turning.

Charleville was a big town. The streets were full of people and as we drove to a parking spot at the Corones Hotel, Ken said this was one of the best western pubs, so we might as well have a quick counter lunch, if we were not too late. Ken ordered the fish of the day. I said I would have the same, and pulled out $5.00 to pay for it, telling Ken that it was only fair, seeing he was giving me a lift to 'Brissie'. He would not have a bar of it, saying it was a dutch shout. I had to ask what this meant and was told each pays for his own.

We had a couple of beers while we waited for our meal and I took time to notice the grandeur of this famous hotel. The bar was in the middle of the room, so everyone sat or stood in a huge circle. The pictures on the wall were of past footy and cricket teams, prized rams and bulls and one of a rodeo rider riding a bucking horse, which took my eye.

Back in the ute, feeling full and a bit drowsy, we headed east for Roma. Ken wanted to keep talking to stay alert while driving the next 268 kilometres. We had already covered about three hundred to Charleville. Ken said he had to meet a few chaps at the School of Arts in Roma and would be staying the night. That got me thinking. He didn't seem the sort of person interested in the arts and having a School of Arts in a western town didn't make sense. I wondered if he was an art buyer as well as a cattle buyer. I wouldn't make a fool of myself by asking, but tonight was going to be interesting.

Ken went round to all the cattle sales in Western Queensland, buying cattle for a big meat works company. He would assess the dressed weight of each bullock on the hoof and be able to fill an order for a week's kill. He also arranged the trucking or railing of the cattle and teed up train drovers. All very knowledgeable, but I have just repeated what Ken told me. He liked the travelling and had mates in every town. I was surprised when he told me he was looking forward to getting back to Brisbane to see his wife and three kids.

The drive was starting to get a bit hairy. In the twilight with the sun behind us, it was the time for kangaroos to be hopping across the road. A few times we had to stop the car as mobs of about twenty hopped in front of us without much warning.

I said to Ken, "You wouldn't want to hit one of those big ones."

"That's why I have the bull bar on the front, but they still can cause a lot of damage. I had one on the bonnet and it came through the windscreen, and a small one got caught under the car. Its claw ripped my radiator, which left me stranded out Quilpie way for a couple of days.

"But the worst thing you can hit is a wild pig – look out!"

Ken hit the brakes with the back tyres smoking.

"Well, I'll be buggered," said Ken, "talk about pigs, and a bloody big boar runs right out in front of you. Boy, they can put your car out of action for weeks; the bastards can rip your sump out."

We came to the lights of another big town after passing a few small ones. Ken told me that once there was a town or stop every twenty-five miles for the Cobb and Co coaches. The town was Roma, our destination for the night; I had to smile to myself as we parked outside the School of Arts Hotel in the main street. We walked into the busy main bar and Ken's mates were waiting for him, shaking hands, smiles all around, a few slaps on the back and then I was introduced.

"This is Jack. We are travelling together to Brisbane. Jack, this is Tom, Roy, and Phil." We shook hands and said our good days, even though it was evening now.

"Let's start a fresh shout. You all having beers?" Ken slammed a ten dollar note down on the bar, and soon five beers were pulled. Even though it wasn't meant, I was left out of the conversation as it started out about cattle markets, scoring against other cattle buyers, then about mates they all knew and what they were up to. Then the yarns started.

I murmured a few 'really', and 'you didn't', 'fair dinkum' and 'I never knew that', trying to be part of the group. One thing I noticed, they all had dirt under their fingernails and so did I.

I was starting to feel I was one of the men.

But I had a big worry. I was down at the end of the line, which meant I had to consume four beers. Then it was my shout. How in the hell was I going to be able to drink five beers? I could handle a glass or two of wine, a sherry, and a liqueur, even three swigs of rum from the train drover. But I did have two beers for lunch, and four the night before. To be honest, I really didn't like the stuff all that much. A couple of glasses on a hot day were fine. I was going to find out if I could hold my liquor or not.

My other problem was money. I knew at lunchtime I only had $4.65 left, and it was Saturday tomorrow, so the banks wouldn't be open. So what was I to do? If I spent all my money tonight, what would I have over the weekend? Problem solved.

"Oi, George, can you change a cheque for us?" a customer called to the publican.

"Yeah, no problems, Bill."

It was my shout next.

"Five beers please," I said, holding my hand up, showing five fingers, as the noise of the Friday night drinkers was drowning out any normal conversation. As the five full clean glasses were put down in front of us, the barmaid asked whose shout it was.

The boys looked at me and said, "It's Jack's, the quiet one."

"Yeah, can you cash a cheque for me?" I asked the bottle blonde barmaid.

"It all depends. How much, darl?"

I pulled my fortnightly pay cheque out of my wallet and unfolded it. It was only for $26.00 and handed it to her.

"No worries, darls," she said as she turned to the till to change it. After she put the change on the counter, I never checked it, as I had never seen any of the other men checking theirs.

That was one problem solved. The other at the time was of

more a concern to me. I had consumed three and a half beers and started to feel bloated. In front of me was a glass and a half. I managed to get the half down. But just as I had finished, Ken, who started the shout, was starting the second round. Two full glasses of beer in front of me, I accidentally on purpose knocked one glass and lost half its contents. Then I managed to swallow the other glass down. It sank and rose a few times in my gullet before it rested on the other litres of grog in my stomach.

I had to have a leak.

"Going to strain the spuds," I said to no-one in particular and made my way to the gents.

I stood up to the urinal, unbuttoned my fly and just let it all hang out. I raised and folded my arms and leant them against the wall with my head resting on them. I pulled my buttocks back to give the urine a good clean flow. I must have been there a minute before the relief started to flow through my body. I just wee'd and wee'd like I had never done before. I didn't care about anyone or anything at that urinal; I just had to get rid of all that beer. Giving it a good shake and buttoning up, I felt so much lighter, but the door shifted a bit when I tried to open it. The barstool moved too, as I nearly missed the seat, and my elbows didn't quite connect to the bar top.

What the hell! In front of me were four beers lined up just for me. I forced two down and then my gullet refused to take the rest. It just wouldn't open. Then, "C'mon Jack, it's your shout."

I paid for four and told the barmaid I had enough in front of me to down; she seemed to appreciate my situation and I was spared another humiliating full glass lined up in front of me.

My head was being split open. My neck was stiff as a board, my mouth felt like number three sandpaper and my feet were freezing. I was sick. I wanted to die, trying to get my bearings. I was jammed up in the front seat of a car, my right arm was trapped through the steering wheel and my feet were sticking outside the window, one shoe and sock off. Where was I?

Getting out of the car, I went all dizzy and the world started to spin. I promptly sat on the dewy grass, getting a wet bum. I heard movement in the back of the ute.

"Is that you Jack?"

I answered saying, "Where in the hell am I and gee I feel crook."

Ken's head appeared over the side of the ute.

"You got yourself pissed last night and I had to drag you out of the pub semi-conscious. Then we drove out of town for a camp."

He crawled out of his swag and told me to freshen myself up over at the dam in the nearby paddock. I took my towel and soap, crawled through the barbed wire fence and did something I never thought I would, and that was, strip off all my clothes and jump in to the brown muddy water. The shock of the freezing water made me gasp for air and did not make my splitting head any better. I washed myself and added some more fluid to the dam before wading out and drying myself on the banks. I am a very modest fellow, and for me to be butt naked in the middle of open surroundings a few metres off a main road will demonstrate how I was feeling that Saturday morning. Definitely not myself.

"Its 6.30 A.M. If we get a move on, we can have breakfast at Miles. It's only another 150 kilometres, and we should be able to do the other three hundred to Brisbane and be there by two o'clock. That suit you, Jack? And where do you want to be dropped off?"

"Oh, anywhere in the city will do. I have to find some lodgings. That would be great, thank you."

"Well, I have to go through the city to get to my family at Windsor. I will drop you off at Upper Edward Street. There's a few good boarding houses you could stay at. And by the way, I got your money that you left at the bar last night. 's in the glove box."

"Gee, thanks Ken. I had forgotten all about it." I opened the glove box.

"It's in the brown envelope," my companion advised. I stuck it in my pocket, not wanting to count it as I didn't want to seem untrusting, but I was worried how much was left.

"A good greasy breakfast of bacon and eggs and sausages with some black coffee will do you good." I was told at the diner in Miles where we were checking the menu out.

Ken was right. The smell nearly made me puke, but I didn't feel too bad after I finished my meal.

"Look Jack, it's none of my business, but do you mind if I give you a bit of advice? You're a great bloke and you will make it out west, but don't leave all your money on a bar. Only enough to cover what you're about to drink. Keep more in your pocket than on the bar, and you will always have money. And Jack, when you have had enough and given it your best shot, whether it's drink, a fight, a job or a woman, call it quits. No real man would condemn you."

We made it to Brisbane by 2.30 P.M. Back to a noisy, smelly city. Ken dropped me off at *The Alexander's*, a good boarding house. I thanked Ken for giving me the lift down and saving me and my money at Roma last night. We shook hands and said our goodbyes, and then he drove off with a toot of the horn and a wave of his hand.

C.9

The Ekka

Down & Out, Lostmans, The Interview

The boarding house wasn't posh but it was clean. You knew that by the smell of cleaners and disinfectants that had been used.

"No meals, front door closes at 10 P.M., alcohol and friends not allowed and a week in advance, thank you, and that will be $10.00." All said in one breath, by a very large woman who filled the front door entrance. My room was on the first floor, overlooking the street. It had the essentials, a made-up bed slightly saggy with a rather loud floral bed cover, dressing table, wardrobe, bedside table with lamp, curtains for privacy, a square of carpet on the linoleum, and the bathroom down the passage. Yes, there was a further order of not spending more than ten minutes in the bathroom, 'as one has to think of the other guests.'

I paid the woman the $10.00 out of the brown envelope Ken had put my change in from the pub last night. I counted what was left. A slight sickness took my stomach, as there was only $9.35 left.

Pay cheque was $26.00. Paid my accommodation $10.00, breakfast 80c, a packet of Rothmans, 50c. Where in the hell did the other $5.40 go? I could not have spent that much at the pub, could I?

How in the hell am I going to live on $9.00 for the next week and that is if I get a job straight away? The $20.00 emergency money put in the bank before I left for Blackall was still there, but that was for a dire emergency, and I was not going to ask for help from home. Never!

I decided on a strict plan. Find a cheaper place to stay, roll your own smokes only, have fruit and cereal for breakfast, no lunch, a healthy dinner, find a good cheap place for meals, and not to spend a cent on anything else. Today being Saturday and the Ekka not starting till the following Thursday, I had to survive in a strange city for five days and had nothing to do.

Walking down Edward Street, passing the Saturday night crowds, I remembered a little café under the People's Palace building, looked at the small menu. The pie and mash with peas suited my budget at 30c and that included a cup of tea. The other occupants were definitely not part of the evening crowd going to the restaurant and the theatre. They were people like me - poor.

I did find a cheaper place. It was called Lostmans Motel, off a little side street from where I was staying, but at this time it was not for me, so I stayed at the Alexander for the week.

I kept to my plan. There is nothing to talk about regarding the next five days. They were boring, reading old newspapers and magazines, washing and ironing, writing letters and sending them without stamps. Telling my mum I had found a better position and would notify her of my new address soon. Long walks, keeping well away from shops in case I weakened, exploring the nooks and crannies of Brisbane were my only activities that week.

Thursday at last, the start of the Ekka. A lean, hungry chap with slicked down hair, ironed shirt and trousers paid his way into the Ekka. It was me. As I passed through the turnstiles, I thought this was the gateway to my future. May it be good. The building where all the agents were situated was near the cattle pavilion. Walking in the front door and down a passageway with the agents' shingles hanging each side of it, I found Mike Chudley's office and asked the young man at the wooden counter if I could see him.

"He is not here now, its best you call around lunchtime about 12.45. Who may I say is wanting to see him?"

"It's Jack Alexander and yes, I will come back at lunchtime."

That gave me three hours to fill in, so an exploration of the great Ekka should fill the time nicely.

It wasn't really crowded as it was the first day and stallholders and exhibitors were putting the final touches to everything. The cattle pavilion was nearby, so I checked it out. Young men and women were grooming massive bulls, curling their hair with curry combs, others outside were shampooing the beasts. They all looked impressive, but I just couldn't imagine them out in the paddock at Blackall. They were just too fat, but what do I know? I was interested to see some Brahmans with their big humps and large flappy ears, probably to keep the flies out of their eyes. They were new to the show and supposed to be the upcoming breed for Northern Australia.

The smell of straw, cattle, country, and Queensland were all there in that pavilion. And to be honest, I did envy those young men and women, their casualness and confidence around those huge animals, tanned, fit, healthy and fun loving and working with animals. They were my goals. Next the horse stalls. No way was I interested in the craft and cookery pavilion or even the vegetable stands. I had my share, dragged around as a kid, spending hours of useless life in pavilions at the Royal Melbourne show with my grandmother. Okay, a few minutes with the animals and sideshow alley but we always had to leave before the night-time rodeo.

I loved the horses, big, small, grand. There were haughty types that looked down at you as if you were a lower life, nippy little ponies with, oh so darling, looks, and the congenial gentle giants - the draught horses, and everything in between. Slim girls in tight riding britches with bouncy ponytails, big bum girls that could throw a full-grown man and every type of human for every type of horse. I was amused that with the big draught horses, only small slight men were in their attendance. Smells of leather, polish, straw and horse poop were pleasant aromas to me, even though I was slightly scared of these large animals, or should I say, had a healthy respect for them. I knew then, whether I liked it or not, horses would play a large part in my life.

Back at the agents' building at one, I saw Mike Chudley chatting to a typical grazier type. I waited for them to finish and as the grazier left, and Mr Chudley turned into his office, I said, "Excuse me, Mr Chudley?"

He turned round and said, "Yes?"

"Uh, the name's Jack Alexander. I spoke with you a couple of weeks ago and you said you could help me with a position as a jackaroo on a stud at Meandarra."

"Oh yes, I remember, as a matter of fact I spoke to the owner, Mr Short, about you and he seems interested and would like to meet you. He has the flu and said to meet him at the Hereford stand in the lower cattle pavilion at 10 A.M. sharp on Monday morning. The stud's name is Tee Tree. Can you be there?"

"No worries, I'll be there and thanks." I hoped I didn't sound too disappointed, but another four days to survive on limited capital? Hell!

I went without lunch, tightening the belt another notch, and thought I was here now, so I might as well spend the rest of the day at the show. I tried to educate myself. I sat on tractors and bulldozers and tried to work out what all the levers and pedals did, without the motors going. Seeing the farming implements and making a fool of myself asking what this machine did and what that one did. I did not care because they didn't know me. I learnt about windmills and pumps, and so many things that I forgot most of it by the end of the day. There was side show alley with fairy floss, monkeys on sticks, kewpie dolls, whistles, masks and fake spiders on strings.

I stood outside Jimmy Sharman's boxing tent hearing the decent thumping of the drum and, "Anyone wanting a go? Ten dollars. Who can go a round with Slasher Jack?" yelled Jimmy Sharman.

For a mad second, I thought I would have a go. Ten dollars was something I needed very badly. The showman noticed my interest and pointed at me and said, "Here young fella, you want a go? Step up here."

Boom, boom went the drum as the crowd looked at me. "C'mon fella, step up here, see if yous can go one round and ya earn yourself a tenner."

For another mad second, I had a silly thought. Then I remembered the only fights I had were with my sister and she always won. Slasher Jack would have murdered me. I smiled at the showman, nodded my head, and pushed my way through the crowd to escape to a more congenial sideshow.

There was one which advertised, 'Come and see the man-eating shark'. But I read in a discarded newspaper afterwards. they closed that show later in the day, as it was a con. You paid 20c to see pictures of man-eating sharks and in the ring was a man eating a piece of flake, which is the name for shark meat. I was tired by the time I walked back to the boarding house; I had a shower, my last smoke, and went to bed without dinner. I was thinking I would have to move out of this accommodation in the morning and see if I could get a bed at Lostmans Motel, which didn't excite me one little bit.

I was starving. I got up early, walked down to the Salvation Army's café and had a good breakfast of cereal, scrambled eggs, a double helping of toast and a pot of tea. On my way back, I called into Lostmans Motel to enquire about a room for the next five days. The unshaven two-day grey growth on the short bald man with the brown knitted jumper unravelling at the elbows, seemed surprised to see me.

"We seldom have your type here, but we can let you have a bed here for 25c a night. That okay by you?"

"Could I see the room?" I asked.

He led me through the hallway with the frayed carpet, the wallpaper starting to peel off and sticky flypaper hanging from the ceiling with its catch of flies and insects on them. He opened the door on the left and showed me into a room with six beds, six small bedside tables with ashtrays and six small wardrobes, two standard windows, four sticky fly papers and a lonely light in the middle without a shade.

"You can have the bed beside that window." He pointed to the far wall. "We change the sheets when you leave and all the other beds are in use." Then, closing the door, he led me to the bathroom and toilets at the back of the house.

"It will cost ya three cents for a hot shower. Just put it in the meter. Now you stayin' or going?"

I didn't have a choice. I said I would pick up my things and be back later in the day as I handed him a precious $1.25 for the five nights.

I gathered up my things from the boarding house, tried to get a refund for a day but all I got was a finger pointing to a sign saying, no refunds given. I said goodbye as I turned toward the door but my host had already disappeared.

The bed was old but not too saggy, the lino was old but clean, the furnishings matched the rest of the décor and the bedside table was covered with cigarette burns and stains. I didn't know it then, but I was going to experience another type of life I had never dreamed of, would hear words that I had never dared utter. Experienced things that made me thankful for my life and frightened me out of my wits about what life could be all about.

They started coming in about ten o'clock. Some drunk, some stumbling around cursing, some shuffling to their prospective beds, hoping they wouldn't be noticed. They all entered without switching the light on. All had 'roll yer own' butts hanging out of their mouths, some alight, some not. All undressed to their underwear and socks and slipped into the paper-thin sheets and the two old grey army blankets that wouldn't keep a dog warm on a summer's night, but the room was warm now with six bodies breathing in the dusty air.

I can best describe the events of the first night as the same as every night I stayed at the Lostmans Motel. Bill, a large man with a huge gut on him, was the first bed on the sidewall nearest me. Little Norm was in the next bed beside Bill. Don was on the other side wall nearest me, then Eric and Ralph were on the opposite wall where the door was. I could observe all my roommates from my position and thank god, I had a window. I propped it open a bit so I could get some fresh air. The adventure of the night about to unfold before me was to prove my action of opening the window was one of inspirational forethought.

We all settled down to sleep with grunts, mumbles, burps and farts, tossing and turning, punching pillows, yorking up a golly from the depths of the inner throat and expelling it on the floor. It was enough for me to be thankful that I went to the toilet beforehand and wouldn't have to negotiate the slag on the floor. I was amazingly asleep when I was woken up by, "You bitch, you fuckin' bloody bitch, you bitch, I oughta jam your rotten mouth with hot bitumen, you slut!"

I opened my eyes to see where the sound was coming from and I could see Bill in the moonlit room, sound asleep, lying right on the edge of the bed. His whopping stomach over the bed's edge. How he stayed on the bed without falling on the floor beats me. It would only take the slightest of breezes to send him crashing to the floor. Yes, it was him talking in his sleep. I guess he was on the very edge of the bed to be far as possible away from the imaginary wife beside him. "Ya bitch, you rotten stinking bitch."

Then Eric started whimpering. "I didn't mean it, oh god, I didn't mean it. Killed you all, all of you. Oh god, how I loved you. I didn't mean it." He started sobbing again. I later learnt his wife and two young children were killed in a car accident twenty years ago and that he was driving. Norm then started getting out of his bed and walking around, opening and shutting the door. I wasn't sure if he was awake or not, but he did this, if not six times a night, at least ten. I think being in a German prison for a few years during the war started the habit. Ralph, I think, was a bit simple. He giggled and his little body shook as he giggled. He giggled in his sleep, he giggled when he was awake and he giggled in the toilet. Don was always drunk. He mumbled about women; he mumbled about pig iron Bob Menzies. He told us we were all curried turds and swore at us all. He was the one who vomited at least once a night. The liquid puke would snake across the floor, picking up snot and spit on its way towards me.

All night long, it was cursing, crying, giggling, banging doors and footsteps, spitting and vomiting, rustling, and snoring, mumbling and yelling and it was the same every night. I used to stay awake most of the night seeing if Bill would fall off his bed, but he never did.

I listened to the cries and sounds of men who were dealt a rotten blow in their lives, needing love, help and companionship. I found out later, Bill's wife, by stealth, had taken a lover. His news agency, his house and possessions had been left to him by his parents. While he was doing early morning deliveries and running the business, he let his wife run the financial side of things, much to his regret.

You know about poor Eric losing his young family and never recovering, and Norm, who went through hell in the war. Giggling Ralph was a mechanic and the hoist gave way while he was working on a car and he suffered brain damage. His family couldn't cope with him and threw him out. There weren't many social services in those days. Don's family rejected his disgusting, drunken ways. He had been a successful businessman and family man that became an alcoholic and bankrupt. I learnt a lot from these broken men and their stories. I swore to myself that my life was going to have rules in it that would never let me end up in a Lostmans Motel ever again.

There were two other rooms in the motel, which were the same as mine and I guess housing the same type of characters. The men all rose early, about six, I think, to get in early to queue up for their free breakfast kindly donated by the Salvos. I would be tired after watching and listening to the antics of my fellow roommates, so with my nose toward the open window for fresh air, I managed a snooze for the next hour or so. Then I would get up, walk, no tiptoe on my toenails, the childhood ballet lessons came in handy after all, to miss the nights goo on the floor. Paid my three cents for a great hot shower, made my bed and got out of the rooms before eight thirty.

The cleaning woman came in at 8.30 A.M. She was old and cranky and very wrinkled, with extremely bandy legs. I often wondered how she put her knickers on in the morning. She washed and mopped the disgusting floor till it was presentable again. That was all she did. Washed and mopped the three rooms every morning and gave the showers and toilets a quick wipe over. The men always made their beds and kept their meager belongings very tidy. They took their time, painfully slow, making sure the blankets were just folded right, ends tucked in, shoes evenly put under their beds and clothes, old and threadbare, were treated as if they were of the finest silk. Why? Because it helped fill in the long days of absolutely nothing to do. Rolling a cigarette was the greatest of pastimes. The whole process could take up to forty-five minutes.

First, you have to arrange all the equipment. Take out your old, dented log cabin tin, look at it, then take the lid off and gently place the tin and lid on the table. Then search each pocket carefully until you find your Tally-Ho or boomerang papers and place these next to the tin. Another search to find the matches and place them beside the other implements. Now the exciting bit, a feel of the left-hand shirt pocket will produce butts. These would have been lovingly picked up the day before from the gutter or footpath and saved. A count and a second count to make sure you have them all and to see if it beat yesterday's collection. Each butt is carefully unwrapped from its chewed paper, or the filter tip taken out and the contents are placed in the open tin. This is done with shaky fingers and care that one does not lose one strand of tobacco. When all the butts are emptied, the leftover bits of paper are brushed to the floor.

Then very slowly, a paper is pulled out of the Tally-Ho packet and inspected for the thin bit of glue on one side. This is then placed onto the lips, not too far, as you don't want the paper wet. Then a pinch of tobacco kneaded into your left palm with the closed bottom of your right fist. Taking the paper from your lips and again inspecting it for the glue side, you place the tobacco in the creased middle, gently playing it out along the length of the paper. Then you gently roll it without any tobacco coming out each end. The tip of a pink tongue moistens the paper and the job is done, except for getting a match and poking each end in to make sure no tobacco is lost. The cigarette is then put behind the ear. As the utensils are put into their prospective pockets, a feel in the right-hand pocket ends up finding a good size butt, which is duly lit with a sigh of satisfaction. The one just rolled, now behind the ear, completely forgotten.

I often talked to the men. They seemed pleased with my companionship and I got a lot of advice from them, as it was very rare for young people to end up where I was at that time. I found out where the best restaurants and cafés were for handouts at the back door, *tips I didn't use,* where you can get cheap tobacco, *got some, as I was desperate* and they told me where to queue up early in the mornings for a free feed, *which I did.*

To keep myself occupied for the next few days, I took long walks to the botanical gardens and read left over newspapers. Once I went to a doctor's surgery, *waiting for someone, so I said,* and read some magazines to fill in time.

Monday morning at last. Spruced up, I walked to the show grounds and wondered how I could get in without paying. I noticed families would go through the turnstiles and the father would go last and hand the attendant all the tickets. I sneaked into the queue between some kids and their parents, talking to the kids about what they were going to see and what sample bags they were getting. I managed to pass through the turnstiles, thankful for my younger than age looks and my small stature. They didn't notice. I said, "Have a good time," to the kids and hurried away, leaving a father arguing about how many kids he should pay for, to be on time for my ten o'clock appointment with Mr Short at the bull stalls.

I got there at 9.55 A.M. and found the stud. They had a big banner with Tee Tree Hereford Stud and lots of blue and white championship ribbons decorating it. There were two men standing there. One was about thirty, big and tall with a ruddy red face and ginger hair receding, and the other, an elderly small man dressed to the nines with a moustache face that looked as if it had been squashed by a vice.

I said in my best manly voice, "Mr Short?"

The small man turned and looked at me and replied with a curt, "Yes, what do you want?"

"My name is Jack Alexander. Mr Chudley said that you might have a jackaroo's job for me."

He looked at his watch and said, "You are five minutes late. Come and see me tomorrow at nine o'clock sharp. This time be on time." I looked at my watch, which I had thoroughly checked by other clocks, and I was still two minutes early. But he had turned away, ignoring me and finishing his conversation with the ginger-headed bloke.

I walked away in despair, with a sick feeling in my stomach. Gosh, I was in no position to be mucked about with. Here am I, desperate for a job at the lowest position I have ever been in my life. *Why, why should I put up with this?* I thought. *Go to some other agents. You're sure to get a job with one of the hundreds of graziers at the show.* But I did not think of that. I was like a drowning man clutching a straw. I wasn't game to let go and try something else. This was my only hope.

With my rejected feelings, I walked the inside of the show grounds fence, the best I could, going around buildings, the railway station, and obstacles. Then I did the same on the outside. The purpose was to find a weak spot so I could sneak in tomorrow again without paying. It was good to get my mind off my real problem and the walking and exercise did my body good. At the eastern side of the grounds, the fence was not as high or barbed like most of the rest of the fence and I noticed cars were parked beside the weakest spot. If it was the same the next day, I could climb on one of the cars and get myself over the fence. I prayed it wouldn't be a sports car or one with a soft-top parked there or I would be in strife. I don't think I mentioned that you had to be out of the rooms I was staying in by 8.30 A.M. and were not allowed back until 4.30 P.M. I felt like the other men, doing things slowly to fill the day in.

Showered and spruced up again, a free breakfast at the Salvos and a walk up to the back of the show grounds, I arrived nice and early to be on time. But alas, too early, as there were no cars parked at the spot I selected to get over the wall. I dared not wait till one came. Panic set in, as I just couldn't afford to pay my way in. If I did, I wouldn't be able to have my only other meal for the day. Walking back down the road, I spied some trucks and horse floats with horses in them, going through the gate. The drivers showed their passes to the attendant as they went through to the show arena. It wasn't any clever thought on my part, it must have been survival instinct, I jumped on to the back of the last horse float just balancing on the thin edge with my toes, hands holding on to the top of the back door like grim death. There must have been some mental telepathy between me and one of the horses because as we were passing through the gate, he swished his tail over the back door and covered my top half with his tail. I was very thankful for this, but I wished he had not done a sloppy one beforehand as his tail was covered in it. Besides the digested grass and oats splattering my face and my hair, my white shirt was flecked with the brown stuff. I got into the grounds again without paying for the second time. Finding a drinking fountain, I managed to clean my face and hair up with my hankie, but I just made it worse when I tried to clean it off my shirt and jacket. Well, what the hell, I smell like country.

I was in the cattle pavilion at 8.40 A.M. I saw the big ginger-headed man and told him I was to meet Mr Short. He introduced himself as Tom, the bull groom for the Hereford stud and told me Mr Short would be sometime and to wait, and wait I did, till he arrived at twenty to ten. I felt like looking at my watch and saying, "You're late," but being polite and desperate, I just said, "Mr Short, I am here about the job."

A grunt was all the reply I got, then, "You will have to come tomorrow. My wife's gone shopping and she will want to talk to you before I make a decision. Be here at eleven sharp." And then he just walked away.

I was seething; I was mad; I was scared; I was all screwed up. Another day, another night, another payment for my bed, another boring twenty-four hours to fill in and just one dollar twenty in my pocket. Will I make it? Will I get the job? Or horror of horrors, will I have to confess to my family I cannot make it on my own? Never!

With a heavy heart, I walked my way down to Queen Street and withdrew $10.00 of my precious $20.00 emergency fund from the bank. I felt guilty and a failure, because when I deposited the money, everything was rosy only three weeks ago and now I was hungry and desperate and not very pleased with myself. I passed the café where I had my congratulatory dinner after getting the job at Blackall. I stopped. Bugger it, why not? I needed a lift, so I went in, ordered a mixed grill with the lot, one of them cappuccino coffees and a packet of Rothmans, please.

While I waited for my order, I glanced at the other diners. An old couple looked familiar. Could it be? Yes, it was Harold and Gladys. The first Brisbane-ites who kindly shouted me tea and pikelets when I first arrived. I slid out from my seat and approached them, really needing someone to talk to.

"G'day, it's me, Jack Alexander, the chap wanting to be a jackaroo." They both looked up, a bit startled, and then Harold smiled. "Well boy, it's good to see you. What, no job yet?"

So I told them everything, getting the job, the sack, all except where I was staying and how broke I was.

"Oh Jack, where are you staying? And have you enough money till you get a new job?" enquired Gladys, with a very concerned expression on her face. "You know we have a spare room. Harold, Jack could stay with us, couldn't he?"

"Of course he can if he wants to, but dear, I think Jack's on a mission. Jack, here is our phone number." He scribbled it on a serviette. "Please give us a ring when and if you need a feed or accommodation. Gladys and I would welcome you anytime in our home."

The waitress brought my meal over after looking around to see where I was. "Well, Jack you have had an adventure," continued Harold, "now you are sure of getting a job with Mr Short this week?"

"Oh, no doubt," said I, full of confidence, "I believe it's somewhere near Meandarra, wherever that is."

"That's just north of where our daughter Lucy is. She lives at Goondiwindi, isn't that right Harold?"

"Yes dear, it's not far from Meandarra," said Harold, giving his wife an admiring smile.

We made small talk, then the old couple excused themselves as they had finished their tea and had an appointment to attend to.

"Well Jack, all the best for the new job and don't feel too bad about losing the other one. Experience is the best educator, and you are going through one of life's educational processes, if you get my meaning. You are a fighter, son, and you will get somewhere one day, I am sure," said Harold, giving me a firm handshake.

"Jack, please give us a call if you need a bed, anytime! Now you have our number, haven't you?" said Gladys. I said I would and how pleased I was to see them again.

I stood up as they left the table. "Thanks for being here." I don't know if they realised how important it was for me to meet them at this time. I watched the elderly couple, arm in arm, as they made their way to the cash register, thinking 'God bless them.' I wanted to take up their kind offer of accommodation, but no, I had to do this by myself. Harold was right, I was on a mission. Yes, a mission to be a man!

I felt so much better; my stomach was fuller than it had ever been in the last two weeks. The luxury of a tailor made and my spirits had picked up no end. I even noticed a bit of a bounce to my step, as I must have been starting to shuffle like my roommates. I went to the news agency and bought a reader's digest and a phantom comic, went to the gardens and read and smoked till the lucky people were leaving their jobs and hurrying home to their loved ones after the day's work.

It was 10 A.M. Thursday morning. I have always been honest and tried to do the right thing; I felt so guilty sneaking in to the showgrounds without paying. I approached the attendant at the gate where I snuck in on the back of the horse float yesterday and said, "Excuse me, but I am seeking employment as a jackaroo. I must see my prospective employer in the cattle pavilion. I can't afford to pay. Will you let me in?"

The grandfatherly type wrinkled his already wrinkled face with a smile and said, "Son, I am going to look at that truck over there. When I turn around, I do not want to see you again." He turned. I scooted past into the grounds as fast as I could, feeling so much better for being honest.

I was on time and so were they. Talking to Mr Short was a tall woman smartly dressed, hat and white gloves, black hair tied back in a bun with a few wisps of hair on her forehead, a long pointy chin matching a long stern-looking face. This had to be Mrs Short.

"This is the lad I was telling you about, dear," said Mr Short as he and his wife proceeded to sit on bales of straw, which were placed on their sides as a border between the bulls and the thoroughfare. So here was I, standing facing, not only my two seated prospective employers but also the backsides of four massive Hereford bulls, with the hairy end bits of their tails beautifully fluffed out, inches away from the backs of the Shorts.

I was asked my age, where I went to school, what my mother did – librarian – what my father did – salesman. I told them they were separated when I was young, *big mistake*, and what was I doing in Queensland? Who was I running away from and why did I want this job? I thought my answers were satisfactory and were honest. Yes, I could milk a cow, no I couldn't kill, and yes, I have had some experience with horses and sheep in Victoria. Then I was ignored. I felt as if I was a slave standing in front of them as they discussed me.

"Well dear, what do you think of him?" asked Mr Short.

"Well, I don't know. Is he strong enough for what you want?" said the wife.

"Well, he has to work for you too," said the husband.

"But it's your decision," said the wife.

"I don't like taking on a kid from a broken home. They always cause trouble, what do you think?" said the husband.

"As I said it's up to you dear, but he does look a decent type, but will he be experienced enough for what you want?" said the wife.

As I was being discussed, I was looking from one to the other as if at a tennis match. This indecision going back and forth was starting to drive me crazy. Would I get the job? Would I not? Would I get it? Would I?

Then, to my utmost dismay and unbelievable horror, I noticed one of the bull's tails starting to lift, directly behind Mrs Short. I could see the anus starting to take action. I opened my mouth to shout a warning, but not a sound came out. Frozen on the spot, my eyes expanded as the aperture of the bull's anus expanded. They noticed my mortified look, turned round, and moved out of the way quickly, standing up just in time to miss the expelled gravy, grain and hay.

Mr Short said, "We will give you a month's trial. Be here at 9.30 on Saturday morning and you can help Tom, the bull groom, load the cattle and come with him back to the property."

As he spoke, Tom came from nowhere.

"Tom, we are going to give this young fella a go. This is Tom. What's your name again?"

"Er, Jack Alexander," I answered and put out my hand to shake Tom's.

"As I was saying, we are giving the young fellow a go and he will be here at 9.30 A.M. on Saturday to help load the bulls."

Tom and I acknowledge the order. Tom went to get a fork to clean up the unexpected mess. The Shorts dismissed me by turning and walking out of the pavilion and I went the other way.

I should have felt exhilarated. I felt some relief as I walked away, but I worried that the future was going to be a little tough for a while. I had a job, that was the most important thing. I was a functioning human again, and I only had to spend two more nights at the motel. It passed my mind to get other accommodation and spend some money on some much-needed things as I did not know how far out of town I would be and what opportunities I would have to buy some necessities. Having no idea on wage or conditions, and the feeling of not obtaining the best position I might have, it was decided that I would keep to my budget until my financial position was much more secure.

I managed to sneak back to the motel well before the 4.30 P.M. opening time and sorted all my gear out. I did some washing in the old Pope washing machine with the ringer on the top. I had previously spied it in a room next to the bathroom. Whether it was for guests' use or not, I didn't know, but I badly needed to properly wash and iron my clothes. Previously, I would hand wash what I was wearing the day before, while in the shower the following morning and hang them out on the prop clothesline out the back, to dry.

That's something Queensland weather was good at, drying clothes in a day. In Melbourne, it could take a week. Surprisingly, I knew and felt that my gear was quite safe. I did not have anything really valuable, but it seemed while I was at Lostmans Motel my personal property was just that, and for a roommate to borrow or steal from a fellow boarder, could end up in a death. There was a strong code of ethics amongst the men who had nothing.

Friday passed slowly. I shouted myself to the pictures that evening and arrived back at the motel the same time as the other boarders. I told them I had a job and that I would be leaving in the morning. They nodded and wished me luck. Bill came over, shook my hand and said, "I never want to see you here again."

Don told the curried turds to shut up, and Ralph giggled. Another night of grunts, swearing, farting, vomiting, and calling out to ghosts. I got up early, showered and packed my things and went outside for an early morning stroll down to my old breakfast place underneath the People's Palace. When I got back to pick up my things, all the men had gone. I felt I should do something for them; I had a second chance and I will have more in my young life. These men will never ever have another chance; they are doomed until they are dead. I went to the corner shop and changed $3.00 into 20c pieces then I placed 40c and two Rothmans into my last six envelopes, sealed them and putting a roommate's name on the front, I left an envelope on each of their beds. Those men in their way taught me about life, a life I may never have learnt of if our paths had never crossed. I often think of them when I am down or depressed, for without fortitude, direction and sticking to the rules of good living and luck, by the grace of God go I.

C.10

Back to the Bush

Bulls, One of the Stock, The Shorts, Liver

I was employed. I paid my way in and got to the cattle pavilion with all my worldly processions. This was no small feat, as the show grounds were a good two uphill kilometres from the motel. With my rucksack bulging, my boots hanging from the outside, and carrying a small TAA airbag with my sleeping bag attached to the handles, I struggled to make my 9.30 A.M. appointment, but make it, I did. Flustered and exhausted, but I was there! Mr Short or his missus were nowhere about, but Tom was.

"Look mate, you didn't have to be here this early. There is not much to do until we start packing up and we are not allowed to move from the grounds till after twelve noon. Come with me and I will show you where to put yer gear, 'cause things walk here."

He took me to the end of the stalls where there was a very small, locked room full of show halters, gray dust coats, buckets and forks, feed bags, grooming gear, bales of straw and a swag. There was hardly an inch of room to put my gear, but I managed.

Tom grabbed one of the gray dust coats indicating for me to put it on, saying, "While you're waiting, you might as well keep your eyes on the bulls. Make sure no cheeky kids pull their tails or stick an ice cream up their bum. That really makes 'em go mad, and pick up any droppings with this fork and put it in the pile over in the corner." He then told me he wanted to get into town to buy some things before we headed off to Meandarra later that afternoon.

Well, ain't life funny? Last week I was enviously looking at the grooms and jackaroos of the stud cattle, and blow me down, here I was now one of them. I was a proud man looking after my charges, picking up an occasional dropping and answering questions from the curious city passers-by. Not knowing the answers, as I was no wiser than they were, but because I had the dustcoat on and leaned intelligently on the manure fork, I just had to make up what I didn't know.

"Why do the bulls have rings in their noses?"

"Because they didn't fit on their finger!"

I went busily away, fluffing up the straw around the cattle. There were eight in all, four bulls, two heifers and two bull calves. I enjoyed myself that Saturday morning and I felt comfortable being around the cattle. It was the same feeling with the horse and dogs at Farlee Station. It was as if I had been with animals before, maybe in my last life? I don't know.

Tom came back in a hurry. "Listen mate, go and get yourself a quick feed as it will probably be the last one you get today. And get back as soon as you can because we are allowed to move out of the pavilion/ I have parked the truck ready for loading."

There was a food place just near the pavilion, so I ordered a hamburger with the works and chocolate flavoured milk and a roll of peppermint lifesavers for afters. Only being away less than twenty minutes, I was amazed how quick the little room was emptied of all the gear. Even mine was gone. Tom came back around the corner with another man; he was introduced to me as Gordon Hand, the new cowboy for the stud. There were going to be two new employees then.

Gordon did not fit my image of what a cowboy should look like. He was tall, blond, and gangly, with long blond fluff on his red and marked face, a bobbing Adam's apple, a hooked nose and squinty blue eyes. How old he was, it was hard to tell, maybe twenty, maybe a lot more. He had one of those ageless faces. Gordon was not the best dressed either. A checked shirt that looked if it was washed in muddy water, a pair of unironed cotton drill trousers which billowed out at the knees, as if he had spent a lot of time sitting down and a pair of black lace-up boots which hadn't seen polish since they were bought. Shaking his hand was like shaking a wet slimy eel. He smiled, showing surprisingly white even teeth and said, "Glad to meet you."

I answered, letting his hand go quickly and wiping mine on the dustcoat. "Yeah, and I am pleased to meet you, too."

"We've got all the gear on the truck, including yours, Jack. All we must do is load the cattle," said Tom as he handed me and Gordon a lead rope. "We will load the bulls first and the heifers and bull calves last. Jack, you get Sid, Gordon, you get Fred and I will lead Mansfield. Now have you led bulls before?"

We both nodded a negative.

"Well, that's okay, all you have to do is clip the lead I gave you to the nose ring, undo the lead rope from the ring in the wall that's connected to the halter. Then walk beside the beast's shoulder with both leads slightly loose. If the bull gives any trouble, they won't, all you have to do is give the lead rope connected to the nose ring an upward jerk. You both got that?" *So that's what the nose ring was used for.*

We nodded a yes.

"Well, what are you waiting for? Let's go. I will lead the way, then Gordon and Jack can follow up behind."

To tell the truth, I felt a bit nervous as my bull Sid was the biggest of them all. He was massive indeed. He won a championship ribbon for best all breed bull of the show. I clipped the lead on to his nose ring, undid the rope from the ring on the wall and waited till Tom and Gordon had their charges ready, then followed behind them out of the pavilion.

I was surprised this huge beast walking beside me wasn't lumbering or moving in an agitated manner but was actually gliding. It reminded me of some ballroom dancing classes I was conned into going to when I was about fourteen years of age. The teacher was a huge German fraulein with bosoms to match; she admonished me about not holding my partner close. I could not. My partner had nice little budding breasts, but I had something budding somewhere else. This very large teacher grabbed me, pressing my body close to hers, my face jammed in between her large breasts, my bum sticking out as much as it could to save me from mortified embarrassment. But I also remembered how such a big woman could feel so light as she waltzed over the dance floor. It was that same rhythmic motion that Sid the bull had as we walked together toward the Bedford truck.

The first three walked up the ramp without any trouble and were tied by the lead rope of the halter to a rail in the truck's crate. Tom told Gordon to stay and watch the three bulls while he and I got the others. I brought up the last remaining bull, Keith, while Tom brought up one of the bull calves. There was a dividing gate in the truck's crate. When the bulls were in, the dividing gate was closed. Then the heifers and bull calves would have the rear section for themselves. Everything went well until the last heifer had to be loaded. She just refused to walk up the ramp and be with her mates. She pulled back, tossed her head sideways, trying to get out of the halter and being a real problem. Gordon and I were told to go to the back of the heifer, one each side, clasp hands, and with our arms at the beast's backside, push her up the ramp while Tom pulled on the lead rope. We got her there eventually, tied her up, lifted the ramp up, which was part of the back door of the truck's crate and locked it in to place.

Now we had a problem. The eight head of cattle were nicely tucked into the truck with a thick covering of sawdust and straw to stop them slipping on our long journey. There was a rack at the front of the crate that was full of halters, rugs, manure forks and shovels and all the gear required for eight head of cattle for ten days at the Brissie Ekka.

So where was my gear? In the truck cab. Where was everyone else's? In the truck cab. It was so jammed, there was just enough room for the driver.

"Tom, where are Gordon and I going to fit in?"

"In the back with the cattle, mate."

Tom opened the door on the driver's side and got behind the wheel of the eight-ton truck. Gordon and I climbed into the crate and stood with the bulls at the front. I don't know how Gordon felt, but I felt like a bit of purchased merchandise bought at the Ekka and chucked in to the back of the truck with the other goodies from the show.

The old Bedford crossed the Story Bridge on its way to Tee-Tree stud, about a six hour, three hundred kilometre trip. We left about 2.00 P.M., so we guessed we would arrive at our destination about 8.00 P.M. It was a pleasant sunny winter's day, but the wind created by the moving truck was cold and I was thankful for my fur lined flying jacket. Gordon, wearing his only shirt, was ducking down behind the cab. But the straw and sawdust were blowing little eddies, getting into his eyes, nose and mouth, so eventually he stood up with me, stuffing straw into his shirt to try and stay warm out of the wind. We thought of getting in between the bulls for warmth and shelter, but we changed our minds when Tom slammed the brakes on to miss hitting a car in front, who had decided they couldn't make the yellow traffic signal and stopped suddenly. The bulls lurched forward. If we had been in between them, we could have been squashed by tons of live meat. As it was, we were almost squashed, but as the brakes came into effect, the cattle lurched backwards and saved us.

The sun was beginning to lose its warmth as it started to slide down the western horizon. The wind had a feeling of ice as we passed the city of Toowoomba and started to make our way through the famous Darling Downs. Gordon banged on the roof of the truck, making Tom stop. His head shot out of the window as he yelled, "What's the matter?"

"Could you stop at a café so we can get a coffee? It's bloody freezing up here, or better still, stop at a pub so we can get a nip of rum," yelled back Gordon.

"It ain't worth my job," said Tom. "The boss wanted the cattle home before 7.30 and we are running late. It's not worth my job to be delayed any longer. If you're so cold, climb up to the rack and get some of the spare bull rugs and drape them around you."

This we did, as Tom took off with a grating of gears. The rugs were good and kept the wind out, but our faces still copped the icy blasts as we both tried to find the best part of the front of the truck to try and make ourselves more comfortable. With our backs to the wind but standing up, so we could move out of the bull's way when the truck lurched or went over a bump. We couldn't talk as the wind whisked our words away and even if we could, our now chapped lips and numb brains would not have cooperated.

It was dark now and even with the spare bull rugs we were cold, tired and miserable. Our legs were tired from standing up on the swaying deck of the truck. Our hands and arms were tired from hanging on and our now empty stomachs were crying out for soup or hot food or something, but the truck droned on. The cattle swayed and ground their teeth.

We passed a large, lit town, which Gordon said was Dalby and that we had about another hundred to go.

To be honest, I don't remember much more of that trip. I think my body just gave up and went into a semi-conscious state. There was a sharp turn, a dusty, dirt road, lots of bumps, the cattle were getting more restless, the truck stopping, a gate, truck starting, more gates, more jerking, more stopping and thank God at last we had arrived.

Tom backed the truck up to a large shed that I found out later was the bull stalls. We led the younger stock to a different yard with a small covered-in shed, unloaded the bulls and put them in to their own individual saw dust covered floor stall. Tom said, "The boss wants you up at the house Jack, so find yer gear and take a hike up to there. Gordon and I will feed the stock and bed them down."

I offered to help, but Tom insisted I go to the house straightaway as the boss would be waiting and it was late already. He turned to Gordon and said, "You can help me, then I shall drive the truck over to our quarters where you will be staying."

I walked up the hill, past two metal silos and approached an unimpressive farmhouse. Oh, it looked all right in the moonlight, but I had my heart set on a Queensland homestead with wide verandas, like I had seen in books, but this wasn't one of them. Tired and struggling with all my gear, I knocked on the back door. Soon the porch light was switched on and Mr Short appeared, opening the door. He was wearing a dark blue woollen dressing gown tied at the waist by a cord with tassels at the end, a pair of brown, kinder checked velvet zip up slippers and flannel pyjamas underneath.

The greeting. "You're late. What have you been up to? Where are Tom and the cattle? Did the cowboy come too?"

I answered all the questions the best I could and mumbled something about I didn't know we were so late as we hadn't stopped anywhere. I was then invited in. Shown past the kitchen into the dining room, told to be quiet, which was difficult, carrying all my gear in without any offer of help. Down a small passage and into a very nice bedroom. It all looked so new compared to the rest of the house and, as I suspected and found out later, it had been added to the homestead only a couple of years previously. I didn't have time to properly observe my new room, as I was told to put my gear down so I could be shown the bathroom and toilet. So back through the kitchen, past the back door I had entered from, and continuing through another door into another small passageway that led to the bathroom and toilet.

It was a very sparse room, just the basics: a bath; a wash hand basin; porcelain toilet and a small shaving cabinet with a mirror in it, a couple of towel racks and that was all. The floor was wooden and the walls were unlined ripple iron, a very cold room indeed. I guessed this was my bathroom and the family one was in another part of the house.

Tired, hungry and cold, I could not believe what I was being told.

"You are in the country now, so we don't waste water here. I've drawn a black ring around the bath, look see here lad."

I saw a ring drawn inside the bath about two hundred millimetres from the bottom, not even enough to cover my skinny legs, if it was filled to the line with water. Mr Short continued, "And the hot water comes from the wood stove so there is not much to waste there either".

He turned around and walked out of the room. I followed, walking through the kitchen he then said, "You can have tomorrow off, breakfast will be at eight, don't make a noise or disturb the family and you better go and have your bath now." and left me, for another part of the house. Nice sort of welcome, I must say. Nothing about food, or helping yourself in the kitchen or, you can make yourself tea and toast. No, just have a bath and be quiet till breakfast at eight.

The room was nice, even better than the one at Blackall. Built-in cupboards and wardrobes, two single beds nicely made up with fresh linen and new warm blankets. It was nicely painted in a pastel pale yellow and blue. New lino with a couple of attractive scatter rugs on the floor. I had mixed feelings, a nice room, *a palace compared to Lostmans Motel,* but Mr Short seemed a very gruff sort of person indeed. I unpacked a few things, got my toilet bag and pyjamas and went and had my bath. I put in the plug and ran the hot water, but it wasn't hot. It was lukewarm, so there was no need to run the cold tap. It took forever to fill to that black line. By then it was cold, just the chill had been taken off. I lowered my tired, aching, hungry body into the puddle of tepid water and proceeded to wash the dust and grime off from the six hours of being in the back of the truck with the cattle.

Suddenly, the bathroom door burst open and there was Mr Short checking on me to see if I had not filled the bath over his black line. The indignity of my new boss looking at my naked body and checking up on me was so humiliating. I didn't say anything. What could I say? He said a gruff goodnight and walked out, leaving the door open. As I dried myself, I thought, *Jack, you are going to have to learn a lot of patience, a lot of diplomacy. You're going to take whatever is dished out to you, and keep your mouth shut or you will be back at Lostmans Motel and on the street before you can say, 'you bastard'.*

I tumbled into the nice new sheets and was asleep just as my top eyelids touched my bottom ones.

The kookaburras woke me with their raucous cackling and laughter. My body felt stiff and sore, as I tried to take stock of my surroundings and where I was. I pulled back the blankets and sat up on the bed with my feet resting on one of the scatter rugs. Yawning and rubbing my eyes, I tried to get my thoughts together. Which parts were dreams and which were reality? The morning was cold and fresh. My large silver alarm clock told me it was 6.15 A.M. and the night sky was receding as the day was getting ready to welcome the sun. I think the Aborigines say the kookaburras laugh to wake up the sun and give the day a happy beginning.

I had to go to the bathroom because of my bladder. Was there really a black line drawn around the inside of the bath? Diving into my backpack, I pulled out a pair of clean strides, a work shirt, undies and socks. Getting dressed quickly, I donned my favorite flying jacket and proceeded to the bathroom with my towel and toilet bag. Creeping past the kitchen and into the cold, uninviting bathroom, I switched the light on. It glowed very weakly and hardly threw any light. I thought, *we must be on thirty-two-volt power with a generator charger, which must be the same as at Blackall.*

Yep, the line was there all right. I tried to rub a teeny section out, thinking I may be able to make another line a bit higher. But no luck, it was painted on, a good scraping with a knife would be the only way to remove it, and that would leave a tell-tale mark, anyway. After a good healthy piddle, I had a shave in the cold water, brushed my hair and cleaned my teeth to freshen myself up. I arranged my toiletries in the small cabinet where I found a section of velvet soap that supposedly was for my use and hung my towel on one of the racks to dry.

Gee, I was hungry, as the hamburger I'd eaten at the Ekka yesterday had well passed its usefulness. Then, I remembered my roll of lifesavers. Sneaking back to my room, I got them out of my trousers pocket that I'd worn yesterday. I gathered my Rothmans and matches, picked up my lace-up boots and headed for the back door. Sitting on the steps outside, lacing my boots on and drawing in my first smoke of the day, I slipped a lifesaver into my mouth. It helped my hunger pains but didn't solve them.

Looking around from my position, I could see the sun peeping over the tree line in the distance. A rooster crowing, a cow mooing and birds of a feather chattering away, fluffing and preening their feathers to catch the first warmth of rays from the new morning sun.

To my right were a couple of small buildings side by side. I got up from my step seat and went to investigate. The first was in two parts. One was a laundry with a Malleys washing machine, a set of concrete troughs with a hand ringer clamped on the dividing wall of them, a built-in copper with ashes spilling out of the bottom fire place. There were packets of Rinso laundry soap and bars of velvet soap on a ledge, a basket full of pegs and other paraphernalia you would find in a laundry. The locked, partitioned part of the laundry held my curiosity and I tried peeping into some cracks to see what was there, but to no avail. Behind this building was another small shed. All these buildings had painted white weatherboard walls and corrugated iron silver roofs. That shed had the lighting plant in it. A stack of six-volt lighting batteries, *they looked like car batteries to me*, were stacked side by side, joined together by lead clamps. There were twelve of them. A green Lister engine coupled to a generator was the charging plant. The other small building on the other side of the laundry had a large silver thing with a big handle on it, mounted on a square post in the middle of the floor. I actually knew what it was; a separator to separate the milk from the cream leaving skim milk. I found that out at the Ekka.

Silver cones on racks, stainless steel bowls with long spouts on them, a stainless-steel bucket, all turned upside down on a large bench at the side of the building. There were two twenty-litre square kerosene tins with the tops cut out, hanging up on wire handles with a bit of green garden hose threaded on to them. I didn't know it at the time, but these make-shift buckets were going to put some muscles on my arms. Beside the bench was a large metal washing up trough, with a tap and a five litre tin of detergent. A broom was in the corner. I guess to keep the concrete floor clean.

Venturing out past a tired strip of garden which bordered the concrete pathway and through the small gate in the garden fence, there was a big wood heap on my left and further away, what looked like a large fowl run. To my right was a small building with a steep, pitched iron roof. The top half of the walls were untimbered, but gauzed in. This I knew was the butcher shop, where they killed and dressed sheep, hung overnight for the meat to set before being cut up in the morning. I did learn some things at Gold's place.

Walking up the hill past the large grain silos toward me was Gordon, the new cowboy. We exchanged greetings, and he offered me a tailor-made Craven, a cork-tipped cigarette, which I accepted.

"I am supposed to come here to the house for breakfast by eight, but it's a bloody long walk," he said.

"Where did you have to come from?" I asked, turning around as he pointed.

"See the bull stalls we unloaded the stock from last night? Well, cast your eye down the road past them and to the hay shed and machinery shed. See the road turn to the right and through an iron gate?" I followed his finger in his indicated direction.

"Then see that clump of trees in the distance, not there, over there," as he directed me in the right direction, "well there's an old house but you can't see it, I guess it's two kilometres from here, or more."

"Those cigarettes are banned here. Put them out now!"

We both jumped and turned around quickly. We hadn't heard the boss approach from behind us.

"And why can't we smoke? We aren't hurting anyone," said Gordon indignantly.

"Because tailor-made cigarettes burn to the butt, even if you are not smoking them, which is a fire hazard. We haven't got a problem with smoking roll-yer-owns, except all smoking and smokes are banned around the bull stalls, because of the sawdust and anywhere near the hay sheds, you got it?"

We both nodded as we stubbed our fags out on the ground with our new boss looking to check if we had done the job properly.

"Well, breakfast is on. You better get up to the house before the cook does a 'micky'," said the boss as he trundled beside us toward the garden gate.

The kitchen was warm, mainly because of the Crown combustion stove, with a steamy pot of porridge to the side of the hot plate and chops sizzling in the fry pan. Mrs Short was sitting beside the open fire door of the stove, making toast from the heat of the fire. She was dressed in a plain cotton dress with a knitted lime green woollen cardigan that had seen better days, but I guessed it was her favourite. Her hair was untidy, pulled back into a wispy bun.

"Good morning boys," she said in a bright tone, "just help yourself to the porridge. Gordon, you eat in the men's kitchen." She indicated a small room at the side with table and chairs. "In future, would you mind coming in by the men's kitchen entrance and not the way you did this morning?"

She said it politely, but Gordon mumbled something under his breath, grabbed an empty bowl from the side bench and ladled in a good portion of porridge, turned round and walked to the men's kitchen area.

"Jack, you're the jackaroo, you eat in the dining room with us," she said as she put the toasting fork down and handed me a bowl. As I was dishing out my share of porridge, she turned to her husband and said in a rather tense voice, "And where are the other men? I've cooked enough for eight. Where are the other three men? I've told you often enough to let me know if the men aren't coming for meals."

The boss calmly said, "Dear, it's Sunday. They never have meals here on a Sunday or Saturday. I have mentioned this before."

"Well, you might think that you have told me, but I don't recollect any such conversation. Now, what am I going to do with the extra food?"

"Give it to the chooks if the boys can't eat it," suggested the boss.

"Have you ever seen chooks eating chops?" was the retort.

I took my porridge into the dining room, sat down at the laid table with the green glass jug of milk with the fly veil over the top. Silver sugar and salt containers and tomato and Worcestershire sauce in small bottles which fitted into a silver patterned container, specially made for holding them. There were four places set at the table. I wondered if this couple, my bosses, had managed or even been blessed with children. A quick observation of the room showed me the house was an old farmhouse, clean and tidy and freshly painted, but nothing special about it. The dining room was large with a high plaster ceiling; two shaded lights hung from chains from the ceiling to a height of about two yards. The dining table was off side to one of the lights, the other was in the other end of the dining room where there was a fabric couch and two lounge chairs with wide armrests, the sort you sink into and can't get out. An AWA radiogram was in the corner tuned to the ABC and giving out the state weather report region by region. A low coffee table was full and overflowing with Country Life newspapers, Hereford Stud monthly and rural magazines by the port full. A small table beside one of the chairs had a couple of Women's Weeklies and New Ideas, but not many. Three walls were panelled with stained ply wood halfway up, then plaster to the ceiling. The wall behind me had six sash windows with small floral design curtains hanging from each one, with views out past the silos down to the bull stores.

For decoration, there were plenty of pictures around the wall in heavy scrolled frames. These were of bulls and cows with champion ribbons round their necks and being held by a beaming Mr Short or a beaming Mr and Mrs Short, proudly holding some large silver tray or trophy beside one of their beasts. There was a long sideboard nearly half the length of the room opposite where I was sitting patiently waiting for the boss and his missus to sit down before my porridge got cold. The sideboard had a sliding glass door and the array of silver trophies were packed in. Displayed on the top were more trophies, as well as some china figurines of Herefords and one small-framed picture of two little girls in plaits. It was easy to see who was most revered in this household and it wasn't humans.

At last, they came into the dining room. I stood up and waited till both were seated.

"You haven't eaten your porridge, Jack; you didn't have to wait for Mr Short or myself."

Now she tells this starving boy with a shrunken stomach that he need not have waited. You're not always rewarded for having good manners. Pouring a little milk on to the porridge and a sprinkle of sugar, I started to eat. The first spoonful created a war in my insides. Everything was ready for food and boy, I didn't realise that I was so hungry. The boss sat at the head of the table, leaning down over his bowl, slurping and shoveling his meal into his mouth; his moustache managed to catch a lump of oats that he wiped with a napkin, which made it worse by smearing it through the bristles. The missus was the opposite. She sat bolt upright in her chair opposite me, lifting her spoon all the way to her mouth and delicately dispatching the contents without any dribbles into the bowl or onto the tablecloth. She had a very discreet few black hairs on her upper lip, but these always remained free of food. Finishing my porridge well after the boss but before the missus, I waited to take their bowls as I had done at the Golds' place. I was told thank you, but they weren't cripples and they could manage to take their own bowls out and get their second course themselves, but would I make a pot of tea while getting my chops?

During the second course of neck chops and toast – *thank God for the toast as the chops were all fat, bone and gristle* – the boss said, "You can have the day off, look around and familiarise yourself with the property. We don't want you going out at nights with the men as you will be too tired to satisfactorily complete your chores the next morning. This includes the weekends. However, when you're invited, you may accompany the family if they choose to spend an evening out, as long as you're on your best behavior." He continued in his abrupt manner, "You will be paid slightly more than a first-year jackaroo's wage as we require you to work six days a week and chores that you will be given to do on Sundays."

My answers were just nods. What could I say? I finished my toast and cup of tea, picked up my dishes, excused myself from the table, scraped the quarter-eaten chops into the waste bin, and was just straightening up when a female voice behind me said, "You must be the new jackaroo?"

I turned around and saw a tall, slim girl, about twenty-three with fair hair, blue-green eyes, dressed in riding jodhpurs with a blue shirt opened at the neck and a navy jacket over the top. Her facial features showed who her parents were, but she had a lovely smile and I guessed a personality to go with it.

"Yea, my name is Jack. Do you know if I am supposed to do the dishes or what?"

"If you know what's good for you, I would get out of the kitchen as soon as I can."

I took the hint and made for the door, turned and said, "Thanks."

She replied, "My name is Fran, and I think we are going to get along alright."

Not being very confident with the fairer sex, I mumbled, "I hope so, and what time is lunch?"

"Oh, about 12.30 or so. Mother or I will strike the gong when it's ready, why where will you be?"

"Oh, I just want to check everything out and go and see the bulls and that."

"Okay, see you at lunch then," said Fran, as I went down the path towards the bull stalls.

The sun was warm, but a slight breeze from the west kept a chill in the air. I walked past the hay and machinery shed housing a huge red McCormack tractor and a blue Fordson major tractor. There was an array of ploughs and farming implements which I had a very slight knowledge of after my informative hours at the Brisbane Exhibition only a day or so ago. Passing a large cattle yard on my right, I noticed there was a cow bale in the corner. *I knew about them!* A pen to the side, which was rather large, it had a corrugated iron roof with rails on the side with only small gaps between them and a strong-looking gate. I guess the pen would be about two metres high, three metres long and about the same wide. I wondered what it was for. Still puzzling it out, I came to the stalls, which was a large timber building with a small round yard to one side and another larger yard at the end.

Entering through a side door of the building, I found myself in a large room with a platform in the middle, stacked three yards high, with bags of milo and oats. Against one of the sidewalls were three large storage bins that could handle a couple of bags, each of grain with hinged lids and a few smaller ones. And blow me down, on the wall were written menus for each animal and they were all different. For example - Sid, Breakfast: four tins of milo, four of oats, five of chaff, one of bran, two teaspoons of minivite, three of linseed two of calcium one of salt and ½ of vitamin A. Lunch: two biscuits of hay. Dinner: the same as breakfast. Wow! Then through a doorway to a passageway with six stalls on either side with sawdust on the floor. Here were some of the bulls we brought from the Ekka the previous night, plus a few more. I walked up to Sid, the bull that I'd led yesterday. He was lying down and I said in a loud voice, "Get up, Sid, you lazy beggar."

I did not realise he was asleep and he woke with such a start that he tried to get up in a hurry.

"Shhhh, keep your voice down and don't frighten the stock." It was Tom, who I hadn't heard come up behind me. "You must be quiet when you enter the stalls, especially in the mornings or when they are asleep. The bulls are so heavy that if they get up in a hurry, they can break a leg and that's $16,000 down the drain, and no one would be pleased."

"What does everyone do on the place and how many workers and such?" I asked.

"Well, I am the bull groom and I am in charge of all the stud animals," said Tom importantly. "I feed them three times a day their special feeds, clean and rake out the stalls, take all the sawdust out and replace it with new every week, clean their water troughs, and groom them. I also drench them, spray them for flies and lice and train them to lead and so on. One of your jobs is to help me when I need it."

"Well, do you know what I have to do?" I wondered.

"You're the jackaroo, so I guess you will have chores before breakfast, like cut the chops for the meal, lay the boss's table, then after breakfast you have to foster-mother the calves, milk cows, separate milk, feed the chooks, chop wood for the stove. Then do whatever the boss wants. He is tough, but fair."

"If I have to do all that, what's Gordon have to do"? I asked, rather dismayed about what was expected of me.

"I shouldn't tell you this," said Tom, lowering his voice, "but you are both on trial and whoever works out the best keeps the job while the other goes. I will help you as much as I can, as Gordon kept me awake most of the night with his mumbling and snoring, and anyway he has an odor problem and my room stinks already."

"Gee, thanks Tom, but what are his jobs?"

It seemed to me I had a heavy workload already and if Gordon had a string of chores and jobs like me, and if he goes, I might have to work twenty-four hours a day.

"Gordon would have to work the vegetable garden, kill, *I knew that meant kill a sheep for meat,* be in charge of garbage and be general gardener and handyman," recited Tom.

"Then there is Bill. You won't have much to do with him. He does all the farming, ploughing, seeding and pasture improvement. And I must not forget old Barry, the stockman. He looks after the sheep, and I doubt if you will see him much either. Now, is there any more you want to know, Jack?"

"Only about Fran."

"Well mate, she is too old for you and anyway she is engaged to Peter, the jackaroo you're replacing. Jenny is home on school holidays and I wouldn't have anything to do with her. She is a feisty one that."

I didn't say anything, but it looked like there was another family member in the house I hadn't met.

"Thanks for the info, Tom," as I turned to go and explore some more of the property.

The rest of the day passed pleasantly. I met Jenny at lunch, and she had a pretty face with tied back brunette hair, a body that fitted perfectly into her slim jeans and a checked shirt. I thought she was a bit of *awright*. Lunch was a mutton roast with some vegetables and junket for sweets; tea was only bread, jam and cream.

Wouldn't you know it, that was pretty well the diet and menu the whole time I was there at the stud. Breakfast was porridge, two chops, two pieces of toast and a cup of tea. Lunch was usually boiled brisket taken straight out of the boiler and dumped on the plate, a fatty, watery, grisly mess, with one potato, one slice of pumpkin and a spoon full of peas. Sweets were either jelly or junket. Tea at night was bread and butter. On Sunday, you could have cream and jam. Lunch was a leg or shoulder of mutton. There were other dishes, but the above were pretty normal. No morning or afternoon teas or smokos. I don't remember seeing any fruit. And it would be seen later, what the diet did to me.

Gordon the cowboy did not last long. He had a mind of his own, *doesn't everyone?* and he wasn't frightened of saying what he thought. Once a week he would have to kill, and I was told by the boss to watch and learn. Mrs Short always asked for the liver. Gordon hated liver, so he gave it to the dogs. One night at teatime, she asked Gordon where the liver was.

"The dogs got it, Missus."

"Now Gordon, don't tell me the dogs got it. Where is the liver?"

"Well, I can't tell you, 'cause you told me not to say the dogs got it."

"Oh, we are smart, aren't we, young man? Well, answer me this, did you give the liver to the dogs? Or did the dogs take the liver out of the sheep when you weren't looking?"

She stood glaring at Gordon, hands on hips, her right leg thrust forward, full of verbal fight. "Well?"

"Err, Missus, the dogs got it and that is all I am saying."

Mrs Short twirled around at me.

"Jack where is the liver?"

"All I saw was the dogs fighting over it. I didn't see whether he gave it to them or not," I gushed. It was the truth. I didn't actually see him give the liver to the dogs, but I knew he had.

At lunch the next day, we were dished up our water-logged boiled meal. Gordon took the dish in his hand, walked straight to the trash bin, putting his foot on the pedal, which lifted the lid up, with one elegant swipe of his knife he scraped his lunch in to the bin saying to Mrs Short, "This ain't fit for the *dorgs*." Gordon left the kitchen and the property right there and then, with Mr Short's hand clamped on to the back of his collar, forcing him out the fly screen door to goodness knows where. We all admired Gordon for his complete honesty and courage regarding the meals. I am getting a bit ahead of myself, so back to my chores. Tom was right, I had to cut the chops for breakfast. What a mess. I missed several times and mangled them with the chopper, but no one said anything, and I did get better with practice.

It was Monday, my first day on the new job. I set the table and eyed Jenny off while she helped her mother do the toast in the firebox of the combustion stove. After breakfast, the boss told me to get the milk bucket and the two twenty-litre kerosene tins out of the separator shed and meet him down at the cow bale.

C.11

Tee Tree Stud

An Argument, Nearly Castrated, Tar Boy, Death

It was the large cattle yard that we walked to, the one with the head bale.

As we entered through the small wooden gate, I got a better look at the beasts inside. There were four big dairy cows. They were called A.I.S. or Illawarra Shorthorns and were they not the great old dames. Huge and brown, with a certain air about them, large udders and teats to match. They walked majestically, slightly swinging their full udders in such a way as to say, "We know our job. We are the best. You better respect us, you little human, as we are not to be trifled with. We are the best of stud cows, so there!"

In the pen that was part of the yard I observed yesterday, were four young Hereford bull calves only three weeks old. They had been taken off their poor mums and now had to be fed by these stately foster cows. And that was my job.

"Don't let 'em have too much milk or they will scour," said the boss. Scouring was where young calves with a sudden change of diet that was too rich, got diarrhoea and it was hard to get them back to normal.

"But how will I know when they have had enough?" I asked.

"Well, that's your job, but you make sure they don't scour! Then milk the rest out of the cows. You should nearly fill both these twenty litre drums. When you have finished, let the cows out in that their paddock." He gestured, pointing to the right of the yards. "Leave the calves in the yard, and the pen door open and bring the milk up to the house and ask for me." Then he promptly left me to it.

Being the expert now that I was, I put some feed in to the trough and brought the first cow to the bale. She put her head in, waited till I baled her up, then put her hind leg back, ready for me to tie it. Yep, I had to agree she was a pro. I called her Madam. Cunningly, I thought, *four cows, the boss said about forty litres of milk in the buckets, so that's ten per cow, so I will milk them first and let the calf have the rest of the cow.*

Grabbing the log to sit on, milking bucket between my knees, I proceeded to milk. The bloody tits were so big and fat I could hardly get my fingers around them. Using all my arm and hand muscles, I managed to squeeze the milk out. When I got my ten litres, I tipped the bucket into the drums, opened the pen door and all the calves ran out fighting for a teat.

Well, Madam kicked as the calves grabbed what they could. I was in the middle, trying to get three of them back in to the pen. I knew it was one calf for each cow. What a shambles. Luckily, Tom must have heard the melee and came over to help. He then showed me how to get each calf out and told me their names.

"This is Russell, that's Morrie and Leskin, and over there is Victor."

He must have seen my puzzled look and said, laughing, "I know they all look the same to you, but you will soon get to know them," and I did.

They got to know me, too. After a week or so, I could open the pen gate and say, "Right, Russell go get 'em," and out he would bound and latch on to one of Madam's big teats. They all knew their new mums and their turns. I loved this job even though my arms ached, especially the forearms and wrists, but hell, so what, I had to be building some manly muscle.

Every day, the calves got bigger and bigger, and the bigger they became, the more randy they were. I was surprised to learn they even masturbate by rubbing their penis inside their sheaf. I took special interest in their eyes. They didn't seem to get white spots in them or go blind, and as far as madness, they seemed quite happy. All this was a tremendous relief to me personally. Being from a family of women, I didn't know what to believe or not! As the bull calves got older and fatter and not only on milk, but a diet of grains and minerals, they got randier. One day when they were about six months old, I just couldn't bend over in their yard or turn my back on them. They were really frustrated.

The boss lost his glasses in the yard one day and went down on all fours to find them. This was too good for Morrie, the oldest bull calf. He raced up, mounted the boss with his front legs over his shoulders. The boss tried to crawl away; Morrie pulled him back with his front legs into his groin. The boss was crying for help and all us workers just happened to be there at the time. Gosh, it was funny. We laughed and laughed, but then felt sorry for him, so we went to help. We all got the sack.

"Get off this property now!" was all the reward we got. But we were reinstated again that afternoon.

In the mornings, we start on the dot of 6.00 A.M.

"Animals like their meals on time," I was told by his lordship.

When I got my babies up for breakfast one cold morning, lo and behold, each one had a kitten curled up on the calves' forelegs, little cheek against a biggin. A purr from the cat and a snore from the sleeping beast.

After my first morning milking, which took a long time, I struggled up to the house with the two full twenty-litre drums of milk and a milk bucket on my back, with the handle over my head and a few drips running down my back. How else was I going to carry the three items? The wire handles with the hose over them didn't help the cutting sensation in my hands or the stretching of my arms. The further I walked, the more stooped I became and the more rests I needed, but I made it. The boss answered my call with a gruff, "You took your time. You will have to be much quicker because this must be done before breakfast. You have other chores, then a day's work." He glanced over to where I continued to wait.

"Well, what are you standing there for? You know how to separate?" I pleaded ignorance.

"Well, come and I will show you."

I won't go into the detail, but you have to more or less build the separator, as everything has to be dismounted for cleaning after use, which was also my job. I was sure I would have muscles like Atlas when I was finished this jackarooing. Just starting to hand wind the separator took all my strength; it got a bit easier the longer I went, but it was still hard. The milk was poured in to the large top basin; I wound the handle and cream would come out one spout and skim milk out the other. Then the boss started to give me my daily chores.

"When you have finished cleaning the separator, the disinfectant is over there and all you need to wash everything thoroughly that is here.

"Then feed the chooks the skim milk and bring the cream to the house, chop the wood, and fill the wood box by the stove.

"I expect you to lay the dining room table for breakfast, cut the chops and place them in a covered basin beside the stove, then feed your calves and milk the cows.

"Breakfast is 7.00 A.M. sharp, then you have the separating to do, the chooks and the wood. And be finished by 8.30 ready for a day's work, got it?"

I nodded a 'yes' and wondered what a day's work entailed, as he walked down to the bull stalls and left me doing the separating.

These were my daily chores; I had a couple more after Gordon left and that was killing a sheep when required and cutting it up. Yes, I learnt to do that too. I made an awful mess the first few times. The bloody sheep wouldn't die and gurgled blood for ages. The skinning was not the right word, as I took most of the meat with the skin. The guts, the smell, the shit and piss, I hated it and then had to eat the thing. But I ended up becoming competent and efficient at it, like all the chores, I managed and thought I did a good job. But there are those days when things go wrong and animals and machinery are uncooperative as they don't have watches on, or work to a time.

One such day, I was running late, which happened occasionally. To save time, instead of walking the one hundred metres or so to the chook pen, clean their dishes and pour the skim milk out, I just heaved it out behind the separator shed. Saved me ten minutes, it did. Well, as I was saying, this day, I hoyed the milk out then went on to cutting the daily wood after that, putting it into the wood box. Now this wood box was a two-way box. I filled it from the outside from the wheelbarrow and the missus took it for the stove from the kitchen side.

"Jack, did you give the chooks their skim milk this morning?"

"Er no, Missus."

"Well then, could you sensibly explain why not?"

This conversation was taking place through the wood box, with Mrs Short kneeling on the kitchen floor, while I was outside starting to fill it up.

"The chooks don't drink all the skim milk and it goes off in their dishes and smells the chook house out."

"Now Jack, don't be like Gordon. You know what happened to him. So, you were asked to do a chore and you didn't, I want to know why."

As this intense conversation was going on, I continued to fill the wood box, because if I was one minute later than the eight thirty meeting with the boss at the bull stores for the day's work, there would be hell and more to pay. So as Mrs Short nagged, I filled the wood box, slowly covering her knees, her waist, her chest, her chin. She kept nagging. I really tried to explain my actions nicely, but I realised she was going to give me heaps till the sun went down, no matter what I said or did. I put more wood in, covered her mouth but not the sound, more wood, covering her eyes and forehead, then the lot of her.

I sneaked away with the barrow so I could be on time with the boss. Then I heard a bang, an explosion. I spun around and wood was flying in all directions from the wood box. The missus must have sat on the floor and with both feet, kicked all the wood out, surprisingly with a lot of force, or more probably rage. Then a head appeared through the wood box.

"How dare you walk away when I am speaking to you. How dare you!"

I listened to the tirade till she had nothing more to say. I refilled the wood box after she left, finishing with, "Wait till Mr Short hears about this."

I knew I was dead anyway as I hurried down to meet my fate.

"And where have you been, Jack? It is now three past nine," the boss enquired in his abrupt tone with his little Hitler moustache quivering.

"With your wife," I replied bravely.

His moustache quivered more as his voice raised slightly.

"And what, may I ask, were you doing with my wife?"

I said we had a slight misunderstanding and she had lots and lots of words to say and I had some difficulty getting down here on time. A very slight hint of a smile on just one-quarter of his mouth appeared as if he might have been in a similar situation that I had just come from, once or twice himself.

"Jack, never rock the hand that rocks the cradle. Now hop in the car. We are checking and cleaning some water troughs today."

My favourite times were with the animals, especially the bull calves and their foster mums. I loved them; they were my charges. There were dogs, but you can't play with working dogs. The Shorts were strict with me and very hard on discipline. If you were asked to do something and you didn't run, you were given a slight but firm tap with the bull cane on the legs. I made the mistake of telling them at the interview that my parents were separated. It was a view widely held that someone from a broken home was trouble, a larrikin, a problem child, and a child without discipline. So I wasn't allowed out unless it was with the family, no fraternising with the hired help. 'We are going to train you as a human being,' or that was the attitude.

But that was the job. I worked hard, did my chores, as well as painted yards, stick-picked, burr hoeing and spraying, which was walking around with a twenty litre tank on my back spraying poison on burrs. Opened gates for the boss, cleaned out calf pens and bull stores, stacked one hundred kilo bags of grain, sorted feed, put out licks, sprayed the bulls with me on a stirrup pump.

"C'mon Jack, work harder on that hand pump. We got to get the spray through into the skin." My poor arms again.

I learned how to dig post holes, repair and strain fences, oil windmills and so on, but alas, no horse work. That was left to Fran and old Barry the sheepman, it wasn't fair. I always seemed to get the job of stacking hay.

One terrible day, a truck load of hay arrived. Two men in their thirties were in the truck, big strong bushmen, done hard yakka all their lives and by the look of their huge biceps and the hint of their rippling stomachs, nothing would be trouble to them. They were on top of the stack, throwing the bales down while I was stacking and busting my gut, trying to keep up with them, but still giving a bit of cheek, which I do occasionally.

Then the crisis happened. I saw one wink at the other and with all his might, threw a bale of hay directly at me, knocking me down. They both leapt off the truck and in a vice-like grip, held me down flat on the ground. They held me so tight, all I could do was bat an eyelid. Then, between the teeth of the tallest one, I noticed a castrating knife.

"We got you now, you little bugger and we are going to cut your balls out and give 'em to the crows, not that it will be a feed for 'em."

And then, as one kept me from moving, the other with the knife was trying to undo my strides. I had never been so scared or helpless in my life. There was nothing I could do, and I could not even call out, as my mouth was bone dry with fear. Then my pants were pulled down and only the thinnest of cotton underpants protected what manhood I had.

The one holding me down released his steel grip on me saying, "That's enough Bruce, we have had our fun. We better get this unloaded and get another load for Fritz up the road."

Bruce clasped his knife as he got off me. He laughed as he got back on to the truck. "We really could have done it."

I got up, pulled my strides up and went back to stacking, keeping a constant watch on them, ready to bolt at the slightest hint of trouble. I made a rule to myself there and then that nobody, just nobody, will ever take advantage of me again.

I loved hard work. My body seemed to thrive on it, as if it was waiting to bust out of this child's frame and make me a man. At night, while waiting for sleep, which wasn't long, I could feel the muscles growing in my arms, shoulders, legs and body. I would feel myself and wonder at the transformation my body was taking. I was always bullied at school, being the smallest and weakest, and sometimes now I think it wasn't a bad thing, as it didn't break me. I learnt from it and ended up being able to take and handle the bullying that life hands out to us all at times as we grow through the years.

It was shearing time and I was going to be a rousabout, Tom would do my chores, as I would be spending the next two weeks in the shearing shed. I was excited. The bleating of the sheep, dogs barking, shrill whistles from the penner-upper, the slow thump, thump of the single piston Southern Cross engine, a shrill noise as the sparks fly and the red circles the comb makes, as the expert sharpens them on the emery discs. Clatter, clatter goes the ratchet as the presser presses the wool in the old Warrigo press, the whirl of the hand pieces as the shearers oil them, the swish of brooms and the occasional voice of men hard at work.

Dust, smells of sheep shit, wool, lanolin, jute from the wool packs and ink from the stencil blocks, human sweat, oil and diesel and dags; these were some of the sights, sounds and smells of the shearing shed. Outside in the yards, dust and a whirl of confusion as woolly sheep were drafted and shorn sheep branded. Chemicals, jetting engine, more dogs and more yelling from Fran and Barry who were bringing sheep in and taking shorn sheep back to the paddock.

"Get me the raddle, the raddle, not the fuckin' rattle."

If you are like me and do not know the difference, raddle is chalk for marking a particular sheep. A rattle is a half dozen log cabin or champion tobacco tin lids threaded on to some fencing wire to make a noise to get the sheep moving. Very hard to hear the difference in a noisy shearing shed. My job as a rousabout entailed keeping the wool away from the shearer, picking up the wool fleece and throwing it on to the skirting table to get rid of stains and burr, help keep the sheep pens full and most importantly, I was in charge of the tar pot. When a sheep was cut it was, 'Tar here Jack.' Just as it is in the song, *Click goes the shears boys, tar here Jack!* That was me!

"One minute to go," shouts the boss of the board, thirty seconds, fifteen seconds, then he rings a bell and everything goes quiet as the shearers stop shearing. Everyone stops work for smoko. Even the sheep stop their bleating. Only the clatter of their cloven hooves on the slatted floor of the pens can be heard.

I had a go at everything except the shearing and the sharpening of combs and cutters. I needed help on the press, as I just wasn't strong enough to get the monkey or the wooden slab on top of the wool, which two cables are attached to press the wool into the bale, right down. It was a busy, exhausting, interesting time. I had never slept so easily at nights and felt so stiff and sore in the mornings, but hey, I was a Queensland jackaroo, I could handle this.

The cattle work I enjoyed too; calving was a special time. Of course, that was after mating. I loved how the bulls really looked 'lovey dovey' and the cows being served had quite a sheepish look, as if to say, "I really shouldn't be doing this, but I don't mind, really!" Yep, the seasons changed from cold frosty mornings to beautiful sunny days. Now it was spring, the barn cats were having kittens; the bitch was having more puppies, again! The birds were singing, the roosters crowing and the cows calving.

Some of them had trouble and Tom and I were on calving duty anytime day or night. We carried our delicate instruments, a piece of strong rope about a yard in length, a piece of broom handle about foot long, a bottle of Dettol, water, clean rags and a hand towel and, of course, a torch for night time. The first one I assisted in was not the most pleasant experience. Tom was there as well as the boss, and boy, was he worried, as it was one of the best stud breeders.

Here were the calf's back legs sticking out from the cow's vagina. Tom said, "It's a breech."

"I know it's a bloody breech. You don't have to tell me, just get the calf out," said the boss. Two loops of each end of the rope on the calf's back legs, the bit of broom handle twisted into the middle of the rope and a gentle pull down should have done the trick. We were really pulling.

"It's no good," said the boss, "you will have to try and turn the calf internally."

Tom said, "Give it a rest Jack, and I will see what I can do."

Slipping both hands into the cow up to his elbows, his face turned redder and redder and the look of effort and concern showed how hard he was trying.

"Well Tom, have you freed it yet? Because the cow is not straining, she must be exhausted and given up."

"It's okay Boss, I have freed the front leg. It was caught in the side of the pelvis. I think Jack and I can get it out now."

We pulled and pulled and something was starting to give.

"C'mon Jack, pull, pull, it's coming." And out slid the calf with a good thump on the ground. It just lay there. I just stared, thinking it was dead. Tom went on his knees quickly, started to rotate the calf's leg and massaging it on the chest.

"Jack, just clear that membrane from his mouth and nose so he can breathe."

It looked yuck. I tentatively went down to wipe the stuff off.

"It won't hurt you, for Christ's sake. Just clear the airways now," yelled the boss, who never did a thing but give orders and panic. As I cleared the muck away, the calf took a breath.

"It's alive, it's alive!" exclaimed Mr Short.

"I knew it would be," confirmed Tom as he let the cow lick the calf all over, clearing the membrane with its rough tongue and getting the circulation going.

"Look, it's having another," I yelled. "Look what's coming out now."

"That's the afterbirth, go and pick it up before the cow starts eating it. Get the shovel out of the ute and bury it," directed the boss.

Trying to pick the muck up on the shovel, the purple slop kept slipping off and to be truthful, the birth was okay but this stuff was making me feel ill.

"For god's sake, Jack, pick it up in your hands and go bury it. We haven't got all day. We want to leave the cow and its calf in peace now the ordeal is over."

I tried, but the stuff just oozed out of my arms. Bits through my fingers kept sliding back on to the ground as I tried gathering it up. It was like trying to carry a gallon of slimy jelly. I just managed to gather it up off the ground for the third time and started to walk with it over to a place I had decided to bury it, when I tripped. I wasn't sure, but I think the boss did it, because he laughingly said, "That's your initiation Jack. You won't be so worried about afterbirth next time."

Indignation, anger, revulsion, sick and disgusted would describe some of my feelings. I had afterbirth all over me, my hair, face, clothes, everywhere. If it happened six months ago, I would have cried. Tom said afterwards it was a mean thing to happen to me, but the screwed-up nose and the look of horror, when I was told to pick the mess up, showed I needed a bit of toughening up.

Killing kittens and puppies because there were too many, sheep to eat, killing 'roos and emus for dog food, having sport with pigs and eagles, castrating, branding, earmarking, blood and guts and a host of other tortures and mayhem seem to be the norm in country life. I felt somehow that I belonged to the animals and wondered whether being part of all this was right. Would I toughen up and take life as it was, or would I end up as some pathetic nerd as far as animals were concerned? Time would tell.

As summer approached, with its hot days and westerly winds, rain and more rain, melon holes full of water, mosquitoes by the thousands, snakes by the bag full, redback spiders and young Jenny finished school and came home. All were dangerous and one had to be aware. For examples you had to be aware of sunburn, dried cracked lips, needing a water bag, flooded creeks, and slippery boggy roads.

Then there were death adders in the kitchen, brown snakes in the bull stalls and tiger snakes after the kittens in the hay shed, redback spiders under and in everything. Then there were the mosquitoes. Let me tell you about them. You couldn't have a bog, crap or shit in the paddock as your bum would be just covered with the little monsters, and they weren't that little. Scotch grays as big as grasshoppers. Fair dinkum, a bit of bare skin was black with the insects before you could blink.

Now I suppose you are wondering about my social life while at the Tee Tree Stud. Well, that's the next chapter, but I will give you a hint of what's to come. It was one of those nights when I sneaked out with the girls, Fran and Jenny, and I think I might have had a touch too much to drink at the party we were at as, on the way home, I got terribly game or more likely bloody stupid. Fran was driving, Jenny was in the middle and I was on the passenger side. For some unexplained reason, and very out of character for me, I started to run my hand up Jenny's skirt. I didn't get very far; I wouldn't have known what to do if I had. About nine centimetres past the knee, I felt a whack! She smashed my hand with the back of her hardback plastic hairbrush. I howled as I quickly retrieved my wandering hand.

"What happened?" enquired Fran, who was concentrating on driving on a very slippery black soil road.

"Oh nothing," I replied, still in great pain. Jenny piped up, smirking, "Just keeping the hired hand under control."

I was in agony. I was late for breakfast the next morning as I could only milk the cows one handed. My poor hand was so badly bruised and swollen, I could not even move my fingers. Mrs Short noticed at breakfast as I tried to eat my porridge with the spoon in my left hand.

"Whatever happened to your hand, Jack? It looks nasty."

"One of the bitches whacked it," I answered.

The two girls glanced at each other with a hint of a smile.

"Now Jack, there is no need to swear, and you really shouldn't call the cows that word."

I smiled inwardly, wondering if she knew she just called her youngest daughter a cow! I did notice I was starting to swear a bit. If I had said even 'damn' back home in Melbourne, it would have been frowned upon. As I have now explained, summer and its creatures can be very dangerous.

I was dropped off in the bull paddock with my cut sandwiches and water bag and told to hoe the entire Bathurst burr invasion around and near the turkey's nest. I had never seen a turkey's nest before, and come to think of it, I hadn't seen any turkeys. I wasted a good third of the day looking for their nest but could not find it. I hoed the rest of the day round a dam which had a lot of burrs. How was I to know that the shape of the dam is called a turkey's nest? Derr!

The learning process took a while for a city kid, but I was getting there. Under one large Bathurst burr I hoed out, was a fully grown fat death adder, about sixty centimetres long. It was coiled and ready to strike, as it was angry at being disturbed. I calmed it down with a whack that took its head clean off! I then decided to skin it, as it would make a fine hatband. The skin was beautiful with soft feathery scales. Squatting down, taking my premium stock knife out of its pouch, I proceeded to cut the skin away from the neck muscle, enabling me to peel the skin off like a stocking from the snake's twitching body. And would you believe, the head of the snake, only centimetres from my bare legs, tried to strike at me. It must have been nerves, but the head jumped at least ten centimetres toward me with mouth open and fangs at the ready. I suddenly fell backwards with the shock of it all; the body of the snake sailed through the air. Getting up quickly, I smashed that head to smithereens with the hoe till it was like a squashed strawberry, then I went and found the rest of the snake and finished skinning it. When I got home, I cured it with Brigalow ash and left it hanging in a tree beside my bedroom window. It did make a fine hatband and drew a lot of comment that made me feel good.

Mr Short was carted off to hospital eighty kilometres away. He had asthma and sinus trouble and was always snorting and sniffing, particularly at mealtimes, which didn't make the fare served up to me any easier to get down one's throat. The girls went with their father, as did Mrs Short. I rather think they all went on holidays while the boss suffered in hospital at Roma. I was now chief cook and bottle washer! The men usually didn't have meals at the house. Tom, Bill and Barry usually went into town for evening meals and had their breakfast and made their lunches at the cottage across the creek where they lived. They reckoned it was much better that way than trying to stomach the meals at the house; they felt sorry for the girls and me. They decided that now I was the cook, they would try me out. I did all right with roasts and grills and fries, had a few very successful puddings and cakes and a few disasters. The men congratulated me, but I couldn't help noticing that by the fifth day they went back to their old habits of having meals at the cottage. I could only cook what was there. The storeroom was always locked, but the girls showed me a place where you could pinch a bit of contraband food such as biscuits and tin fruit. Gosh, they were the daughters and yet they suffered from the limited menu that I suffered from as well. And I did suffer. Being a city kid and a fussy eater, I only ate vegetarian. Sausages and pies were all right, but fatty meat steaks and chops were not on. So when I ended up with a main diet of fatty mutton and boiled vegetables, my body reacted. In the first weeks or so it was not uncommon for me to vomit up the fatty glug. But the body needed fuel and it learnt to handle this fare in its own way, but it did suffer, as you will see later on.

The Shorts were back only a few days when a double disaster happened. A wild storm erupted from the west. Thunder and howling winds with sheet and forked lightning everywhere; it was the start of the big wet. We were having dinner at the height of the storm when there was a huge crack and an explosion. We were all literally thrown from our chairs on to the floor. Dazed and in shock, we struggled to regain our feet and awareness of our surrounds.

"We've been hit by lightning!" said Mr Short in a burst of knowledge. "Is everyone alright?"

We all nodded an affirmative.

"Jack, go outside and report the damage," said the master as he resumed his seat at the table and started to waffle down his dinner. Crikey, the storm was still raging; all hell was breaking loose and I had to go outside? Not on your life.

I went to the bathroom and sat on the dunny for a while. After five or so minutes, I splashed water on my hair and chucked it over my shoulders and opened and slammed the back door. Then went back into the dining room, explaining in a voice that met the situation.

"Gosh, Mr Short, it's wild out there. There's broken trees and stuff everywhere, but I didn't see any damage," I lied.

"That was very brave of you, Jack. Go dry your hair and come back and finish your meal," said Mrs Short.

I dried the hair, but finish the meal? Oh no, it was cold and all the fat had congealed on the plate. I just said I didn't feel well and could I be excused.

"You're not much of an observer. Look at the damage and money you have cost me by not having a good look around last night," said the boss the next morning. "You were pretty quick; I think you just went around the house and didn't check the rest of the buildings."

The boss and I were standing by a roof that had blown off a large metal silo hit by lightning, causing all the grain in the silo to be saturated by the rain. The roof was only yards from the house, the silo at least 150 metres away. The lightning bolt that threw us on the floor the night before was probably the one that caused this damage. As the boss was muttering about the damage and the costs, I kept very quiet, just nodding in agreement.

Tom came running up from the bull stalls. Something was very wrong indeed. "Boss, come down to the stalls quick. A terrible accident has happened!"

We rushed down. Even the boss managed some form of an excuse for running. We entered the stalls and saw the calamity. It was Sid, the prize stud bull I had led on to the truck at the Ekka. Somehow, he had got his head jammed in the rails between the two stalls and had slipped and broken his neck. He was dead. We all stood and just looked with our own thoughts, as he was a grand bull and we all loved him. But evidently not as much as the boss. He had a tear in his eye, abruptly saying, "It's all your fault Tom. You should have been with the bulls during the storm, clean up the mess and don't ever let this kind of thing happen again. And Jack, go and get Bill and sort out about the silo."

Then he about turned and marched back to the house. Tom was terribly upset; I think it caused his nervous breakdown and his leaving a month later.

At the house, for the rest of the week, blinds and curtains were drawn; we tiptoed around the house and whispered to each other, because a close, valued member of the family had died. They mourned for a bloody week over that bull. Okay, we were all sad it happened, but fair dinkum, to mourn like it was one of your very own kids? We even had a large photo of the bull draped with all his ribbons and two small vases on each side in the centre of the sideboard in the dining room. Yes, and a candle was lit as well. I honestly think he loved and looked after and fed those bulls better than his own wife and daughters. In fact, I'm sure he did.

C.12

The Social Life

Escape, A Girl, Christmas, Exodus

Fran did all my washing. Everything was folded and put away nicely, and she was a great kid. She was going to marry Peter, the last jackaroo that was here. Tom reckoned it wasn't for love, but to escape the place. Peter had a job up north and I only saw him twice. Once I came home to get a dry pair of pants and I interrupted something that was going on in the spare bed in my room.

"Psst, nick off Jack and leave us alone, will you?"

I closed the door and spent the rest of the afternoon in saturated trousers. That night, you could smell the sex in the room. The second time I saw him was for Christmas dinner, not much of an engagement.

Talking about smells in my room, my bedroom was next to the storeroom and even though I never saw one bit of fresh fruit while I was there, the room stunk of mangoes. There must have been a crate of rotten ones in a corner of the store that had been forgotten, except by me. I have never eaten a mango since and never will. That smell haunts me to this day.

Poor Fran, she was always in trouble with her father. She just could not do anything right. They had terrible rows about the miscounting of cows and sheep in the paddocks and not doing exactly as she was asked. She was treated miserably. We all felt sorry for Fran.

Now being stuck in a place seven days a week and only going out very occasionally with the boss was not healthy for a young 'un like me. I used to escape through my bedroom window on a Friday or Saturday night, bolt down to the bull stalls where Tom was waiting for me in his FJ ute to hit the town. The main street was dusty. Electricity hadn't reached the small town of Meandarra, and shop windows were lit with candles, hurricane lamps and carbine lamps. It reminded me of the old western movie towns.

There was the clatter of 32-volt generators; the pub was well lit with its own large 240-volt job. The pub clientele were ringers in their high-heeled riding boots, gray moleskin duds and khaki shirts with hats that had their own special bash in them, and the wide brims with a few earmarks from the lamb marking pliers. Shearers in their gray woollen singlets, their leather moccasins and denim pants. Then there were the labourers, hairy arms and chests poking out of Jackie Howe singlets, and drifters, every type of man you could think of. Oh, there were women, but not many. The barmaids, the shop owners' wives and a few tarts. The bush people didn't mix with the townfolk, they seemed to be a different breed.

But it was all right for us young 'uns to mix with the local stock agents and bank johnnies. These were blokes my age. They either came from Brisbane or large provincial cities doing their country duty before being promoted back to the city. They were the young tellers and clerks from the two banks in town, or the office boys and salesman from the four stock agencies and a couple of very young teachers in their first year. We drank too much, told the dirtiest yarns, and told massive lies about all the women we rooted and more bull dust than could be imagined. We played snooker, cards and arm wrestled. I always wimped out on these sorts of contests. We just let our hair down. We caused no one trouble and kept to ourselves. I was learning to hold my grog a bit better but some nights, or should I say, early mornings, my mouth and feet would not cooperate with my brain. As was the case when I was sneaking back into my room in the early hours of the morning.

One time, I tripped over a sack of potatoes, with me banging the wall as I went down. Spuds rolled everywhere; it made a terrible din. I sobered up quickly and changed into my work clothes. I was walking out of my bedroom when the boss, tying his dressing gown cord around his waist, accosted me.

"What in the hell is going on here, Jack? Explain yourself!"

"Sorry Mr Short. I tripped over this bag of potatoes. I was worried about the calves in the pen."

"It's bloody three o'clock in the morning," said the boss.

"I didn't realise it was so early. I just dreamt something terrible happened to Russell and wanted to check up on him. I'm sorry I woke you," I lied.

I think I got away with that as he just said, "I am pleased you're conscientious about your job, but please don't let this keenness disturb the rest of the family at this time of night." Then he shuffled around the corner and went back to bed. I got my buckets and went down and slept with the calves for the next three hours. I didn't trust myself to go back to bed.

Because there wasn't a dog or horse that I was allowed to have, I found my own two pets to play with and enjoy, but both ended up dying in a most tragic way. Limey was a slow worm. They look like a little snake but if you inspect them carefully, you can see little legs on their belly. They don't use them, but they are there. He, *or was it she?* had a very pointed nose and I kept

Limey in my shirt pocket, feeding him on the tiny insects and moths the lights at night attracted. I also had Glen, a frill-necked lizard that ate the bigger insects. Alas, he ate Limey as well, and I missed my little slow worm. I also missed Glen, too. He must have been in the doorway when the wind slammed the door shut. Poor bugger, that is what you get when you eat a Limey.

Fran did me a great favour; she asked her father if I could go out with her when she went out to dances or parties. Being engaged did not stop one's social life. Her excuse was she needed someone to open gates or help fix a puncture, or if something happened on the roads late at night. She won. Good old Fran, she did it just for me, as she could well look after herself. But there was always a catch. I had to present myself to Mr and Mrs Short every time we went out. I was told to change that shirt, and not that tie, show me your nails and scrape that bit of fluff off your face. Then the manners, do this, don't do that. You are representing the stud. You don't drink alcohol and do what you are told. We were always late as the inspection and lecture always took half-hour or more, but one must pay for small pleasures.

We went to the pictures, which were in a large hall with deck chair type seats with hessian being the main support. You had to look out for the threadbare ones. Now and then you would hear someone hit the floor or maybe it was some wag undoing the lacing at the back of the chair. Anyhow, I enjoyed the flicks. We saw Summer of the Seventeenth Doll, which I liked, but I also had an affinity with it. Nothing to do with the film but with the producer, a famous playwright called Ray Lawler.

Now, as I said, I did a bit of ballet and acting in plays at the National Theatre in Melbourne and the first play I did at the great age of nine was one of Ray Lawler's first. It was called Victoria Regina and I had a small part in it. Unfortunately, I had a bit of trouble pronouncing words and when the elite of Melbourne asked me, "What are you playing in now, Jack?" I would proudly say, "I'm playing in Victoria's vagina" and then wonder about the funny little smiles they gave me.

We saw The Big Fisherman and listened to Elvis's new hit, A Wooden Heart, which was played on every radio. Even Mrs Short said she didn't mind Elvis, which was a surprise.

I met Bonny, slim, and delightful, a luscious brunette, hair down to her shoulders, rosy, red cheeks, big brown soft eyes like a fallow deer, a smile that made something go 'tick' inside of me and a voice that was like a robin singing. She was a bit of *awright*. She was a jillaroo on her father's property near the Morg, that's short for Glenmorgan. I met her when the Shorts and Fran took me to church and introduced us. I never thought much about church but was now getting a different perspective of the benefits of religion. It may seem strange for a bloke that's been brought up by women, but I just didn't know how they worked, I *still don't*, and I felt very uncomfortable around girls my age. Bonny was different. I felt relaxed with her and was able to have a reasonable conversation. I was even amusing sometimes and she would throw her head back and laugh, as naturally as she smiled. Life at that moment seemed wonderful. I was invited to her place the next weekend to a tennis party. I said I would love to attend if I wasn't working. Fran pleaded with her father on my behalf and for once he said "all right" if she went as well.

The week went so slowly, but Saturday did eventually arrive, Fran asked if I played tennis. I had to give her a negative. I had never held a racquet, let alone had any whites. It didn't seem to matter, particularly after the boss offered me his tennis clobber that was yellow with age and made in the thirties. Fran said it wasn't essential to play, that there would be a lot of other activities. Spruced up after Friday's bath night. This was before the rain and we had a water shortage, so I was only allowed to bath on Fridays. The boss had lowered the paint level on the bathtub. Old Spice aftershave, Brylcreem on my hair and my best casual clothes that Mum had sent up only three weeks before. I was ready. Even the boss approved and said I looked pretty darn good, and then spoilt it by finishing with, "For a kid from a broken home."

We arrived at the party; the latest model cars were in the car park. Ford Fairlanes, Buicks, Jaguars, Holdens and Mercedes. This was a right royal do. The green lawns of the homestead contrasted with the dull brownness of the countryside and the homestead at last looked like a western Queenslander, as I had seen in photos. Gentlemen were dressed in Fletcher Jones trousers with kangaroo hide plaited belts, fine checked shirts, pastel woolen ties and highly polished brogues or dress riding boots. No matter the different sizes, they looked healthy, tanned and fit. They were countrymen. The ladies all wore fine straw hats, pretty cotton frocks, little makeup and were perfectly groomed.

Of course, anyone playing tennis was wearing the Persil whiter than white whites and the whitest of tennis shoes. Bonny came out to welcome us. She was just beautiful.

"Oh Jack, I was hoping you could play tennis. You can, can't you?"

"I've never have had the opportunity."

"Well, we will have fun teaching you. I've booked for you to play with me later in the day." My male mind flashed a wicked thought. "Now come and meet Dad and the rest of the crowd and Jack, help yourself to the keg over there if you want a beer or there's punch and lemonade on the table."

I was introduced to 'Dad', an enormous fellow. He had a good, hearty handshake and a booming, laughing voice.

"So, you're the new jackaroo at the Shorts? Well, let's see if you can stay longer than any of the others. He is a hard man, but fair. Jack, make yourself at home, enjoy what we have to offer and do have a fun time." He then started to make his way inside. Fran introduced me to other jackaroos and station owners' sons and daughters. We swapped yarns, and I listened to exciting stories about pig hunts, rodeos, the latest cars, brake horsepower in bulldozers, timber treatment and so on. I was really interested in everything that was said and started to realise how much was in this grazing game that I had chosen as a career. I lost at snooker, won at table tennis, lost while balancing on one chair in a handstand.

Then there was Bonny, who was busy being the perfect hostess, making sure everyone had a drink, passing the savouries around, talking to everyone and playing tennis. I loved watching her move around, especially when she was on the court. Her hair bounced about, her legs danced the dance and every now and then I got a sneak preview of her snow-white briefs covering a little gorgeous bum. "C'mon Jack, it's your turn to put these tennis shoes on I've found for you and we will have a hit." I pulled off my boots and quickly put on the tennis shoes. They were a bit tight but who cared? She grabbed me by the hand, an electric shock ran right up my arm. I was dumbfounded that a touch from another human's hand could cause such a reaction. She played tennis, I hit the ball now and then and everywhere, but I had fun and she made me feel like a Lew Hoad. Late in the evening when the oldies started to go home, Bonny was sitting beside me while a group of us were yarning and telling stories. I felt very naïve, as I was well and truly out of my depth. These were bush people born and raised. Here I was from Melbourne and four months ago I had never seen a sheep, let alone know anything about the bush. Bonny must have noticed my quietness and started to ask about Melbourne and what I used to do. This time I had the floor, while everyone listened to my exaggerated stories about city life.

Fran came and spoilt everything by saying, "Jack, we better go, so we won't be late home and get into trouble with Dad."

Everyone seemed to understand that I had no alternative but to leave. Bonny saw us to the car. Not feeling very manly with Fran getting into the driver's side. But once again, Bonny made me feel good by saying, "I was glad you could come, Jack. I sorta like you and hope I can see you soon."

I blurted out, "Me too," as Fran put the old vanguard into first gear and started the long drive home. I had pleasant dreams that night.

Fran and I went to the local 50/50 dance a few weeks later and I was praying Bonny would be there. But alas, they were shearing for the next month and nobody goes out when shearing is on. I had to be content waltzing and quickstepping with the local maidens and their mothers. Touched everybody's sticky, sweaty palms during the barn dance and rocked and rolled a bit. It was a bit hard with the band of four, a piano, piano accordion, the sax and violin, all played by people in their fifties. There was one other, a young drummer that used to rub the brushes on the drums for the old-time dances, but when they announced *Rock Around the Clock*, he really went to town. After that dance, the band had a break and I think the older members gave the young fella a bit of a talking to about the noise or something, as he was very quiet when the dances resumed. I had a few dancing lessons in the city, but I was surprised how the little kids danced beautifully and knew all the moves. They were good.

Bonny, when would I see her next? I started to see the hopelessness of the situation. If only I had a car. If only I didn't have to work most weekends. If only I had more money. My lousy $15.00 a week, paid monthly, did not give me a bank account that would make me feel adequate in squiring a grazier's daughter around. She could ride a horse, muster, brand, crack a stockwhip, play tennis, water ski and goodness knows what else. Here was I, a poor humble city boy that was way out of his depth. What chance did I have? A fat chance, that's what!

I thought of Bonny constantly, but did I phone her? No, because phones were on a party line and no way was the community going to hear my romantic conversation. Perhaps a letter. No, I was not good at writing and spelling was a disaster. I wasn't going to let myself down further. I saw Bonny twice more, again at church when we managed to get ten minutes together and at her place for New Year's Eve, but that was another disaster as Mr Short had too much to drink and we had to go home early. I never saw Bonny again. I used to think of her a lot. I believe we were two very close, loving people in our last lives. It was a tiny bump in the passing of this one.

The mailman came but once a week. I always looked forward to mail from home. Mum wrote regularly and sent things up that a fella would never think of, like underpants, socks, and hankies, something warm in winter and something cool for summer. It was Christmas and I got lots of parcels. I was a spoilt brat as far as Mr Short was concerned. Two books from my sister, clothes from Mum, a nice jacket and shirt with little goodies like The Sporting Shooter, The Man on the Land, and a host of other magazines. Sweets and chocolates that melted on the way and best of all, a home baked Christmas cake from Gran. A bloody cake. I hadn't had a cake since I left home. I wasn't sharing it with anyone. I cut a man-size slice every night for three days and then it was gone, but gee, it was great. My father sent me a $20.00 note in a card, which was a surprise.

I bought Fran a frypan for her glory box, Jenny, who was never home as she stayed with relatives in Brisbane to go to uni in the New Year, I bought her a writing set and the Shorts; I got them a set of six mugs. They were the new thing out. Fran gave me a kangaroo-plaited belt and the Shorts gave me a book, Famous Hereford Studs, of course, with Tee Tree Stud getting a big mention. It wasn't a bad day; we had roasted chook and vegetables and plum pudding with three penny pieces in it and I was even shouted a beer. But I still had to do all the chores: the cows; the separating; the wood and all the rest.

After New Year, things at the stud started to deteriorate. Fran left without telling anyone. I think she ran away to be with Peter, or that's the gossip. Jenny was down in Brisbane and Tom, with his nervous breakdown, left for good. The Shorts were very short with me and things just weren't hunky-dory. I was given Tom's job, feeding bulls three times a day, raking and cleaning twelve bull stalls as well as grooming, sorting feed and keeping the flies to a mere thousand or so as well as my other chores. They employed another jackaroo to help me. He was hopeless. Came from a farm somewhere and couldn't kill a sheep and was flat out milking one cow. *Don't know where they get them from these days!*

I was not feeling very well. I felt lethargic and had to force myself to get my jobs done. I had no youthful energy and had these horrible weeping sores on my arms, legs and hands.

"It's nothing," said Mr Short, "it's just Barcoo rot. Everyone gets it."

But I wasn't happy. I missed Fran and Tom. I never saw or had much to do with Bill or Barry. Mr and Mrs Short weren't a barrel of fun either and seemed to pick on me as if I was a permanently blocked nostril. Things were not good at Tee Tree Stud.

It was inevitable that it would happen. I was cleaning the stalls and was accused of not doing them properly. One of the bulls was losing weight and did I regularly clean their water troughs and could I be a bit quicker? But then, what can you expect from someone from a broken home?

That did it. I was sick, tired, working thirteen-hour days, seven days a week, no breaks since Tom and Fran left and to cop that. I stopped what I was doing and said very calmly, "Mr Short, I wish to give a fortnight's notice."

"You young whippersnapper, how dare you! You can get off the property now."

Putting the fork down slowly, I said, "Very well, if that's your wish," and started to walk out of the stalls toward the house.

"Er, just a minute Jack. I might have been a bit hasty; do you really want to give a fortnight's notice?"

"Yes, I do, Boss. I really mean it," I calmly replied.

"Well, we will see, but maybe we can talk about it when we have both cooled down a bit. You can get back to work now." I returned to my job raking the sawdust as the boss walked out of the stalls.

There was a great transformation with the Shorts. They were so nice to me and the food seemed a bit better. There was more conversation at mealtimes and Mr Short said what a good job I was doing and how hard it was to get devoted workers these days. I was going to leave. I was not well and the Shorts were working me hard with no relief, nothing about a few extra dollars since I took over Tom's job. I felt I would not progress any further in my career if I stayed here and I had a feeling I should go home. Not that I was homesick, but needed to see if leaving the city was the right choice, or maybe it was to say goodbye forever to the boy, as I felt soon I could class myself a MAN.

A week after the row, I said to the boss, "I understand I will be leaving this day next week?"

He exploded. "You little bastard, leave the bulls without a groom? Leave Mrs Short and I with the lot. How dare you! How dare you!"

He was frothing at the mouth and he was shaking like a leaf and I thought he would either have a heart attack or kill me there and then with his bare hands.

"Right, you have fifteen minutes to get off this property or I will call the police and have you charged with trespassing."

I left him fuming, raced to the house and started packing my things. I seemed to have collected so much more in the six months I was there. I had trouble fitting it all into my knapsack and airway bag. I rolled what I couldn't fit in, into a long sausage like a swag. It took me a bit longer than fifteen minutes, but I guess not that much longer. There was a knock on the door and Mrs Short entered with tears in her eyes and a tissue held to a sniffly nose.

"Oh Jack, I am so sorry it's come to this. Mr Short has had a lot of problems of late and he did look on you as the son we never had."

She blew into the tissue and then rolled it around to find a dry spot, but there was still a drip from the end of her nose.

"I see you're determined to go. We are both sorry you're leaving and I would like to say on behalf of Mr Short and myself," she started to get really teary then and sniffled some more and her chin started to tremble, as did her voice. "As I was trying to say, Jack, thank you for all you have done and we have appreciated it. Barry will come and pick you up and take you to town. He shouldn't be long."

She slowly turned away, shoulders hunched, still sniffing in to that tight rolled ball of a tissue. I was feeling pretty emotional myself but kept my feelings in check. I had made my decision, whether it was good or bad, I was sticking by it.

Barry pulled the boss's Vanguard up to the back gate. Opening the back passenger door, I placed all my belongings on the back seat. I shut the door and started to get in beside Barry, wanting to get off the place without any more emotional scenes. Mr and Mrs Short appeared at the gate.

Mr Short stepped forward saying, "Well, this is it, Jack," as he handed me an envelope. "Here is your cheque son and all the best."

I took the cheque and went to shake his hand, but he turned around and took the few steps back to Mrs Short. Barry grated the gears and as we headed off down the road, I turned and saw two very lonely pathetic figures. He in his baggy bib and brace overalls, his arm around Mrs Short's waist and she was still with a tissue giving a hint of a wave goodbye.

We didn't talk much travelling the eighteen kilometres to town. Barry never spoke much anyway and I was deep in emotional thought. I did not have a chance to say goodbye to my now rather big babies or the kittens, which were now cats. I wanted to say 'seeya' to Madam and the other cows that had built up my forearms and biceps; I didn't like leaving the Shorts that way. Perhaps they were not that bad. Years later, I realised, even though he was tough and rather aggressive toward me and treated me a bit like an eighteenth-century slave, he did toughen me up. It was known that any jackaroo who lasted at the Shorts for more than four months would end up successful in the grazing industry. He moulded me from a rather feminine city kid to the beginnings of a useful young man. I give credit where it's due.

"Where do you want to be dropped off?" were Barry's first words on the drive in to town.

"The pub will do thanks."

"You shouldn't have left like that; you know the boss will have a lot of trouble finding someone else. You young ones can't seem to take it."

End of conversation and end of the lift. We pulled up outside the Meandarra pub. I struggled getting my gear off the back seat, and Barry just sat in the driver's seat.

"Well, you got all your stuff?" he said, as he grated the gears once again and took off, the back door of the car closing with a bang by itself. I gave a wave to the dusty backside of the disappearing car yelling, "Thanks Barry," but I doubt if he heard.

C.13

There and Back

The Fight, Prostitutes, Melbourne, A Job

I slept on the bank floor that night. That's upstairs where the bank johnnies had their quarters. Dave chucked down a mattress for me and said, "We all had a bet and I won $5.00 that you would last six months at Tee Tree stud, so it's my shout at the pub."

The next morning, I said goodbye to all my townie friends and hitched a ride to Toowoomba with none other than Bruce, the one that nearly gelded me. But there's always a condition, and that was on the basis I helped him load forty bales of wool. That was the reason for him going there in the first place. He was quite chatty on the long drive and even let me have a go at driving the loaded truck while he snoozed. He taught me how to double the clutch and use the diff button for another range of gears.

Gee, I felt great driving the large body truck, especially seeing I only had a Victorian car license. We arrived at the second biggest city in Queensland at the ungodly hour of 12.30 A.M. and we both managed to get a room at Cleweys Motel even at that late hour. Bruce woke me up at seven and asked if I would give him a hand to unload the wool at the railway. I said, "After breakfast."

"I will pay for your bed if we go now," he said.

I was easy, had nothing else to do. As Bruce paid for our night's accommodation, I booked for another two nights as it seemed a reasonable tariff.

We unloaded the wool. Bruce went on his way, and I went mine to the nearest café and ordered a countryman's breakfast, which had the works and filled my very empty stomach. I was walking up the main street towards the motel and who should I see but Tom. I was so pleased to see him and I expect he was to see me. We chatted excitedly about him starting a new job up at Bundaberg running a sugar farm, or was it a mill? And the two months of rest helped him recover from his breakdown. He was pleased I'd left the stud, as he was sure I would find a better job. Then he asked me if I would like to go with him as he was on his way to visit friends and had just stopped off to pick up some grog. I said fine and helped Tom get the grog, then went off to his friend's place. It was a big mistake. It ended up in a very heavy drinking session, giving Tom a sendoff. I was drunk, real drunk.

Someone, I don't know who, dropped me off in the main street. I can only remember weaving and stumbling along the street, yes, and falling down. Somehow, I found the motel and my room. How I got the key into the lock beats me. The bed was revolving, the room was spinning and I was somewhere in between. I was crook, my head, my body, everyone was making such a din. I wanted to die. I swallowed two Vincent powders, a glass of bore water and had half a Rothmans. That was breakfast. I slept most of the morning, could have killed the maid that disturbed me wanting to make up my room. She understood and left quietly.

Arising from my sick bed at two, I went and had the longest shower I ever had and spruced myself up. Then down town for lunch and putting my washing in at the same day laundry.

"Won't be ready till tomorrow, luv."

I looked for a job at the unemployment office and the stock and stations agents, no luck. Booking another night at Cleweys as the drinking binge, the exit from Tee Tree Stud as well as my health, was taking a toll. I picked up my laundry and some Larry & Stretch cowboy booklets. The next day, I stayed in my room, sorted my packing and got everything ready for an early start in the morning. I had planned to hitchhike to Sydney, then train it to Melbourne.

I got lucky with a ride to Warwick, the Roses and Rodeo City of South East Queensland and spent the day in this fine town looking for work. Alas, nothing. Stayed at the Royal Hotel that night ready for another early start for the big cities down south. Lucky again, a lift got me from Warwick to Stanthorpe, the coldest town in this northern state.

"You wanna earn a dollar?" the rough voice behind me said as I was thumbing another lift. It gave me a start, as I didn't see the tall lanky man approach.

"Yea and what doing?" said I with a suspicious voice.

"We are short-handed loading apples and pears out of the cold stores on to the train. I'll pay you $4.00 a day for your trouble."

"You're on, where do I go?"

I followed him to a huge shed nearby and he took me to the basement where there were racks and racks of wooden boxes of fruit.

"This here is your section. If you can empty all these boxes on to the conveyer belt and clear this section, you will get your $4.00."

He pushed a lever on the frame of the conveyer belt to get it started, and then he left, saying a whistle will blow at lunch when all work will cease.

There was about sixteen centimetres of ice-cold water on the floor and everything was cold. Even as I lifted a box on to the moving belt, it would just break and the fruit would go everywhere. But as usual I managed.

The whistle blew and the belt stopped. I found my way out of that freezing dim lit basement in to the warm sun. I saw other men in gumboots and heavy roll neck jumpers and thick trousers eating their lunch, leaning or squatting by the storeroom wall. We all must be working in different sections, as there was no one near me in that basement.

Me, I had no lunch. "Sorry lad, the nearest shop is twelve kilometres away in town."

I walked, jumped, rung out my wet socks and let them and my boots dry in the late February sun. The siren went, the wet socks and boots went back on and back down to that wet cold hell. We finished at 4.30 P.M. I got my money.

"You did a good job today. Wanna come back tomorrow?" I gave a frozen smile and said, "No thanks," and found a quiet place to change my wet clothes. I was far from town, so up comes the thumb as the warm sun goes down and I'm looking for another lift down south.

It was about an hour later that the big semi, with a mixed load of a car, steel and crates and goodness knows what else, pulled over with a whoosh of its air brakes.

"Where you headed, son?" yelled the driver, leaning over to the passenger side of the huge Mack rig.

"Sydney, but anywhere on the way will do," I replied.

"I am going all the way to Sydney. If you can keep me awake and help with the rig, you're welcome," said the now smiling driver as he pushed open the huge door inviting me into the warm cabin. "Chuck your gear in the sleeper behind you. I am running late. It's nonstop to Sydney if it's alright by you? The name is

Jim," he said, extending his right hand.

I shook the beefy paw.

"The handle is Jack," I replied. I got that from the Larry and Stretch western I had just finished, "and thanks a lot Jim for picking me up."

We must have gone through a dozen gears as the rig got up to cruising pace. We talked and talked. I told him of my adventures and what I was doing on the road. He told me about his loving wife and three kids and how he hated leaving them. He would also like to stop interstate driving so he could spend more time with them. He said he had three sets of books under his seat so the police would not be able to know if he had the regulation rests or not. He wanted out, but the more trips meant more money. The sooner he could leave this job and be with the wife and kids, the better.

We stopped at Wallangarra for a quick feed, then on the road again.

"Yer nodding off, Jack, you're the one supposed to keep me awake, not the other way round," said Jim, giving me a nudge. The long day, the cold of that storage basement, the warm cabin, the full stomach, the drone of the Detroit engine. Hell, what was I expected to do but sleep? But a bargain is a bargain. I apologised for not doing my job and so what did he want to talk about?

We were just starting to climb a steep range with the road winding its snaky way up. Jim kept changing the gears down. I started to count the changes; the truck was going slower and slower; the engine was getting louder; my hand was resting on the door handle. In my very bravest voice, I enquired, "Err Jim, what do you do when you run out of gears? 'Cause I don't think the brakes would hold her."

"Oh, you just jack-knife the truck in to the bank," said Jim calmly. I looked at the narrow steep road ahead. *Would the truck fit on the road if it were jack-knifed?*

"Well, that's the last gear I got," said Jim, changing down once more. "We are in the lap of the gods now." He turned to me with a wicked look on his tough Easter Island looking face. "Look Jack, that's poor Bill's rig down there. Poor bastard never made it."

I looked out of my window down the sheer cliff face. I was sure the truck's wheels were only centimetres from the edge. And there, halfway down, was the burnt-out wreck of a semi. Our truck was going so slow, I was sure for every two metres we made we slipped back one. I was now wide awake and feeling rather uncomfortable.

"Jack, look there. See that wreck way down there? That's Fred's, he survived that. You wouldn't believe you could survive a crash like that. He is in a wheelchair, though."

The truck was not going to make it. I was so sure I would be a small legend down the bottom of this range. Bloody Jim pointed out another three wrecks before, with the grace of God and his entire angels, we made it to the top. We had a good coast down the range. Jim changing gears and applying the air brakes, stopped the truck and broke me the news.

"It's your turn to drive now, Jack. I am going to have a kip or two, so wake me before we get to Maitland."

He hopped out and appeared at the passenger side door. Opening it, he said, "Well, move over, Jack. You told me you drove that bloody truck full of wool, so you can drive this. I will help with the gears."

I shifted over to the driver's side, getting a bit tangled with the gearshift caught between my legs, but I managed. Wow, it felt great sitting up so high and in control of this monster. The gears were more complicated than the body truck as it had a preselector on it, which confused me for a while, but what the hell, I was now a truckie. It started to get a bit tricky driving; Jim was snoring (that alone was enough to keep me awake) and kept leaning toward me, his lolling head against my shoulder. I tried to push him over to the other side, but his body was determined to stay where it was.

I managed to change down and apply the brakes as the sign was telling me we were about to enter Maitland. Jim woke up with a start, rubbing his eyes, yawning and said, "Get out Jack. I will take over now, and thanks, I needed that."

I got out and jumped up into my side of the cabin while Jim was more successful than I, sliding into the driver's seat and with a gear change, we were on our way again. We stopped again just outside Wyong.

"This is an old truckie's trick. You have a quick shuteye before the sun comes up, and an hour later, when it's daylight, you go again."

"You see," continued Jim, "it fools the body. Go to sleep when it's dark, wake up when it's daylight and you feel as if you have had a good night's sleep, but it's only been for an hour."

We settled down in our respective seats and soon we were both sound asleep. The starter motor turning over the big eight-cylinder engine woke me.

"We are just waiting till the air builds up and we should be in Sydney about half seven," Jim was saying as he rumpled his hair and had a scratch of his crotch at the same time. "Where do you want to be dropped off? I am going right through Sydney to Kingsford, where I unload this lot and pick up another load, then back to Brissie."

"Oh, anywhere will do, somewhere near Pitt Street if you can. But Jim, aren't you going to see your wife and kids before you head back to Brisbane?" I asked.

"I will try. I must see how long it will take me to unload and load up again. I might be lucky and be able to just change trailers, who knows? We have a small house at Rooty Hill, which is a bit out of the way, but I will give her a call, anyway."

I thought it a bit strange that if he loved his wife and kids so much, he would at least spend a couple of hours with them, but it wasn't my business, so said nothing.

The traffic was starting to get heavy as we passed Hornsby and Jim was busy with gears, brakes and muttering about bloody car drivers. 'didn't they know how long it took to pull up a heavy rig?' The tall buildings were showing on the horizon with the sun rising behind them and then we were in the thick of it, Sydney Town. Jim dropped me off on the corner of George Street and Martin Place.

"You just have to walk to the next block for Pitt Street."

We then said our goodbyes and wished each other the best for the future, hoping all our dreams would come to fruition. With all my gear on my back and in my hands, I felt conspicuous as I walked through the growing early morning workers along Pitt Street to my destination, the YMCA, where a feed, a shower, and a bed was of the utmost urgency.

"Could I have a single room for a couple of days, please?" I asked the middle-aged woman at the reception desk.

"We haven't any singles left, only doubles. Will that do?" she answered, rather short.

"Okay, as long as I don't have to share for today, as I have been up all night and need a good sleep and want to be by myself for the day. If you can manage it, I would be most thankful," I pleaded with her, using my 'how can you resist my doggy-eyes' expression.

"Alright then, mister, sign here, but tomorrow I will be putting someone in with you. We are very busy now."

I signed the register and made it to my room. The long, hot shower was pure bliss on my tired, aching body. I cleaned the sores on my hands and limbs with antiseptic cream, and it didn't help much but felt better. Gee I was tired. The trick of Jim's worked for an hour or so and that's about all. I locked the door and fell on the bed with just a towel around my waist and promptly fell asleep.

I felt pinned to the bed. A weight was on top of me, heavy breathing in my ear, a raw body odor. Perhaps I was dreaming of that terrible day when Bruce and his mate were going to cut me. Hey this wasn't a dream, this was real! Adrenaline surged through my body as I suddenly woke up. Some bastard was trying to root me. With all my strength, I rolled to the left, toppling the rapist and myself to the floor. I was incensed. I was mad. I had made a promise to myself that no one would ever take advantage of me.

This over fat peachy young man with his red pubic hairs and his small, half-erect penis was going to get a lesson he would never forget. As he started to get up off the floor he said, "Oh that was fun, ducks! You ready to play some more?"

I hit him. I hit him in his fat, porky guts as hard as I could. I had often dreamed of being in a fight, but my arms seemed weak and my punches felt like little powder puffs on my opponent's face and they just laughed. His knees buckled. A right cross to the jaw straightened him up for a second before he hit the floor. Dear Madam and her girls did put the strength in my arms from my hours of milking. I waited till he regained his feet.

"C'mon you queer, you did want to play, didn't you?"

Oh, I was mad, mad as hell; I think all my life's frustrations and hurts rose up from some hidden depths in my body. He rushed at me; he wasn't good enough; the adrenaline was surging; the hate was hating; the body tuned to kill. I did a *pas d'elevation*, gave two quick jabs to the midriff, a quick *pirouette* to miss his pathetic onslaught. *The ballet lessons were coming in handy, after all*. I confused him with an *epaulement,* then another right cross and finishing with a beautiful uppercut. He went sailing backwards into the three-ply wardrobe, smashing the doors and ending up half in it. I just glared at him waiting, waiting for him to get up.

"C'mon have a go," I taunted. "You haven't touched me yet, and I don't think you can."

He was quick, I will give him that. He shot out of that wardrobe like he had been fired from a cannon. In a half crouch, he head butted me in the chest and with the acceleration of his charge knocked me into the opposite dressing table causing one of its legs to break, leaving me and it sprawled on the floor. I was surprised I hadn't felt a thing. Then he kicked me as I was getting up. The blow got me just below the ribs and knocked the wind out of me. He grabbed the table light that had fallen off the dresser and tried to bash my head in with the heavy brass base. I rolled away just as he brought the base down to where my head should have been. The force and my sudden movement caused him to unbalance and he grabbed the dresser to steady his fall. Before you could say, 'Jack be nimble' I was up behind him, waiting for him to turn around and when he did, it was a one two to the body, a *tour en l'air*, a left to the jaw, a right cross to the body, a *pirouette*, a left and right jab to the solar plexus. Another right cross and a haymaker that sent the creature flying across the room to finish off the wardrobe he had half smashed before. He lay there out like a light, his revolting nude body slumped against the debris that had once held clothes.

I sucked badly needed air into my lungs. My rage was evaporating. I took stock of the room and its damage; something made me turn around and there in the doorway was a crowd of people that a few seconds before I had been completely unaware of. How long they had been there or what they saw, I didn't have a clue. Then, to my utmost horror, I realised I was in the nude facing all these people at my doorway.

"I'm calling the police and I'm having both of you homos charged. We don't have people like you at the Y."

Finding my towel on the floor and quickly putting it around me to cover my nakedness, I said, pointing to the now groaning pervert, "That bastard tried to rape me. You can call the police, 'cause I will charge him with attempted rape and assault."

The small, fat, balding man with the half reading glasses on his nose, who was the one initially going to call the police, now stated in an authoritative voice, "Okay folks, the show is over, you all go about your business now, I'm the manager here."

They were slow to move. He turned, his already red face got redder, his eyeballs bulged and he yelled, "Scram!" Everyone did without the slightest hesitation.

The queer was slowly getting to his feet. He reached across to grab a sheet to cover himself and to wipe the blood from his torn lips and bloody nose. He spoke with a painful voice and a bit of a whimper, "There's been a bit of a mistake."

"Bloody oath, there's been a mistake," said I, still with a bit of fight in me.

"Now then, let's all calm down and tell me exactly what happened," the manager said as he moved into the wrecked room, shutting the door behind him as my opponent sat himself on my bed.

"I was sound asleep on my bed because I was up all night and the lady at the front counter said she wouldn't put anyone in my room, so I thought I was by myself. Then this bloke jumped on me and tried to rape me and all I did was protect myself." I explained in one full breath.

"And what have you to say for yourself?" the manager turned to look at my aggressor.

"Oh, it's a terrible mistake. I thought it was Basil's room."

"Just a minute, I know you. You have caused trouble here before, haven't you?" said the balding manager, looking more closely at my victim. "Yes indeed, you're Phillip Grosevner, aren't you?"

A slight nod of the head was all the manager needed.

"You come with me now, are these your clothes in the corner here"? Phillip hobbled across, picked up his clothes and barely giving me a glance.

Then the manager showed him the door. "You just wait here and I will be with you in a sec."

He shut the door behind my guest as he was leaving.

"Listen, son, we don't want to involve the police. We will look after this internally. I think you have given that Phillip bloke a lesson he won't forget. I will find the maid and make sure you get another room; I am sorry this has happened in our establishment. But you should always make sure your room is locked and bolted. That's what they're there for. If you had done that simple thing, nothing would have happened." He abruptly turned, opened the door, grabbed the sniffling Phillip by the elbow and escorted him down the passage. I heard the manager say, "You're out of here, young man and you're a liar to boot. There is no Basil staying here. You got what you deserved, now get out."

I shut the door and felt drained and exhausted. Another shower and a feed should perk me up. I wondered who was going to pay for all the damage. I looked at my watch; it was 12.15 P.M. I walked down the passage to the bathroom with a clean set of clothes, locking my room door behind me and double-checking it. I didn't want any more surprises, thank you. The shower stung the few lacerations I suffered and my left side was stiff and sore already from that bastard's kick. The shower seemed to relieve some of the stress and shock that came from the fight. I even noticed I was shaking slightly and my breathing was a bit uneven. I turned the hot water off and let the cold water run over my body, which seemed to refresh me. Vigorously rubbing myself down with the thin white towel with the blue stripe that had YMCA printed on it, I scraped the bum fluff off my face with the Gillette, got dressed and headed back to my room.

The door was open. I was sure I locked it. Cautiously, I entered, and it was only one of the maids.

"Boy, you boys made a mess of this room. The whole building's talking about it. I always miss out on anything that happens around here. The boss said you were to have room thirty-five, which is one of the best I might add. It's just up the hallway and turn to your right."

She was a slight, wispy thing, her mousy hair tied in to a rather unsuccessful bun. About thirty I would guess. I thanked her and got all my belongings together and stuffed them into my haversack and bags. The sooner I was out of that room, the better. After dumping my gear into thirty-five, which was a larger, better room than my last, I went downstairs and out into the smoggy February sunshine to find a café for a good, decent meal.

Everyone was in a hurry. If they didn't get to where they were going in record time, the sun would fall on them or something stupid like that. I was propelled down Pitt Street by the humanity. If you didn't keep to their pace, I'm sure one would be trampled on. I found an eating place just round the corner in Margaret Street. I ordered, "A pie with vegetables and jelly and ice cream for dessert, thank you, and could I have a vanilla milk shake as well?" The foreign-looking waiter with black, greasy hair down to his shoulders – didn't like that much. Men have short back and sides, don't they? – took the order, and his time, moving to the kitchen to place it.

The milk shake was okay, even though I must have waited ten minutes, and the meal, umph, was more like an entrée. A tiny pie with seaweed or something mixed with the mince and a lousy dessertspoon of vegetables nicely decorated on the plate. I ate the lot in seconds and it cost me a whole $2.50. They should be locked up. How they can justify that amount beats me. Look what I had to do, a bloody day's real work to get that amount. It was counter lunches for me from now on.

I walked around a few blocks without getting harassed too much by the population. Bought some smokes, a Phantom comic and the Sydney Morning Herald even though it was the afternoon and made my way back to the Y. That evening I met a young fellow from Perth, he was on his way to Broken Hill as he had just got a job at the mines there. He said, "Hey, did you hear about the ruckus that happened here this morning? Some homo fella tried to rape this bloke. And got into an awful mess when he was bashed up. They reckoned the whole room was smashed to pieces."

The lad's name was Peter, fair-haired, about my age but taller. We met in the lobby as I was looking in the brochures for something to do tomorrow.

"Yea," he continued, "the manager threw one of them out and charged the other for all the damage. They say $100.00 worth. Struth, I would hate to be that bloke."

I said nothing, but a sick feeling started to rise in the pit of my stomach.

"Nuh, I never heard anything about it," I lied, "my name's Jack, do you want to come out and have a feed?" I asked.

"It's funny you asked, 'cause I am on my way to Kings Cross. They say it's worth having a look, and anyway, I'm told there are some good eating places up there, wanna come?"

So off up William Street we walked towards the Cross. It was a long way. Even Peter commented that we should have caught the bus. Gee, the sights we saw there. Beatniks and flower people, drunks and larrikins, small, tall, fat and thin, but they all had one thing in common and that was they were all queer. We got a window seat at a café so we could watch the fascinating parade of the Sydney-siders. There were strip joints and nightclubs, but neither of us were cashed up enough to visit. I've forgotten what we ordered, but I remembered it was sufficient and a reasonable cost, but I just couldn't believe the different types I was seeing.

I'd only left Melbourne about eight months ago and I am sure we didn't have people like that down there and definitely not in Queensland. After we'd finished our meal and entertainment, I suggested we start walking back, otherwise we would be locked out. I thought the Y closed its doors at eleven or was that in Queensland?

Peter agreed, so we walked around the Cross for a bit, checking out the place, then started heading home.

"Hey look here, it's Palmer Street where the prosos, *prostitutes*, and brothels are. Let's go and have a perv," suggested Peter.

"And why not?" I replied.

Along one side of the street was a large, long, factory brick wall. On the other side was a row of small cottages with little picket fences, some with the front doors open and some with the doors closed. There were dozens, no hundreds, of men with their backs to the brick wall talking, drinking beer from brown paper bags, rolling cigarettes and generally standing around and looking at what was going on. Peter and I started to walk along the footpath in front of the cottages. I was amazed at the girls standing at the little picket gates. They weren't old hags covered in powder, rouge and slap on lipstick with pendulous breasts and split skirts up to the thigh like I imagined prostitutes to look like. No, these girls were about my age, attractive, wore slacks and t-shirts and, believe it or not, I would have been proud to take one home to meet me mum, without the prostitute tag of course. Apparently, the ones with the front doors shut were busy and the ones with the doors open, talking to men over the fence, were negotiating business. You could see right in through the open doorways, a bed with a pillow one end and another in the middle of the sheeted bed, a large towel and a bedside table with a vase of flowers, a box of tissues and a jar of petroleum jelly. No, I did not go in; I was scared stiff. No, *that's not the right word, very nervous, I should say.*

Peter went up and started talking to one of the girls. What was he saying? Was he going in? Was it legal? Could you get locked up being here? Who were all the men standing along the wall? Criminals, murderers, thugs? This wasn't a place for a person such as I. The panic started to mount inside of me. I kept walking down the street, leaving Peter to his business. Then police sirens started, they seemed close. I panicked, I ran, I wanted outta there. I could hear feet, lots of feet running behind me. I ran as fast as I could, hearing the sirens louder and louder. A quick glance behind me showed the whole neighborhood was running behind me. Were they after me? Were they getting away from the police? Oh My God! I'm out of here. I bolted around the corner and back up to William Street and then a very quick walk back to the Y. Phew! What a day. Driving a huge transporter with a heavy load, the fight of my life and the fright of my life. Half a man and yet half a boy. I locked my room, checked it thrice, fell on the bed fully clothed and ended that day of my young life.

I saw Peter down in the breakfast room the next morning.

"Did you get a bit last night?" I asked.

"No, some lunatic started a panic when the police sirens sounded and the whole street did a bolt. I was just getting friendly with a chick, too. She even asked me if I wanted to go inside. Then the rush happened. She just went inside and shut the door like all the other girls did and before you could say, 'Jack be quick' the whole street was empty. Crikey, mate, what happened to you?"

I lied again to Peter. I said, "I was talking to this other chick further down the street, and she was an alright sort when the stampede happened and it was all over for me too. Anyway, what are you doing today?"

"I got to leave for Broken Hill. My bus leaves at 11.30 and I better be on it."

We finished our breakfast. Peter left for the mines and I caught a ferry to the zoo.

The ferry ride across Port Jackson from Potts Point to Taronga Park Zoo was rather exciting, and so were the views of Sydney Harbour and the city from the zoological gardens. But I didn't like the zoo much. The animals seemed healthy enough, but I felt empathy towards them. Their eyes told me they wanted freedom. I had a feeling that keeping animals like this was wrong. Why couldn't they keep them in huge natural parks and let them roam free and let the people view them from buses or cars or some sort of safari vehicle? Perhaps they might one day.

I checked out of the Y and asked if there was anything owing.

"Er, yes sir, you have paid in full for your accommodation, but there is payment due for damages to your room of $100.00."

"Excuse me," I said indignantly to the new clerk I hadn't seen before. "I have just left my room; number thirty-five and I assure you there is no damage to the room. See, here is my key number thirty-five." I think I had him bluffed.

"I think there has been some mistake. The bill is in your name, but for room number twenty-three. Just a moment sir, I will check with the manager." As soon as he disappeared, I went, haversack on my back, bag in my hand. I couldn't run, but by God I wasn't far off it. Ducking around into King Street, back into Pitt Street and a quick march for the next seven blocks or so, till I got to Central Railway Station. I didn't look back once. I just had to concentrate on getting out of there as quick as possible considering the crowds, my luggage and the distance to the station. Then I caught the train to Melbourne. It seemed a long journey and having to change trains at Albury on the Victorian border because of something about different gauge rail tracks.

Melbourne, green trams crashing over intersections, ding, ding of their bells, cars whizzing here and there, the people not as rushed as in Sydney, better dressed, sooo upper-class. This was, or used to be, my town. And the sameness of it all brought back all the images of my childhood. I didn't want to go home and meet the family. So I went to the pictures instead, after lockering all my gear at Spencer Street Railway Station. I saw *The Sundowners*. It was about shearing and the bush and I picked out a few bush mistakes but enjoyed it. I had notified Mum when I left Sydney, so I was expected sometime that day.

Getting off the green snorting bus, walking down the hill, opening the green back gate of the house where I had spent ten years of my young life. Down the concrete path lined with rose bushes; I was filled with apprehension. *Why did I make the journey home?* I knocked on the back door. I waited. I knocked again and the door was flung open and a great welcome from my family, my mum, grandmother, and sister.

It was a right royal welcome all right. My favourite dinner of roast beef and crispy fresh baked vegetables, with chocolate blancmange and raisins for sweets. They wanted to know about all my adventures and I must confess, I exaggerated a little.

"You look so tanned, dear and you seem to have got taller, but you look as if you have lost a lot of weight," said Mother. "But welcome home. You have had your little adventure now, so I guess you will be looking for work in the city after a bit of a holiday."

My guts froze. Gee, they thought I was back here for good. I better get this straightened out right now.

"Mum, I just came home for your birthday; I will be going back to Queensland in a couple of weeks. I love it up there." I said it as nicely as I could.

Mum said, "It's getting late, dear. We will talk about it some more in the morning."

She gave me a peck on the cheek, turned and went to her room. Gran said they were both looking forward to me coming home to stay. My sister said she'd told them I wouldn't be staying. It was an awkward moment; I went to my nicely made-up bedroom and everything looked small. I felt like a boy coming back to the cradle. I had grown in that eight months. I was too big for the cradle now and fell asleep in my favourite bed with my Joseph of Many Colors blanket.

It was frightening to wake up in the morning. All my Queensland adventures seemed just a dream. Was it real that I left home and did all those things happen to me? I explored my arms. Yes, the weeping sores were still there, the grazes on my knuckles were still there and those biceps, thank the lord, were still there. It was real! I went to the doctor's the next day to check out the sores I had and my sick feeling. I expected a prescription or something simple. But the doctor was horrified.

"Where in God's name have you been? You're anemic. You hardly have any red cells in your blood. I can't believe it; you are just like the convicts that were brought in the hulks from Britain. You have the scurvy, son."

"I thought it was Barcoo rot," I answered.

"You can call it whatever you like, but my diagnosis is scurvy. I'll give you an injection that will put something back into your bloodstream and a course of vitamins and you will need to have plenty of fresh fruit and vegetables. A script for the chemist and an appointment for next week. And by the way, where have you been to get yourself in this sort of condition?"

"I have been working as a jackaroo on a Queensland cattle and sheep station," I said proudly.

"Well, I would like the name and address of where you worked, as they should be reported for treating people like this."

I informed the doc that I had left and that was it; I couldn't see any benefit in reporting anything. I made for the surgery door, rolling my left sleeve down to cover the bit of cotton wool on the injection site. It did hurt a bit, but I was the only one that knew that.

My sores cleaned up quickly but left little pink scars where they had been and my general health was vastly improved.

Improved so much that I felt fit and ready to take on the world, well, Queensland anyway. I left home a fortnight later after a shopping spree, some flicks, and some visits to some old friends. Who, by the way, seemed different and after a few minutes of excited conversation, there were long pauses as we all tried to think of something else to say.

A mother of one of my mates asked me where I was working now. I replied, "On a Queensland Station."

She said, "Are you a porter then?"

I didn't feel like explaining it was a cattle station and not a railway station, even though I had been talking about my adventures for the last half hour. Yes, I had outgrown Melbourne, my family and old friends. The trip back home was important. I knew at last where my destiny lay and I was catching the train from Spencer Street Station, Melbourne, for Goondiwindi, Queensland.

There was a farewell from Mother at the station with, "I hope you are doing the right thing? And you can always come home," as she handed me a present of a silver cigarette lighter. I gave her a peck on the cheek and made my way to the Spirit of Progress second class carriage. I was sorry to see Mum so sad as she walked away, but I was a man now and a man's just gotta do what a man's gotta to do. I felt a great relief as the train pulled out on our way to the northern state.

A midnight change of trains at Albury, a quick pie and sauce and a couple of beers thrown down, as one didn't have too long a wait for the next train to Sydney. By the time you were served at the station cafeteria, it was time to go. About an hour and a half after changing trains I felt crook, huge pain in my gut, headache, feeling feverish, dying was on the menu a couple of times. A few other passengers were looking rather pale and groaning, holding their stomachs. We reckon it was the pies or the beer at our last stop, but boy, we were uncomfortable, I can tell you that.

A four-hour delay in Sydney before the next train left for Queensland. I lockered my gear and walked down good old Pitt Street again, looking for a chemist to see if they could help my poisoned body, but it was early morning and most shops were shut. I was desperate. I spied a Chinese herbalist shop open. They said they were good with ailments, so in I went prepared to give anything a try. A little wizened-looking Chinaman was behind the counter, a very slouched frame with a few straggly hairs for a moustache and beard, a small plait in his hair and little beady eyes. I told him my symptoms; he gave a hint of a smile.

"I fix, I fix," he said as he turned to a vast array of bottles and herbs and things that I didn't want to know about. He scurried about, getting a bit of this and a bit of that and mixing it in a small glass.

"Fifty cents, pleeese." Wow, that was expensive for a small vial of liquid, but I was ill so I handed him the money and he handed me the small glass.

"Drink, drink," he said. I tossed the fluid down my throat then the Chinaman said, "Quick, quick, outa shop. Go, go."

He just about pushed me out of his premises. I knew why a few seconds later when a huge, no, massive volcano erupted in my stomach. The lava flow of pie, peas, beer and goodness knows what, spewed from my mouth all over the pavement, splashing my new suede boots and some passersby. I don't know what he gave me, that little ol' Chinese, but I felt my lungs, stomach and intestines were vomited up as well. I couldn't go and hide or be sick anywhere else. I was in the middle of the street making a huge spectacle of myself. I had never vomited or retched for so long and so violently in my life and never want to again. I made it back to Central station exhausted and lay with my belongings on the platform, waiting for my train.

A slow uneventful trip to Wallangarra, where I rolled and jerked with the train, trying to sleep and recover from my Sydney ordeal. A change of trains to Warwick and then a very slow goods train with one passenger carriage and guard's van combined for Goondiwindi. I was the only passenger. Now feeling much better, I smoked and gazed out of the window, looking at the western scenery passing by, thinking, *this is my country*. Goodiwindi was a typical Queensland town with lots of pubs, a couple of general stores, a big council building, stock and stations agents, saddlery shops and garages. There were a lot of Aborigines around, the first I had seen since I was a small boy.

You see, my first three years of life were spent in Bunyip, Gippsland Victoria, where my father had a dairy farm. We had a large family of Aboriginals living in the bottom paddock. They had been kicked out of a big reserve at Lakes Entrance and my father kindly gave them a place to camp on the property. My sister and I spent most of our first years at the camp learning about the Dreamtime and the Aboriginal ways. But alas, my parents had a problem and separated. The farm was sold. Mother, sister and I went one way, the Aboriginals went another and our father went his.

I liked Gundi which, of course, is short for Goondiwindi, and the people seemed nice and friendly. I booked in to the Royal Hotel for $2.50 a night; I also had a healthy bank account of one hundred and ten to my name. It was Friday. A check with the agents didn't give me much hope for a job, but the chap at United Grazers said see them Monday and they might have something, "But nothing definite, mind you."

A weekend of walking up and down the main street, a football match that was a rough and tumble affair. I didn't understand a thing as this was rugby and all I knew was Aussie Rules. The pictures on Saturday night, a few drinks at the pub to know the local scene and soon it was Monday.

"Well, you're in luck son," the United Graziers man said, "there is a jackaroo job going at Lota Plains, near Dirrinbandi. Now the conditions are you must be able to milk, ride and kill, be of Protestant faith and have a GPS education."

I acknowledged that I could meet all those conditions and would be happy to take the position. He asked me to write down my experience, the school I went to and what church I belonged to, and you know what, I could do it all truthfully now. I handed in the filled-out slip of paper and was told to report back that afternoon for confirmation and details at 2.30 P.M. I skipped out the door. Yes, I had a job already. What luck! I went round to the post office to send a telegram to mother to say I had arrived and had a job already. At 2.30 P.M. precisely I was back at the agents, got the confirmation, I had the job! I was to catch the train at midnight tomorrow for Lota on the Dirrinbandi line. Tuesday, I bought some expensive gear, a Bruno semi-automatic point twenty-two rifle, plus some working strides, along with a carton of cigarettes and a few magazines. I was ready for Lota and my new job.

C.14

Lota Plains

A Test, The Family, Dennis, Chores

It was another goods train with the passengers in the guard's van. There were two of us. My travelling companion, I guess by the look of him, was a shearer and he was sound asleep in the overhead luggage rack. The strong smell of whisky gave me the hint he was sleeping off a heavy drinking session. The train left on time at midnight. I undid my sleeping bag and curled up on the seat to try and get some sleep, even though the overhead luggage racks looked more comfortable with their slight curve. I just wasn't game or drunk enough to try them. I soon fell asleep with the rocking motion of the train. We seemed to stop at a lot of stations, but I was drowsy with sleep and didn't take much notice until we pulled into this station with a jerk and bang of the carriage. I looked at my watch. It was 3.30 in the morning. I looked at the station name through the foggy window; it was Goondiwindi! We had been shunting for the last three and half-hours at the rail yards and still hadn't started our journey. My travelling companion might just as well be dead, except for the snoring and the occasional mumbling as he didn't move.

It was a slow, boring trip. They say about Queensland goods/passenger trains, they are so slow you can get out of the train at a station while it's moving, walk across the street to the pub, have a beer, then walk back and get in your same carriage without the train stopping. My companion woke, half fell, half-stumbled out of the luggage rack onto the seat, acknowledged my presence with a nod and a look from his bleary, bloodshot eyes. He searched his pockets for the makings, rolled a smoke and slurred, "Let's know when we get to Dirrinbandi will ya mate?" He answered himself by saying, "Don't bother, it's the end of the line, anyway."

Then he slouched down in his seat, gazing out the window deep in his own thoughts, with his smoke dangling from his bottom lip.

It was lunchtime when the train pulled into Lota, a very small town with just the railway station, a pub, café/general store, garage, primary school, a church and police station. It was the policeman who I first met as I stepped off the train, being the only passenger to alight. He walked up to me with a friendly smile and said, "G'day I'm Tom Marksman, the local constable. Welcome to Lota. Are you staying long?"

He was a big man, dressed in the khaki uniform of the Queensland Police, about two metres in height, looked pretty fit, with ruddy cheeks and a heavy tan on his round, pleasant face. It was typical of the local police to meet the train to see who was coming into their town and what business they had there. I informed him I was a jackaroo, starting at Lota Plains and waiting for someone to meet me and take me to the property.

"Well, welcome to Lota son and here comes your lift now and it looks like it's your new boss, Mr Williams, picking you up."

A grey Peugeot ute had pulled up and a small man with very bandy legs and a huge straw hat jumped out and quickly approached me.

"Are you the jackaroo for Lota Plains?"

"Yes, my name is Jack Alexander."

I put my hand out to shake Mr Williams' extended hand. He helped me get my gear into the back of the utility and apologised for being so rushed, but I was informed that they were crutching sheep and he wanted to get back and have lunch before they started again at 1.30 P.M. It was a short trip to Lota Plains, I guess about four kilometres. I was dropped off at the jackaroos' quarters and told to freshen up, change in to working clothes and come to lunch at the main homestead, "As soon as possible as we need you at the shearing shed this afternoon."

My first glimpse of the property excited me. It was like a miniature town with cottages and buildings down a dusty thoroughfare with a huge two-story homestead with verandas all around situated further down in another dirt road. My quarters had three rooms length ways with a veranda front and back, a shower, toilet and laundry covered in on the back veranda. My room at the end was simple and clean with an iron single bed nicely made up, a wardrobe, dressing table and a small table. I dumped my gear on the floor, ripped open my pack and got my working gear out. I changed, splashed some cold water on my face, did my hair and made for the main homestead, one hundred yards from my quarters. Wow, entering through the side gate, it was like coming out of the desert into the Garden of Eden. A high hedge all around the boundary, sheltering lush lawns and beautiful gardens full of blooming flowers, protected the homestead and huge garden. A small orchard at the rear with a variety of citrus and apple trees with a fountain gurgling water from the centre garden. The whole scene took my breath away. What a beautiful place.

I found the kitchen door and knocked once. "Come in, come on in. There is no need to knock. Just take your boots off first."

I opened the squeaky fly screen door and entered a large kitchen dominated by a huge chrome and mustered coloured Aga stove. And it was there that Mrs Williams and I introduced ourselves,

A slim woman in her forties, much younger than her husband who I guessed was in his late fifties. She had a friendly face with a welcoming smile, a twinkle in her blue eyes behind rather ornate glasses, dark hair with a hint of grey, cut just above the shoulders with the ends curled. She was about my height.

"Jack, we are a bit rushed today. I know you have had a long train trip, so I have cut you a couple of sandwiches and made you a pot of tea over there," she said, pointing to a large kitchen table with a blue and red-checked tablecloth with a couple of meat sandwiches covered with a gauze fly protector.

A cup and saucer and beside that, a pot of tea, a small milk jug and sugar bowl.

"Dan has gone back to the shearing shed, so as soon as you have finished, I will run you up there. You don't have to eat so quickly; you still have about fifteen minutes to finish your lunch."

She left me alone, giving me time to enjoy the freshly cut sandwiches and a much-needed two cups of tea, as I hadn't eaten since yesterday teatime, except for a small snack on the train. The feed made me feel the tiredness of the last few days but I shook myself and reached into my reserves when Mrs Williams, now to be called the missus and Mr Williams, the boss, came in and said, "Ready to go Jack?"

"Sure am," I replied enthusiastically as I stepped out of the kitchen and hopped around, trying to put my elastic-sided boots on in a hurry as she led the way to a rather battered Ford Customline Ute. Driving the short drive up to the shed, the missus said, "We change for tea, which is usually seven o'clock and come in the entrance you did just now, but I guess Dan will give you the rundown on everything."

We stopped at a very large shearing shed, three times the size of the one at Tee Tree stud. I got out of the ute remembering to thank the missus for lunch and the lift. The thumping of the big Lister engine reached right down to my insides and the thrill of the workings of a shearing shed was exciting me. I walked up to the board to find my new boss and get my orders. The smell of oil, diesel, sheep, lanolin and jute hit my nostrils, which made me feel in familiar territory. They were crutching and wigging, which meant they took only the wool off around the crutch. This was to stop the wool from getting daggy and wet, causing fly strike around their bums. The wigging was taking a piece of wool from each cheek and forehead so the sheep wouldn't get blind when it was in full wool. My job was to keep the board clean and press the crutching's. I was familiar with the press and what was expected of me, which seemed to be a great relief for the boss as he left me to it so he could supervise the drafting in the yards. The shed had eight stands, but there were only four shearers working. Because they were only crutching it was only seconds between each sheep. Boy, was I busy, but I kept the wool away. When I was pressing, the shearers just pushed the crutchings towards the pens and every now and then it was, "Tar here Jack!" It didn't seem long before the expert, Fred, who looked after the workings of the shed and sorted the wool out for me to press, rang the bell for smoko. Why they call them experts, which relates to the engine and sharpening combs and cutters, I do not know 'cause the only tools they carried were a screwdriver, hammer, multi grips and a wrench.

"Permission for a woman to enter the shed?" Fred yelled out. No one took much notice and in came a tall, thin, blonde girl. She was about nineteen years old, with sharp features but a pleasant disposition. She was dressed in khaki slacks and a light blue blouse, carrying a large billy of tea in one hand and a basket full of scones and cake in the other. She was the missus' assistant. Her name was Ethel, and she placed the billy of tea and food on the small table in the wool room as the men gathered around with their enamel mugs thirstily waiting their turn to fill them with the steaming strong black tea. The boss walked in, checked what I had been doing and then said, "Ethel, this is Jack, the new jackaroo and Jack, this is Ethel."

We said our g'days and smiled at each other. She checked me out and I her. She was much taller than me and kinda looked down on me. I didn't like that. I preferred to be the looker-down-upon.

I wanted to make a good impression on my first afternoon, so I continued to press some wool so I wouldn't be behind. Fetching another armful of crutchings to put in the press, the men stirred a bit. The boss said, "Leave it Jack, here is a mug, go and have some tea as the men don't like someone working while it's smoko time." Some union thing, I guess.

The afternoon went by quickly. I had managed to keep all the wool away and had some three bales pressed when the knock off bell rang. I walked out of the shed and watched the boss count the crutched sheep out of their pens and put the number of each shearer's crutched sheep in the tally book. It was, in fact, a red Coopers Stockman's notebook and anyone worth his salt on the land had one. I thought I must have one also. I tried counting the sheep as the boss let them out. Some jumped and others raced out to catch their mates. It wasn't easy. By the time we got to the third pen the boss swung around and said, "How many in that race, Jack?"

"Forty-seven," I answered, not so sure. I got a bit of a fright because I didn't think he knew I was there.

"Not bad Jack, from where you were standing, you were out by one. Now, we will finish here. You can go down and settle in. The bell will ring for dinner at seven at the homestead."

I walked down the dusty road lined with eucalyptus, pepperina and willow trees, towards my new quarters passing cottages, some with children playing in the small neat front gardens. A glimpse of a large cattle and horse yards on the top of a sandy ridge on my right. Turning the corner, I came into the Town Square, as I call it, with a tap and water trough in the middle. A range of sheds on one side, including the saddle shed, and opposite were my quarters, some small yards, and the homestead at the other end. Sorting my gear out, I familiarised myself with the surroundings. I had a septic toilet, a shower recess with hot water, a wash hand basin on the back veranda and at the side of my quarters was a lean to with washing troughs and a copper in the yard. Checking the other two rooms, one looked as if it was occupied and the end one seemed empty except for some basic furniture, as was in my room, except for a chair. I grabbed it and looked for anything else I could use, but alas, a chair was all.

A blue Morris Minor pulled up in front of the quarters and a young man in a suit and tie got out and reached for a briefcase from the back seat. I said, "G'day," as I opened the picket fence gate. He turned round and shut the Morris door and said, "Hello, I'm Mick Stainton, the schoolteacher in Lota and you must be...?"

"I'm Jack Alexander, the new jackaroo here," I said as I extended my hand. He switched his briefcase to his other hand so we could shake.

"Well, it looks as if we are housemates then. I board here and that's my room in there," he said, nodding toward the middle room. He was a shorter person than me. That was something. Not much though, with a dark complexion like a Greek or Italian with a round, smiling face, dark brown eyes, slicked back black hair and walked like a duck with his toes pointing out. Age? About mid-twenties, I would guess.

"Do you know the setup here, Jack? They dress well for dinner. Mr Williams always wears a suit and tie. Mrs Williams looks as if she is going to some important do and her assistant Ethel is also done up. Have you a suit?"

"No, I haven't, but I do have a good white shirt and a tie and good slacks. Do you reckon that will do?"

"I am sure it will, but mind your manners and don't ever, ever be late. Seven is the time or else!"

"Thanks for the advice, Mick. Do you know if there is an iron about, my good clothes are sort of crushed."

"There is a kerosene iron in the cupboard in the bathroom."

"A kerosene iron? You're having me on."

"No, it's pretty useless. I'll show you how it works. Coming?" Mick said as he led the way to the bathroom. And there my friend Mick showed me this contraption of an iron. He poured the kerosene into the iron from a bottle and funnel and pumped it with the attached pump. Then he got some shellight and lit that in a small receptacle on the iron to get it started.

"It will take a while to heat up, so have your shower and it should be warm enough by then to get some of those creases out. You know, you pong of sheep!"

"I get the hint and thanks for the lesson on the iron," I said, laughing.

The iron was next to bloody useless, but I managed to get my good clothes in some sort of decent condition.

We were both ready and slicked up when the bell rang at ten to seven. We made our way to the homestead. Taking our shoes and boots off at the kitchen door, we entered with my nose twitching at the aroma of delicious cooking and my mouth started to water. Ethel, her hair done up with a hint of make-up and a floral apron over a cotton dress with a frilly collar, said, "Jack, could you take the plates out of the warmer and take them into the dining room?" She noticed my hesitation. "They are in that bottom section of the oven with the door ajar. Mick, you can take this crock pot with you and show Jack the dining room. Watch it! That pot is hot. Here, take this hand towel and wrap it round the pot so you don't burn your hands."

I grabbed the plates. She didn't worry about my hands, and the plates were hot, but as always, I managed.

Mick led the way to the dining room; it was large with a long dining table with six chairs each side plus two carvers at each end. The table had a lace tablecloth on it with a candelabrum as the centerpiece, a set of salt, pepper, and sauce silver containers at each end of the table. There were five places set with starched embroidery serviettes in silver holders at each place.

"Where will I put the plates?" I asked Mick.

"Just at the side in Mrs Williams' place," he nodded at the right side of the table as he put the crock pot down at the head of the table where the boss sat.

Ethel came in, wheeling a trolley. The serving dishes with china covers were on it. She placed them at the missus' place and said, "Jack, you're to sit to the left of the boss, three chairs down. Mick, you know where your chair is, next to Jack's".

We went round to our places and as I pulled my chair out, Mick whispered, "Don't sit down yet, wait till the missus sits first."

I whispered back my thanks. We three stood at the back of our chairs, waiting. The boss came down the internal stairs at the opposite end of the room, done up in a suit and tie. He had a very bald, bullet-shaped, domed head. He walked to his place at the table, then the missus made her grand entrance. It was like I imagined royalty would be. I soon discovered that on these bigger properties, the old-fashioned manners and courtesies were very strongly maintained, and to be honest, I liked it. The missus sat down, then the boss, then the three of us. Mick had told me the wrong place for the plates. They should have been at the boss's setting, but no one said anything as the missus passed the plates to him. He started serving a stew out of the crock pot onto each plate, then passed it to the missus, who opened the three covered pots and pulled out steaming vegetables and cauliflower with cheese sauce, slightly brown on top.

"Is this enough, Jack?" she said as she handed the plate to

Ethel to hand to me. "It's plenty, Missus, and it really looks and smells good, thank you."

I was the last to be served and started to pick up my knife and fork when the boss said, "Let us pray."

I gently put the cutlery down as I lowered my head for the short grace that was given. Then, to my surprise, the missus said, "Two, four, six, eight, bog in, don't wait," with a smile at me. It wasn't the thing I thought royalty would say, but she broke the ice, showing her sense of humour and I knew my time here should be fun.

The meal was delicious, just like it smelled and I tucked into it. But alas, I was nearly finished when I spied a dead fly in the stew. I hid it under a large, sliced piece of carrot, not wanting to offend anyone. The meal was consumed with relish and silence. Everyone had clean plates except mine that had the carrot on top of the fly with a bit of gravy to keep it there.

"Jack, you haven't finished. I was going to offer you more, but evidently you have had enough."

"It was a lovely meal, thank you, but I am full."

"You mean adequately sufficient, don't you, Jack? Here, hand me your plate."

I handed the missus my plate and to my horror, she scraped the carrot aside and there in the gravy was the fly. She said, "Jack, there was a fly in your dinner. I am so sorry. Why didn't you mention it?" Mick and Ethel were both smiling and the boss even had a smirk on his face.

I found out later; it was a test by the missus with all new jackaroos. The idea was to put a dummy fly in the meal and watch the reaction. If the new chum said, "Look, I have a fly in my meal," it meant he would be a complaining type. If he ate it, he wasn't observant or he was sneaky. And if he did what I did and hid it under some food, it meant I would hide mistakes. If I just put it at the side of the plate and said nothing, that was the best sign of all. Anyway, that was her theory and it looked like I had failed my first test. A great bread and butter pudding finished off a meal that was no exception to all the other meals I enjoyed at Lota Plains. No more Barcoo Rot or scurvy for me.

After dinner, the boss asked me kindly to stay back so he could tell me what was required of me. My chores were to get the night horse in and run the horses in at 5.30 every morning, kill and dress a sheep for the homestead and the men, turn the lighting engine off at 9.30 every night, check it for water, oil and fuel every morning and check the batteries for water.

"That's your chores. There will be another jackaroo starting next week and he will have a different set of chores. Now there is no weekend work, and your pay as a first year jackaroo is $15.00 a week paid monthly. Is that alright with you?"

Wow, no weekend work, and the chores weren't so bad but a 5.30 A.M. start and a finish at 9.30 P.M. was a bit rich, and the pay was not that good, but what a great place and great cooking to be had, I thought.

"Yep, that's fine by me," I answered.

"Well, Jack, you better get to bed now and meet me in the kitchen at 5.30 in the morning. You can find your way out?"

I said, "Yes," and bade him a very good night. As I made my way to my quarters, I realised how tired I was after my big day.

Mr and Mrs Williams, you met. They had four children; one boy and three girls, all away at boarding school in Toowoomba. Then there were Ethel and Mick. Now let me introduce the rest of the permanent staff at Lota Plains. I should add it was a forty-thousand-acre sheep and cattle property with stud sheep and Aberdeen Angus cattle. It carried about twelve thousand sheep, five hundred head of cattle and forty-seven horses. They were horse mad at Lota Plains and had huge pony club camps here.

Back to the staff. In the order of hierarchy down, first there was the overseer, Peter Ford, who happened to be Ethel's brother, his wife Lynette and two small children, about five and seven. They lived in the cottage next to the main homestead. Then the mechanic, Kevin and his wife Sally and two very young children, Bryce and Lana, three and four years old. Kevin is responsible for all the machinery and maintenance. Phil, the gardener, a bachelor and an old ringer of about sixty. He had been crippled from a horse accident years ago. The station hand, Ernie and his huge wife Beatrice, with no children. Then there was old Bill the ringbarker, his mate George, an Aboriginal, and the horse breaker. His name is Bill too. Besides the permanent staff, there were a lot of casuals, mainly Aboriginals who helped with the timber work.

And then along came Dennis the following week, the other jackaroo. He was from a farm at Gatton and had been riding horses all his life. He was a thin, wiry kid, a year younger than me but more knowledgeable about the land and station life. We ended up the greatest of mates. Dennis' chores were to milk the two cows, feed the pigs, chop wood and light the boiler for hot water and fill up the coke flutes for the Aga stove.

The first weekend, Dennis decided to wash his three new pairs of jeans his mum had bought for the job. He didn't like them new and wanted to fade them. He chopped wood all afternoon so he could boil them in the copper all night. He set his alarm to go off every two hours, so he could put more wood under the copper to keep it going. But alas, by morning when he went to get them out, the jeans had burnt holes in them. He forgot to keep adding water to the copper when he stoked the fire. Poor bloke, he wasn't game to tell his mum, so he wore only two old pairs of strides until he could buy some more when he got his monthly cheque.

By the way, Dennis got the fly in his roast lamb and he blew it by saying, "There's a dead fly in my dinner."

He was upset when he was told he held his knife like a pencil and that was not acceptable at the table.

"Can't pick on my work, but whinge about the way I hold a knife," he muttered to me later.

Peter, the overseer, gave me the best present I have ever had. It was a sheep dog called Skipper, about eighteen-months-old, and we adored each other. He was a black kelpie and Peter said he was mine for as long as I stayed at Lota and looked after him properly. A dog is worth three men with sheep and a man is useless working sheep without a dog, I was told. Peter was tall like his sister, but much taller, thin build with a hawkish face and sandy hair. He wore stainless steel-framed glasses and looked more like a student than a station overseer, but we soon realised what a tough, strong man our overseer was. He also gave Dennis a sheep dog, much younger than mine, called Flint, but Dennis didn't have the same rapport with him that I had with Skipper. Flint would follow Dennis everywhere except when he was on a horse.

This day, he was determined his dog would follow. He tied a long, thin rope onto the dog's collar and mounted the horse and started to drag the dog behind with a lot of encouraging words and whistles. Dennis made two mistakes. One, he was riding a young horse just broken in. Two, he never thought out the process of riding a young horse, dragging a young dog behind on a long piece of rope. The inevitable happened. Dennis gave the rope a jerk. This time, the dog obeyed and ran right under the horse. The horse wanted a better view of the intruder, so it twisted its head, putting it way down near the ground and to the side. This action, of course, made the back legs rise in the air. This frightened the young dog who wanted to get away from this monster with whites showing in its eyes. Unfortunately, the rope that was tied to the dog's collar got wound around the off side back leg of the horse. The horse went crazy. So, the scene was of Dennis disappearing into the sandalwood scrub, balancing on the hump of the horse as he bolted and bucked with a yelping dog tied to its back leg.

There was nothing anyone could do, but we felt we should do something, so we split our sides with laughter. The dog, the horse and Dennis survived, but that dog would never go near a horse again and not surprisingly, Dennis never again tried to teach it.

We did a lot with horses. They were our world; they were Mr Williams' world. I believe He had been a light horseman in the First World War and taught me so much about that noble animal and how to read it, ride it and understand it. At 5.30 every morning I would have to run the horses in, walking to the shearing shed where there was feed for the night horse, a white fourteen hand gelding. It was easy to see in the dark. I would then proceed to the small paddock beside the shed where the shearers' quarters were, with a billy of feed and bridle to catch the horse. Once caught, I would hop on him bareback and ride to the square where the saddle shed was and saddle him up, ready for the ride of my life that I had every morning. It was one of the highlights for me at Lota Plains.

We dashed down the slope to the Moonie River, negotiated the narrow crossing and up the other side full pelt, veering to the left of the 400-acre paddock on its southern boundary. Then galloping along to the western boundary, cracking my whip as we went, trying to dodge the sandalwood scrub and making sure my whip didn't connect tree or horse. The horse knew its job. I went along for the ride. With the galloping of hooves, the crack of the whip, it got the horses moving along the northern side where there was a long contour bank they galloped single file along on their way to the yards. Arabs, Anglo-Arabs and Clumpers, liver chestnuts, grays and bays, taffy and buckskins, their manes flowing, tails streaming out in their wake, the rising sun highlighting their shiny colorful coats. The thunder of 360 hooves, the ground trembled. The night horse sweated and I was on a high that one couldn't believe. The horses slowed their pace as they organised themselves across the narrow river crossing, then full gallop up to their destination, bucking and kicking in a swirl of dust as they entered the yard. Sunny, windy, frosty, rain, summer or winter, it didn't matter, the running of the horses was my chore every day. It was a delight, never a chore.

A chore that I hated was the killing. I didn't understand the boss properly when he said I had to kill for the homestead and the men. It meant one sheep for the homestead and half a sheep a week for every other family or workers, which came to an average of six sheep a week, as the Aboriginals got one a week as well. So Tuesday and Thursday nights were kill nights, which I had to do after a day's work. It took me an hour to kill one sheep at the Shorts place. How long would it take to do three? Yes, at the start it was three hours. The first one was okay, the second wouldn't die properly and the third, whether dead or alive, did nothing right. And what made it worse, big 160 kilo Beatrice, the station hand's wife, would be at the killing block talking rubbish to me the whole time. Even after she got her kidneys, liver and brains, she was driving me mad. In the end, as I vigorously swept all the blood and guts off the killing block, after killing the first sheep, I pretended I was so busy sweeping that some of the stuff splashed onto her feet and legs. Ernie, her husband, had a few words the next day to me and I told him if his missus hung around after she got her offal, I wouldn't get it for her anymore. After that she didn't worry me. Not only did I have to kill the sheep, get the kidneys and liver, but the tripe, plus break their skulls open for the brains, then skin a couple of heads in the winter for soup. After a couple of months, I could do one sheep in twelve minutes, but at first, I didn't finish till nine o'clock and missed my dinner, but I didn't care. I just crawled to my room and asked Dennis if he could turn the lighting engine off for me at 9.30 P.M.

We mustered sheep, drafted, sprayed for lice, drenched for worms and lamb marked. Now lamb marking was hard work. It went this way. First, the ewes were drafted from the lambs and placed in a pen by themselves. On one side of the pen were six marking cradles. Our job was to catch the lambs and sit them up in the cradles with a bar holding them in. We would get bindi burrs in our hands, short sharp horns rubbed into our chests from the lamb rams and bending down, catching them and lifting them into the cradle, wore a man down toward the end of the day.

Now on the other side of the cradle were Peter and Ernie. Peter was the first operator and had the knife. His job was to cut the lambs' tails off and when he came to a ram lamb, he would grasp the purse, cut the top off, push down on the purse with both hands and out popped two bloody white testicles. He then proceeded to put his mouth over them and pulled them from the lamb with his teeth. He held them there with blood on his lips, two stringy cords hanging from his mouth, with flies trying and succeeding in getting in on the act. When he came to the next lamb, he spat the testicles out and the dogs would run in for a quick morsel. Ernie followed behind, putting the station earmark in the right ear and two clips in the left to show it was born in sixty-one. I volunteered to have a go; I wasn't that keen, but I thought it would be a macho thing to do, so I did. It wasn't too bad if you shut your eyes. The balls tasted warm with a slight nothingness bloody flavour. I was about to spit them out when I was told I had to keep them in my mouth until I was ready to do the next ram lamb. This I managed to do until Peter gave me a bang between the shoulder blades and I swallowed the balls. Not a pleasant experience as they slid down my throat like oysters.

I had a go at everything; I was keen and I wanted to learn. I jumped in whether I was asked to or not. I even had a go at shearing when the stud ewes were being shorn. I asked one of the older shearers if I could have a go. Things were going well for me until I came to the neck, which is a hard part to get the wool off due to the wrinkles; I dug the shears in too much and cut its jugular. The blood flowed everywhere on the board; the sheep passed away and everyone said, as it was a stud ewe, I would get shot. I carried my victim out of the shed and down to the killing pen. Thank God it was a Thursday. I let one of the killers, *supposed to be killed that night*, have freedom and served the stud ewe up to the homestead instead. No one knew, except the shearers and Dennis.

He thought it was funny to pipe up at dinnertime and said in a mock voice, "What have you done to the mutton Mrs Williams? It tastes so tender."

I could have killed him because we usually kill cast for age wethers, those past their prime, and it definitely was a different taste. I piped up and said it wasn't the sheep but how you killed it that made it tender. Ethel had to have her say, claiming it was the cook who made the meat tender. But that was all that was said. I made plenty of mistakes, but I was learning something new every day, and that included in the area of romance.

C.15

My First Love

The Ball, Romance, Embarrassment, Educated

It started with the 'matchmaker' at the telephone exchange, Mrs Mac. The boss called me to the phone one evening about three weeks after I had arrived. I had told no one the number. I was slightly mystified as to who was calling. I picked up the receiver and said, "This is Jack Alexander here."

"Oh, excuse me Mr Alexander, it's Mrs Mac from the Lota exchange speaking. I have seen you a couple of times in town and seeing you look like a decent lad; I was wondering if you would like to accompany a young lady to an important formal ball at Dirranbandi?"

Now I had a couple of problems. Remember I said I went to a posh all boys boarding school as a dayboy and that I would tell you why later? You see, I was expelled from the state school when I was in grade three. What was my crime? Playing doctors and nurses and investigating something that a little girl hadn't and a little boy had. I am sure she put me up to it. When a big busty spinster of a headmistress caught us, the poor little girl was treated like a wounded princess, me as the bastard rapist. Gosh at eight years old in those days, all I knew was 'tossy was for widdies'.

Anyway, after a severe dressing down from the headmistress in her office, then hauled before the full school assembly to be ridiculed and castigated, I was expelled as a filthy little boy and sent to a private boy's school on the other side of Melbourne. Gee, I was only just eight. Since then, I have had a slight problem with girls. Some brilliant psychologist would probably know why that was one of my problems.

The others I expressed to Mrs Mac.

"Look, that's very nice of you to ask me, but I don't have a car!"

"Oh, don't worry about that. She has a new car of her own, so transport is not a problem, Mr Alexander."

Gosh, how was I going to get out of this? I didn't want to go because I hated blind dates and anyway, if this girl was so desperate to ask the exchange lady, she would have to be a bag.

"That's great, Mrs Mac, but I don't possess any evening clothes. I am really sorry; I do want to help, but that's the way it is."

"I am so pleased you're willing to go. Now, I will make an extra effort to get you a dinner suit. The ball is on Friday week so that will give us plenty of time to find some refinery for you".

What could I say? Except with panic in my voice, "Thank you so much for asking me, and I hope I haven't been too much trouble."

"That's all right, it's been a pleasure. I will give Mrs Williams all the details when they come to hand and she can pass them on to you. Tra lar."

I hung up the phone in despair. *Jack, you're going to have fun on Friday week*, I said to myself as I walked back through the dining room and out of the kitchen.

"What was all that about, Jack? You look a bit worried."

"Oh nothing Missus, just a blind date for next Friday," I replied as I was putting my boots on outside the screen door.

"I think you may be in for a big surprise that night," said Mrs Williams with a grin like a Cheshire cat. Yep, you bet, I had been set up.

There was a parade of strange men the following week offering parts of dinner suits for me to try on. Eventually, after much trying on and getting teased by Dennis, we finally came up with a dinner suit for me. Four different pieces from four very kind gentlemen. It wasn't perfect, but it was the best we could do. The bow tie fitted all right, the pleated shirt was fine also, except for the long sleeves and a yellow stain on the left-hand side. But that was covered by the coat which was a tad large and it wasn't quite the same black as the pants were. They were a bit small and tight round the waist but all together I looked bloody marvellous - like a circus clown.

The fateful night arrived. I was allowed to knock off early as I had to meet this girl in the kitchen at 6.30 P.M., so the missus informed me. Well, I scrubbed up, whacked the Old Spice on and a hint of California Poppy hair oil. Putting on my best underpants and getting dressed in the oddment of clothes that would pass as a formal dinner suit, I realised as I put my brown socks on, *the only good ones I had,* I didn't have any black shoes. I couldn't wear my riding boots. Dennis came to the rescue. He leant me his. Thank god we were the same size and they were black. They were also quilted on top with the biggest rubber ripple sole shoes in the best of Elvis Presley wear. Dennis said I looked great, just the spiffiest man around, which was kind of him, as I felt just the opposite. And Mrs Williams and Ethel were kind and said I looked lovely. The boss walked in, took one look at me and without any expression, turned round and went from whence he had come.

I heard the car and my heart started a slow thump.

"Here she comes now," said Ethel. Then my heart started to pound in my chest. She opened the door and walked in. My heart stopped. My face flushed and my heart started up again, thumping as if I had broken the four-minute mile. I grabbed the back of a chair to save my sagging knees. She was beautiful, no, she was gorgeous, and she did not belong here. My breathing started to suffer. I am sure I was panting. She was tall, sleek, five foot five, short blonde hair, soft and silky as if it were brushed two hundred times a day. Just the cutest pointy nose and blue, dancing, sparkling eyes, lips like, like the best red lips you can imagine and the whitest of teeth to match. She was a goddess.

But there was one small problem. Here I was, dressed in an ill-matched, ill-fitting dinner suit with Elvis Presley shoes and here was this goddess who, by the way, was called Joan Fisher, wearing a nice, tailored woolen suit. Someone got it wrong. We weren't going to a formal ball, just a teenager's dance and me going like this, she must have thought I was mad. This is what I thought until I found out later you never get in to your good evening clothes until you're at your destination as the long dusty roads would make everything dirty and covered in dust.

After the introductions, I escorted her out to her car, a brand new blue and white Ford Angler. She said, "You may drive," in the sweetest of singsong voices. Where did this princess come from?

"Dad owns a couple of stations up the road. One joins Lota Plains," she said. Would you believe she was my next-door neighbour, only eighteen kilometres up the road?

It was a sixty-three kilometre drive to Dirrinbandi, over a very rough dirt road. I hadn't driven much on dirt roads, especially in a brand new little four-cylinder car. I hit every bump, spun in the sand, lots of 'oopses' and 'sorries' between getting-to-know-you conversations. I told her truthfully about me with, of course, a few exaggerations and she about her life at boarding school and home. She loved to ride and play tennis and anything to do with animals. I think we were going to get along fine. It took us well over the hour to get there. We pulled up outside the United Graziers Club for Joan to get changed into her refinery, as a lot of other girls were doing.

I introduced myself to some of the fellas outside, dressed in white tuxedoes and some in tails, waiting for their women. I found it difficult to talk to them. They seemed in a special club all of their own, or was it my dress code? I felt they thought I wasn't up to their class; well they could go and get stuck.

We had a wonderful time. It was just the best. She looked radiant in a beautiful blue embroidered evening gown and we just danced the night away. I had every dance, no one had a chance. She was funny, I laughed. I was funny, she laughed. We waltzed and jived, slow danced and twisted. We did the lot, and we were so entranced with each other, we danced till the music stopped at two. On the way home, we got lost. Fair dinkum, we took the wrong turn and ended up near St George, ninety-four odd kilometres away.

We were late and we were in trouble. Party lines were humming as Joan's parents wondered where she was and what sort of a bloke she had succumbed to. We pulled into Lota Plains homestead just as the breakfast bell rang; there was a huge black car, a Humber Super Snipe outside the entrance.

"Dear, oh dear, that's Dad's car," murmured Joan, "I hope he won't be too cross with us."

I slowed Joan's car gently to a stop near the Humber; a very tall, distinguished man was leaning against the bonnet with, one might say, a disapproving look on his very serious face. I had to get it over and done with. I opened the door and marched straight up to him and said, "My name is Jack Alexander, sir, and I sincerely apologise for bringing your daughter home at this hour. You see, we took the wrong turn and ended up at St George and it took us ages."

Joan, by this time, was out of her car, walked up to her dad, gave him a big hug and said in the sweetest voice, "Don't be cross, Daddy. It was my fault. I told Jack to take the turn. We are both fine and Jack behaved like a perfect gentleman."

"Well, your mother and I have been extremely worried; I suggest you drive home right now and try and calm your mother, who is in quite a state."

I held the driver's door open for Joan to drive her own car back home. I whispered, "I would like to ask you out again, but I don't know what's on or have any transport."

"Pick you up at seven next Saturday. There's a good movie on in Lota," a smile, a gear change, some dust and a wonderful dream had gone.

Turning to Mr Fisher, I apologised again. His features softened ever so slightly as he said, "Jack, Mr Williams said you are a decent lad and I take his word. Now a bit of advice, young man. Get some maps of the district and learn your way around the place. You know women have no sense of direction."

At that, he opened the door and fired the big V8 engine and took off after his fabulous daughter.

Did I cop hell from everyone? They teased me and told me they knew what we were up to. Dennis congratulated himself, saying, "It was the shoes. It was my shoes." Thank God it was Saturday, no work, so off to bed for a good day's rest. The eyelids fluttered, then closed as I dreamt of the night again. The week seemed forever to get back to Saturday. I worked hard and kept myself very busy, hoping it would make the week go quicker, and eventually, Saturday did arrive. I was excited and by 7.30 P.M. I was more excited as she floated through the kitchen door. She was just great. She hadn't changed one little bit except for her clothes; they were a nice fawn twinset with a light tweed skirt.

I drove the short distance to Lota where the pictures were held in the showgrounds pavilion. I think we watched a John Wayne movie and *Three Coins in the Fountain,* but the girl next to me just took my concentration away. We shared chips and a drink of lemon squash at interval. During the second movie, we held hands, and she rested her pretty head with such soft hair on my shoulder. The shoulder started to ache after a while, but it was a pleasant ache and that shoulder wasn't going to move for anything.

We drove straight back to the homestead as soon as the movies had finished, a quick goodbye and, "I will ring you next week," said the princess as she moved into the driver's seat and I moved out. We were definitely going to make sure we were on time after this date.

As I watched her drive off, I wondered if I should have given her a kiss. Just the thought gave me a tingle in the stomach, but then, I had never kissed a girl before. I wondered how you did it and what it was like. I felt great all the following week. Ain't it wonderful to have a girl? Joan rang Wednesday night and we arranged again to go to the movies Saturday week. A whole fortnight to wait.

The day came, she picked me up, we went off to the movies, and the first one was awful. I watched it intently; I was worried and nervous about this kissing bit. I just wanted to be the most romantic lover in the world. If there was a special technique to kissing, I wanted to know it. This woman beside me deserved the best. We decided it wasn't worth staying for the second picture and if we did, it was too much of a rush for her to get home in time for the curfew set by her mother.

We parked that little car under a willow tree on the banks of the Moonie River; the moon was playing hide and seek with one or two small fluffy clouds. I made up a little verse:

The sky is dark blue,

with the pretty stars and the moon

The night is cold but you are warm.

Please don't leave me, stay till dawn.

For I am I and you are you

So let's stay here, just we two.

A gentle breeze rustled the willow leaves, there was the sound of bubbling water jostling in the rapids. She moved closer to me and I to her. A cricket was a chirping and the Willie Wagtail intermittently whistled. Our cheeks touched, the air was hot; we turned slightly, our lips about to meet and then – I farted.

It wasn't a creeping Jesus, it was an, 'Oh my God'. I badly wanted to die. She said, "It's hot in here," and wound the window down.

I said, "I think I better go." I got out of the car, hoping the earth would open and swallow me up, but no, it was going to make me suffer. I turned and gave a slight wave as she drove off, knowing I was doomed. I continued walking slowly to my quarters with my world shattered.

I sat on the bed, had a smoke and gazed at the floor when a small miracle happened. I was gazing at a Reader's Digest. What it was doing there, or how it got there, I do not know, but what was amazing, it was opened at a page with the heading, The Art of Kissing. I picked it up and devoured every word it said. I read about the longest kiss ever recorded. It was during a kissing contest and the winning couple lasted a staggering twenty-nine hours until the judges discovered their teeth braces were stuck together. But what interested me was that a real romantic kiss actually produced so many hundred pounds of pressure, *I forget how many but it really was a lot*, on a couple's lips. There were a lot of other bits and pieces, but I thought I had the message.

Armed with all this information, I wanted desperately to try it out, so a fortnight later, I got game and invited Joan to the next lot of movies. If, of course, she wanted to, and if she could pick me up. She said, "Yes." She had been waiting for my phone call. All had been forgiven.

We left again after interval and we parked at the same place. I was excited. I knew just what to do. The atmosphere was the same, but the moon was brighter, the night was colder. We cuddled, we whispered, we giggled. The moment had arrived. I was going to be the most romantic bloke alive. I planted my lips on hers and if they reckon a few hundred pounds made a great kiss; I was going to use a thousand. The bucket seat collapsed behind her. We both ended up half in the back seat. She was struggling. Was it in ecstasy, or was she urgently needing air?

It was the air. As I released my romantic embrace, my princess struggled into a half-sitting position. She said breathlessly, "I like to be kissed softly."

We got the bucket seat up properly and she used a tissue to wipe some blood off her lips. Damaged by a tooth, I suspect. I confessed and she laughed.

"I don't believe it; at your age you have never had a romantic kiss? Well, I shall just have to teach you."

And the education started right away. *Reader's Digest*, you know nothing.

C.16

The Noble Horse

Bachelor Bill, Winnings, Wild Pigs, Breaking In

If you think after riding a horse for a couple of weeks at the Golds property, Farlee, that I could just go galloping around on horses, cracking stock whips, you're very much mistaken. Even though I had some rapport with animals, and I think the riding came a bit naturally to me, there was still an education process to go through. The first horse given to me was an old clumper, quiet as a lamb.

The boss said, "You're never going to learn how to be a good rider on that horse. Next week you ride Bachelor Bill."

Bachelor Bill was a big, powerful, dapple-grey Arab, at least sixteen hands. Everyone said that weekend I was in for some fun. Dennis, who had been riding all his life and was very confident on a horse, said, "Listen Jack, I haven't ridden the horse, but I am told if you get on smartly and correctly and don't move your arms or legs when you're mounted, you will be fine. If you do and he sees a stray arm or leg out of position, he will buck and keep bucking till you're off-loaded."

"Umm," I said bravely, "I would like to see if he could get rid of me."

Dennis was one year younger than me and knew more than me about horses, which hurt my pride a bit, so I always tried to be as good as him or better, if I could.

Monday morning came. I saddled Bachelor Bill up in the yards. At least they were on a sand hill and if I did hit the dirt, it would be pretty soft. The horse was big and fresh. He walked around and shifted nervously as I saddled him up and tightened the girth. I walked him round the yard to get any air out of his belly and tightened the girth again. Everyone was watching me, that is, Dennis, Peter, the overseer and the boss. It was my job. I had to do this. The butterflies were in the belly.

I reined him up, keeping his head toward me, putting boot to stirrup and mounted so quickly, as if my life depended on it. The horse moved quickly.

"Just walk him round the yard," the boss yelled, "keep him busy, turn him to the right and left, let him feel you are the boss."

I did all I was told. The horse felt frisky underneath me. I could feel the muscles bunch underneath the saddle and the raw power in the animal, but he did nothing and I kept him busy. The others mounted their horses and we rode out together to the ram paddock to get some rams in for drenching and to clip their feet and horns. All was going well. Dennis got off and opened and shut the first gate and remounted. Then he yelled, "Jack, look at that huge red 'roo over there. He must be well over two metres."

I forgot. I turned. My hand and knee went out of place. The horse wrenched the reins, put his nose to the ground, his hind feet to Mars and reversed those positions every quarter second. I saw neither Mars nor ground. I saw whirling and blackness and dapple-grey and mane and hoofs and then the ground, then the stars! I had every breath of air knocked out of me. Everyone looked, even Bachelor Bill. He had stopped bucking and turned around to see what he had done, just like I do when finished in the toilet. I had to get back on again. I wasn't that keen, but as I said before, it was my job.

That horse gave me a buster just about every second day, but it did teach me a lot. How to sit in the correct position, but more importantly to be relaxed and feel the horse and how to lean back and not pull on the reins when he does buck. And most important of all, how to anticipate what the horse is going to do by the feel of him and what his ears and head are telling me. He was a bastard of a horse, but a good bastard at that. Bachelor Bill was the first of many, teaching me the art of staying on and communicating with these wonderful animals.

Bill, the horse breaker, came to break in fourteen young Arabian horses the station had bred. Dennis and I, when we got the chance, would watch him from the rails and sometimes hand him gear when asked. Bill was a tall, straight-backed, neatly dressed man in his fifties; he had a good reputation around the district as a good trainer and breaker. As a matter of fact, he trained a lot of the district racehorses for the various picnic races held in the surrounding townships. One such race day I attended was at Talwood, about one hundred kilometres from Lota and Bill was there. Now, not knowing much about racehorses or betting, I asked Bill, "What should I do?"

He said in his clipped, straight to the point voice, "Put your money on Beau Bell in the first race."

I said thanks and ran off to place a $1.00 on the horse. It won and I got fifteen back. I searched for Bill to thank him again and found him at the stalls where all the horses were kept.

"Bill," I said excitably, "I won a $1.60."

"Shhh, keep your voice down. Never let others know what's going on. Second race, I fancy Tudor Melody."

Off I go again and put $2.00 on the horse and it comes home

by a head. Would you believe it? First time at the races and I pick two winners. Oh yeah, with some help. This happened again in the next two races and I just kept doubling my money. After four races I had nearly a week's wages and I didn't have to sweat, break my back or anything. One afternoon and one week's wages. I saw Bill again for the last race.

He said, "Jack, I dunno this time. It could be Frisky King or Danube. Take your pick," and walked away, leaving me with the decision. Now the sensible thing to do would be to forget about the last race, but money and greed do away with common sense and I put all my money on Frisky King, as it sounded faster than Danube. There were only four in the race. One was miles back, the other eating dust and two were going neck and neck. Everyone was yelling and jumping. The excitement was immeasurable, my horse lost by a nose.

Bill was so highly sought after, he trained horses at some time or other, and all of them, except one, was racing that day. I didn't like losing a week's wages in a couple of minutes, so now gambling with money is not one of my things.

Bill only handled the horses on the ground. Dennis and I had to ride them, which meant we would be the first on their backs. Bill had mouthed them, got the horses comfortable with the saddle, groomed and picked up all their feet and taught them to tie up. It was up to us to teach them the rest. Like not to bolt at a moving leaf; how to move quickly and smartly; how to obey the voice; seat legs and hands; to know a human as a friend and not a foe.

The first young horse I rode was called Noodles. He was a lively, light bay with a silky black mane and tail. Bill had saddled him up and walked him round a bit before introducing him to me.

"Come on son, come and let the young fella have a sniff of you."

I remembered what the boss had told me at breakfast and that was to be confident and relaxed at the same time and have a tranquil air about me, so the horse would feel at ease. Well, that was fine at the breakfast table, but now, approaching the horse, I was having a battle with my confidence, nerves, muscles, heart rate and even my bowel. But Dennis was there and I wasn't going to let him see I was apprehensive. So I walked up to the young horse, let him sniff me as I rubbed his neck.

"Walk round him, stroking him all the time. Stay close to his back legs and let him feel your body against him. I will hold him, but I want you to walk around him twice and let him know you mean the animal no harm."

The horse was quivering. I used every skill I had to keep my body calm and relaxed while talking to Noodles in a friendly way.

"That will do. Now get on. You know how to rein a horse up and mount. I want you to do it swiftly but gently and ease your weight into the saddle. He's all yours now, son."

And then Bill left me and sat next to Dennis on the rail. I also noticed the boss peering through the rails. He must have come up to see how I was going. The show was on; I had an audience and I had a prop now. It was up to me to act. I reined Noodles up. He didn't move. I lifted my left foot to the stirrup. He twitched. The curtain was raised. My right leg cleared the saddle and found the stirrup on the other side.

Noodles braced his legs as I gently eased my bum into the saddle. Nothing happened. I was waiting for an eruption. Noodles was waiting for I don't know what. Here I was, sitting straight, hands down with the horse's legs splayed and quivering underneath me and nothing was happening. It came to me that the poor horse was more scared than I was. He most likely thinking, this weight on my back is some monster going to eat me.

I was just about to stroke him and ruffle his mane and show him I meant no harm when Bill yelled, "Stroke him on the neck and rump and show him you're not going to hurt him."

Well, I did it anyway and the horse seemed to respond and brought his legs back to their normal position.

"Well, let's see some action. Give him the boot," yelled Dennis. Well, not the boot, but I squeezed my legs. Nothing happened.

"Give him a slap with the reins. You got to teach him to move," said Bill. I did and Noodles did a little hop.

"That's the way. Give him some encouragement. Every step is a step in the right direction," more advice from the top rail. Soon we were walking around the yard, no rearing, no bucking, no throwing it self-down like I saw in the newsreels. Just a very frightened horse wondering what was going on.

"Right, you're doing fine now, Jack. All I want is for you to canter him along the back of the yard just once and that will do."

"Shouldn't I try trotting him first?" I asked.

"No, just canter, I don't believe in trotting a horse the first time," said my mentor.

It took a bit of doing, but we did what we were asked. I got off the sweating youngster; he was still quivering, wondering what it was all about. My legs were shaking and I was stiff in the groin. It felt like I had been riding for a year, not five minutes. At Bill's request, I led Noodles into the other yard, where I unsaddled him, rubbed him down, picked up his four hooves, then went and sat on the rail to watch Dennis and his new horse, Moonracker.

As Bill was getting Dennis ready for his ride, the boss told me, "Jack, you have a lot to learn and need a lot of experience, but you will make a horseman one day. I think you may have a gift."

It was great riding the rail watching someone else going through a new experience. Yes, Dennis had done a lot of riding, but never a young horse for the first time. Moonracker was a dapple-gray gelding about the size of Noodles, fourteen and a half hands. Bill came back onto the rail and said, "This horse is more of a mover than yours, Jack."

He then went on to explain, "Most young horses behave like yours, but some do try to get the monkey off their back, while others explode, but you can usually tell, but not always, even when you handle them correctly."

Dennis mounted his horse alright, but as he eased into the saddle, the horse gave a bit of a crow hop. Dennis gave him a slap with the reins. Moonracker did some more crow hops. Another whack with the reins and the horse didn't move. He tried again, but the horse decided enough was enough and it was staying put. Dennis then gave it two good slaps with the reins and stuck in the boot. Moonracker changed his mind and took off. Not at a walk or trot, something a bit faster than a canter. It was so frightened; it didn't see the other side of the yard coming up just before it hit. Dennis bailed out, grabbing the rail.

The horse got up from a half-sitting position, then went crazy. With empty stirrup irons banging its sides, saddle flaps flapping, all the horse wanted to do was get this thing off its back and out of the yards. It bucked and bucked, it reared, it raced around the yard. Bill jumped down off the rail and started to talk to the horse in a soothing sing-song voice. The horse started to realise it was getting tired and the thing on its back was stuck there, so he headed for the only thing he thought was a friend and that was Bill. Moonracker just walked up to him, foaming sweat, and shaking with wide eyes, stopping right in front of Bill. I thought it would run him over, but no, it just stopped. Bill rubbed him down, talking all the time to calm the horse.

"Dennis, you alright, son? Come over here," said Bill, still in a quiet voice.

Dennis didn't seem assured, as he was when he first approached the horse. He walked up to Bill and the horse.

"Now son, you have to get right back on this horse, (a), because it can't have a win and think it can get rid of a rider, (b), you have to get your confidence back and (c), the horse has used up all its energy and won't be inclined to do anything."

Dennis gave me a look as if to say, you're lucky Jack, you don't have to go through this. Bill handed the horse to Dennis and said, "Take him a bit gentler, don't rush him and take your time, kindness will reward kindness."

I could just imagine the turmoil going on inside of Dennis, but he mounted again, eased himself into the saddle and stroked and talked to the horse.

"Okay, that's fine now," encouraged Bill, "just move him on with a gentle squeeze, good lad, get him to walk out, that's it, just walk three times around the yard and that will do for today."

No more surprises. We walked down to the homestead and there were two very sore, but glad to be alive, jackaroos.

Next was taking the horses out in to the big yard – yep, the open paddocks. The feed was good, the horses were in good nick and Dennis and I were fit and game to take on the world. We got bucked off. One horse called Wedgwood threw me five times in the same number of minutes until it was so tired, it just had to submit to me being there. We had bolting horses, horses climbing trees, horses shying and goodness knows what else. The boss said it was our fault being to gung-ho and not working the horses properly, so he checked up on us. Now, we were supposed to ride the horses at a smart pace with the horse on the bit. Encouraging them with our legs all the time, and never to slacken off as these horses had to be ready for a big pony camp being held later in the year. We rode the horses every day.

We had to work twelve of the fourteen young ones that Bill was contracted to break in. After the excitement of saddling them up and three or four hours of riding, the horses and us felt rather tired by mid-morning. The horses were plodding along with their heads hanging down, two young riders also had heads hanging down and shoulders hunched half asleep. Somehow or other, the boss would find us, sneak up behind us on one of his superior chestnut mares, without sleepy horse or jackaroo aware of his presence. Then he would crack his stock whip just above our young charge's rumps. The horses would jump two metres with their hearts in their throats and eyeballs two centimetres out of their sockets, The jackaroos jumped three metres with their hearts in their mouths, hands grabbing reins, saddle, and mane and eyeballs enlarged to the size of table tennis balls. As horses and riders were trying to take control of their wits, the boss would yell, "It's good to see you're all awake," as we careered through the scrub in an uncontrolled shambles.

It got round the district that the jackaroos of Lota Plains were pretty good horsemen. People from around the local stations would bring their problem horses on a Saturday morning for us to ride; it ended up a bit of a rodeo session for about a month until we found ourselves busy with other social activities.

Wild pigs were a problem on the station and we all carried sugar bags and rope on the front of our saddles in the hope we would see and catch some suckers (wild piglets) to put in the sty for fattening. Pork was a welcome change from a diet of mutton.

One day as we were mustering the road paddock, I heard crashing in the scrub and a huge razorback pig came flying out past me, giving the young horse and me a fright. Then straight after the pig came Peter, the overseer, on his horse. As he flew past, he yelled, "Follow me. I want that pig."

The chase was on. The next person we picked up was Dennis, then the boss. We had the huge animal baled up beside a corkwood tree. The boss's dogs were darting in and out, snapping at it. The pig was so big they weren't game to get a hold of it. The pig was mad, its back against the tree for protection, making small charges at the dogs and us, gnashing his huge yellow tusks, ready to use them at the slightest chance it had. The boss had a brilliant idea.

"Jack, go and tie your horse up and sneak up behind the

Corkwood tree and grab one of the beast's back legs. Don't worry, we will keep its attention away from you."

I said, "Ay?" waiting for a reply, then added, "You're not fair dinkum, are you?"

"Don't worry, we will back you up," said Peter.

"Dare you," said Dennis.

I didn't have an option; I rode about twenty metres away, tied my horse to a sandalwood tree and started towards the pig. My brave fellow workers on their horses kept the beast busy, sending in the dogs and riding toward it yelling, the dogs barking.

I was planning my escape if the pig saw me. There wasn't any. All I could see except my horse, was the Corkwood, no low branches and I doubted, even in a life and death emergency, that could I skim up its rough bark.

I was there. The pig hadn't seen me. A decision had to be made, flight or hero. I chose hero, made a dive, and grabbed a left hind leg of that pig with both hands. It was on. The dogs got game, but not that game. Peter and Dennis yelled, "Hang on Jack, don't let it go."

Like bloody hell, if I did, the monster would gore me to death. The boss had another bright idea.

"Try and flip him on his back Jack."

What? One hundred and forty kilograms of wild mad pig? And I an insignificant sixty-five kilogram lad was to throw this monster on its back?!! The pig wasn't waiting for anything. It couldn't turn on me as long as I held the leg firm. It wasn't getting anywhere baled up, so it took off flat as a tack with me being towed behind. Through the scrub, through the sticks, through the big patch of galvanised burr.

"Help!" I yelled, "Help! Bloody help!"

My belly was getting red raw as my shirt had reached the

tattered stage. Then I felt an arm around my ankles. I think it was Peter who was trying to slow the express pig down, but all he was doing was pulling my poor shoulders out of their sockets further. Eventually, the pig slowed down enough for Dennis to get the other hind leg and then the boss was off his horse to give a hand. The dogs, feeling safe now, came and got hold of the razorback's ears. We got him. No, it was a she, a big barren sow, and believe me, sows can have huge tusks.

The boss and Peter trussed her up and tied the animal to a tree to be picked up by the tray back ute after mustering was finished. The boss thought it would make a fine baconer. I turned to Dennis and said, "You took your time giving me a hand."

"Well, I tried, but we had to dodge around trees and scrub to catch up to you while you just went through it, and anyway, we had to dismount and find a place to tie up the horses."

"Yea, I believe you. I know who I can depend on when my life is in real danger."

"Look Jack, it all happened so quick. I will make it up to you and go and get your horse."

"Thanks pal," I replied as I studied my scratches and pulled burr and bindi out of my body.

The boss, Peter and Dennis went to retrieve the pig that night while I killed my Thursday's three sheep for the station. I had just put the dressed carcasses in the butcher shop when the trayback pulled up alongside the pigsty.

"Quick, get the bolt cutters, Jack," was the urgent command from Peter. I ran to the mechanic's shed and grabbed a big pair of bolt cutters, wondering what he wanted them for. I soon found out. Dennis and the boss were holding the struggling, tied up animal on the back of the truck. Peter got the bolt cutters off me, saying, "I'm going to cut those tusks off before someone gets hurt."

As he got near to do the deed, the pig swung its head at him and ripped his shirt with her tusk from the nipple to the navel, while two men were still holding it down.

"Get the bastard in the sty," a very frightened, pale-faced overseer exclaimed. We all rolled her off the truck directly in to the sty and cut the ropes off her leg with one of my sharp killing knives tied to a very long stout stick. Peter said, "Look at this."

We turned and saw his torso, minus his shirt, with a scratch oozing blood right down his belly. He was centimetres from being disemboweled. The pig was found dead in the sty the next morning.

It was very early on a Sunday morning, one I will never forget, when horsemen gathered from miles around to join in the Lota pig hunt. There was the snorting of horses, the jingle of harness, dust swirling as hundreds of hoofs clip-clopped up and down the road, horses bucking, men yelling, dogs barking, excitement in the air as the piccaninny dawn was breaking on this cold and frosty day.

As all this commotion was going on, old Bill, the ringbarker, called me aside. He had four days' growth, his hair looked matted, he was wrapped up in an old army great coat. Sitting on a sawn log, hunched over a sixty-litre open drum with slashes all around the sides, a healthy fire licking out of the sides and top. He was warming his hands as he waited till his billy boiled.

"Sit down here lad, on this log." I did and watched the crimson early morning rays from a lazy sun start to prick the high grey clouds and spread over the horizon. The kookaburra laughed, old Bill in his old-world bush accent started to recite,

"There was movement at the station as the word had passed around."

He recited the whole *Man from Snowy River* poem from Banjo Paterson. I sat there enthralled, listening to him and hearing the background noises of horses, men and dogs in the early morning.

I was there when old Regret got away; I was there down Kosciusko way. Neither actor, nor any play, could ever capture the essence of that poem as old Bill did on that early Sunday morning.

Dennis and I rode horses; we loved the thrill, excitement, and the sheer devilment of it all. But there were dangerous times too. The day I had to swim a horse across the flooded Moonie River. The horse went down; I got off its back and, like the cowboys in the movies, held the horse's tail. A big mistake. All was okay till we got to the other side and as the horse scrambled to get a firm footing on the slippery, muddy bank, he lashed out with his back legs to get rid of the weight stopping him from getting safely up the bank. Sending me swirling back in to the flooded melee of logs and debris with a good kick to the shoulder. It could have been a disaster, but Jack was nimble and made the bank half a mile further down the river.

Lesson – always stay on the horse. If they sink, they will always come back up, alive, or dead. Another time at shearing, I was getting the night horse in and running late. I galloped him bareback toward the saddle shed when I got a stinging pain in my chest and was catapulted from the horse. The bloody shearers had put a wire between two trees for a clothesline. I didn't know and didn't see it in the early morning light; a few centimetres further up and I would have been decapitated. But being young and fit, we jackaroos survived without any serious injuries.

We joined a fledgling polocrosse club and started the game in all the surrounding towns so we could have an inter-town competition. We thought we were pretty smart in our black t-shirts with our white moleskin trousers. My white pith helmet with a black pucker hatband was made especially by Joan with a little three-word message written inside it - I love you. We used to practice every chance we had, in the evenings bouncing the ball on the living quarters' wall and catching and throwing it in our rackets. It made Mick mad, as he couldn't concentrate on the marking of papers and setting up school programs. We also taught our horses to follow the ball, on the ground and in the air. We weren't experts, but we weren't bad either.

We also rode the wild bullocks at the rodeos. It started as a dare between us and then became fair dinkum. Dennis drew the short straw, so he nominated first, then me. I was glad he went first because on other occasions when it came to a dare, I would jump in and do it and when it was his turn, he would change his mind and make up some excuse. We didn't have chaps or cowboy gear, so we rode in our polocrosse clothes, minus the pith helmets, of course. Dennis lasted about three seconds out of ten on his first ride. I had to do better.

"Alexander, chute number four," was my call.

I casually walked up to my assigned chute, practicing my inner self control that I'd learnt from riding young horses. This became especially hard when I realised what I was actually doing and when I saw the beast. It was huge! It had horns. One went up and the other went down and they were both pointy at the ends. On the ground or in the air, Jack was going to cop it from one of the pair! It was a brindle colour, and was bashing the chute and rearing up, trying to get out. The volunteer helper looked at me and said, "You've got a beauty. These brindle ones can really buck. If you can stay on, you have a good chance of winning. You done a lot of riding, have you?"

Keeping my voice steady as I could, I said, "No, this is my first time."

His expression changed from a happy sort of bloke to a doctor about to tell a patient that death would be imminent. He even bowed his head.

I got on.

"Don't sit there. You're not riding a horse. Sit up right on top of the shoulder blades, the further forward you sit, the better you are," advised my helper.

They already had a hemp rope round the beast with a cowbell attached underneath its belly. I slid my hand, palm up, between the beast and the rope and the helper pulled it up tight, so tight it cut all the circulation from my hand. Gosh, it was tight. Then, with the tail of the rope, he wound it around the back of my wrist, then again through the palm. I found with the bulk of all that rope I had difficulty shutting my hand, but I did, as my life depended on it.

The beast was surging back and forth; my legs were getting jammed against the crutch's side.

"Are you ready?" called the helper. "Let her go."

I yelled, "NOW!" wanting to get everything over and done with.

"Keep your eyes on the other end of the arena," shouted the helper as he opened the chute gate wide. The world stopped. The gate opened and I could see the whole of the showgrounds and hundreds of faceless human heads around the perimeters. I could see the hairy back of the neck with the ears and horns of the beast I was astride. All was quiet, all was silent. Then suddenly, as if coming out of a dream, I heard the roar of the crowd, the clanging of a cowbell, the breath, and the grunts of a wild beast. I felt muscles, thousands of them underneath me, heaving me to the east and to the west, then to the north and the south. I glimpsed the head in front of me; it was there, then gone and then back again. Then a whoosh of air as if I was flying, a jarring thud and dust in my mouth. I got up groggily, but unharmed. I knew I'd ridden the beast for a good time. It seemed minutes, not seconds, that I was on the bucking bull. Then disappointment. When my eyes focused, I noticed I had not moved any further than the chute gate.

"Great ride," said Dennis. "You made a whole one and a half seconds."

I ignored him. What could I say? I sort of dreamt that I would win the day but ended up in the shadow of the chute. The thrill of riding the beasts was a huge adrenaline surge to start with and a huge relief when the ride was finished. We both enjoyed our bullock riding and we got better, as you do with practice, but our quarters are shy of trophies. But they will come another time.

Bill had been teased by the townsfolk that he couldn't ride a horse with a hackamore bridle. This was, as far as we knew, a new type of bitless bridle but had been used by the Americans for centuries. Bill had a point to prove, and a bet to win, so the following Saturday he arranged the time and place, saying he would ride the young horse with this hackamore bridle, down the main street of Lota at 2.30 P.M. He, being a man of his word, did just that and rode the young horse, Smoken Joe, from Lota Plains into town. All went well until he passed the pub. He yelled out to the clientele to come and have a look so he could win his bet. The Saturday drinkers rushed out on to the veranda, waving their hats in the air, yelling as loud as they could, "Good on yer Bill."

With the sudden commotion and activity of lots of good spirits, the horse, being bitless, got a huge fright. It had never seen such a scene in his young life before and took off at the bolt to get away from the frightening display. The town dogs took after the horse, chasing it. It was the best entertainment they had had all week. And Bill straight back, long legged in the stirrups, leaning back, yelling, "Whoa there, whoa there," as he disappeared in a cloud of dust heading for Dirranbandi. Poor Bill, he lost his bet. He lost use of a shoulder and had a few broken ribs, but it was great for me, as you will see.

There were two more horses to break in and, with Bill out of action, the boss thought it might be an idea if Dennis and I broke one in each. It was a great opportunity; I was first to have a go because Dennis had to help Peter with some straggler mustering. I ran the horses in as normal this morning and, after breakfast, the men got their horses for mustering. I picked out one of the unbroken horses and locked her in the round yard. It was a rackish bay mare with a slightly haughty-looking face and rather fine features. She wasn't keen to be separated from the mob. I had difficulty getting her by herself in the yard. While I waited for the boss, I got the bag of breaking-in gear, which consisted of ropes, hobbles, halter, extra strong double bridle, old saddle and bits of ropes, straps and harness.

"Well Jack, you have picked a handful for yourself today, so what are you waiting for? Get in the yard with her and use the lasso to catch her." This was the greeting from the boss as he arrived.

I grabbed the rope and hopped in to the small yard. The animal looked at me warily, its ears slightly back, her muzzle slightly wrinkled, her eyes were large and frightened, her stance was ready for fight or flight. I didn't read the signs. I whirled the lasso, trying to get the loop around her neck. When Bill did this and missed, the horse just ran from him. This one didn't. It came straight for me, teeth bared, ears flattened, eyes wild, front hoofs trying to strike me down. I was in shock. It was the first time a horse had attacked me. I panicked and yelled at the creature. I tried bashing it with the rope. I tried to dominate this animal through abuse and slapping. The creature kept coming, trying to strike me down, trying to injure me, even kill me. I did my block, I swore, I cursed, I ran around; I did everything except catch the animal.

When I was totally exhausted, the boss said in a quiet voice, "Jack, step out of the yard."

I was hot; I was sweaty, completely puffed out, and angry, mad and very frightened. The boss climbed into the yard and copied me to a tee. He raced around, yelling and carrying on, looking a complete idiot and making me feel like an absolute stupid fool.

He stepped out of the yard, saying, "Jack, as you have observed, nothing has been achieved. You are worn out, but the horse is fit and as unapproachable as ever. You have gained nothing except maybe a heart attack for yourself. Now, think before you speak and tell me how you are going to handle this difficult horse in a nice, calm, rational way."

After some deep thought, I said, "I am not sure, Mr Williams. I could go and get some feed and place it in the yard and sit there so she will think I am friendly and not try to strike at me. Or I could stay on the top rail without getting in the yard and throw the rope over her, then tug at her with give and take and see how she responds."

"Well, not bad Jack, but your first idea isn't much good because you could be sitting in the yard for days while she is getting lots of feed which will make her fitter and more of a problem. I like your second idea the best and I think you should try it, but before you do, think of the alternatives you're going to use once you get the rope round her neck. Before you start anything, you must have a plan with alternatives and be prepared to follow through, no matter what happens or the time it takes. And do remember that the horse, in its two years of life, was running free and has never been touched by a human hand. Because you have picked a difficult horse, I will help you, but I want to hear what you intend to do before you actually do it."

I picked up the lasso, took a deep breath and climbed to the top rail. The horse watched every move I made. I stood up with a leg on each side of the rail for balance and whirled the rope around and threw. I missed four times, but success was on the fifth.

The rope was snatched out of my hand and I nearly lost my balance as the animal reared up and plunged to get away from this snake on its neck. I jumped down on the other side of the yard, checked to see all the gates were shut and quickly opened the round yard gate to let the horse into the big yard. She saw the opening and took off looking for an escape to get away from the thing that was following her, not realising the other end was around her neck.

She careered around and around the yard till she realised there was no escape for her. She stopped, facing the corner, her sides heaving, and the sweat dripping off her from her exertion.

"Now who's the one running around making a fool of themselves and wearing themselves out? It's not you this time, Jack. Now, what are you going to do?"

I told the boss and he nodded in agreement. I gently walked up towards the horse, talking to it in a sing song voice like Bill did and managed to grab the end of the rope, which was about ten metres from the horse.

I gave the rope a good tug. I expected the horse would resist, but it did the opposite. It whirled around and came for me again. Still holding the end of the rope, I ran around the horse to get away from those killer hooves. The horse turned in the opposite direction and with one thing and another; the rope was caught around its four legs. It went crazy.

Realising it was caught up and with me at the other end pulling, the horse ended up losing its balance and went crashing down, all four legs tangled in the rope.

"Good one Jack, that's the best way to handle a four-legged animal that's acting ornery, and that's for them to lose their footing, but I must admit you have done it in a most unconventional way. Now, what are you going to do?"

I answered truthfully, "I haven't the slightest idea. I suppose, let the animal try and untangle itself and try again, maybe." A nod from the boss in agreement.

As the horse struggled to free itself, I tried to help as much as I could. We were both very aware of each other. At last she found her feet and again. I grabbed the end of the rope; she looked at me trembling outwardly and I looked at her trembling inwardly. Holding the rope, I steadily started to walk towards her. She turned her head, resisting me.

I gave the rope a tug to bring her head round to me, saying, "Come on girl, no more fight. Just come and have a sniff to find out I am not the monster you think I am."

Her ears twitched, but her body language told me to be prepared for anything. I gave the rope around her neck another tug; she took one step toward me. I congratulated her and the boss, from outside the yard, did the same to me. I took my time; she took hers. A tug and release, here a step, another tug and release, another step, until she was close enough to sniff my extended hand with her extended neck.

I talked, she smelt. I tried to put my hand on her neck, again she flinched away. A tug with the rope, another try. After six or seven times, I managed to stroke her neck.

"That's enough now, son. Just leave her there to think about things and we will go and have some smoko. By the look of you, I think you need it."

The mental and physical exertion I had expelled in the last three hours had drained me. "Smoko" was the best word I had heard all morning. Smoko on a fine day, was always in the beautiful gardens of the homestead. Ethel would bring out a tray of hot scones, buttered or with cream and jam, thank you, with nice fine Royal Albert china for a cup of tea. I was always amused to see the boss with his large muscular hands, gnarled from a life of hard work, try and hold the delicate handle of the cup. He always managed, but I never understood just how. Work was never discussed at smokos or meal times. They were for more social gossip that the women could take part of. After a refreshing break and wishing I didn't have that extra scone, the boss and I marched back up to the yard, discussing the next things that had to be done with the young horse.

The horse seemed a bit more settled, even though the rope was still round her neck, with the remainder of it trailing behind her. I went into the yard to pick up the end of the rope when the bitch flattened her ears and had another go at me, but it was a half-hearted attempt and she soon yielded to the tug and release of the rope. Again, we played the cat-and-mouse game, until I managed to stroke her neck and gently ease the rope around it. The next exercise was to be able to take the catching rope off and replace it with a good stout leather halter. This was managed after a very frustrating time, but persistence paid off and by lunchtime, the rope was off her neck and the halter on.

"That's enough for her today," said the boss, "too much and you can sour a horse like this very quickly."

Dennis had a lot of trouble breaking in his horse too, and we both reckoned Bill knew they would be trouble and left them till last. But with the excellent patient coaching from the boss, we managed to get them mouthed, used to the saddle, and us picking up their feet and grooming them.

My horse, now called Sourpuss, let me on her back and didn't buck. But she kept trying to kick with her hind leg, my foot in the stirrup, or striking at the bit with her two front hoofs or turning around and trying to eat my ankle. Sometimes doing all three at once. Dennis' horse, now called Camel because he humped or bucked so much, and if he couldn't get rid of him, just sat down and rolled. They were both really dangerous horses. The boss decided that a good ride out of the yard for four hours would do them good. So on the sixth day of handling, we rode them out of the yard for the first time. Camel started bucking as soon as Dennis got him two metres out. I don't know if he stayed on or not, because that was an excuse for Sourpuss to bolt, striking at the bit all the time. I had no control at all with her head down and front hoofs trying to drag the bit from her mouth. All I could do was lean back and hope God would look after me. He did too, with a bit of humour as horse and rider entered the Moonie River at full gallop. She went over and I went off. No, Dennis didn't survive either, and then I had to get the night horse in to round up all the horses to get our two escaped, saddled mounts back. It took us a lot of riding and a lot of hours, but the horses ended up quite handy. They were always a challenge and they were never fully trusted.

My two favourite horses were One Eye and Horse with no Name. One Eye was a big, strong, 16-hand, bay horse with his left eye missing. So, you had to talk a lot when approaching and especially when you mounted him. He held his head really high; I guess so he could get better vision. In fact, his neck was completely vertical with his mane flowing in my chest. He was as game as Ned Kelly and we had a good understanding of each other. Horse with no Name was called that as she threw the boss and broke his collarbone a few years back. No one on the property could ride her as she continued to throw everyone at will. The boss was going to give her to a rodeo, but I liked her steely gray dapple coat with a silver mane and tail, and a very showy style she had to boot. Do you know what? She never did a thing with me. Never bucked or even pig rooted, a perfectly mannered lady.

Except for one day, I was checking some fences and found an emu's nest. Now it was said that anyone finding emu eggs could bring them home and cakes would be made. Dennis and I had been looking for ages for nests and I was the one who found one. It had fourteen green eggs in the nest and the male emu was not pleased with me stealing them. He was a fair way off, but I kept an eye on him just in case he attacked. I had never heard of them attacking, but it's better to be safe than dead. I placed all fourteen eggs carefully in to the sugar bag that we tied to the front of the saddle. I then tied the bag on to the dee rings on the side of my saddle, where my saddle bag was hitched. With the bag resting on the side of the horse near its flanks, I knew it was a dangerous position, but I trusted my horse as she trusted me. I managed to mount and tip toe the horse very gently back the four kilometres to the homestead. We made it so far without incident. I was dismounting at the saddle shed, rather clumsily, when the horse smartly stepped aside and the bag of eggs banged her side. The noise and the wetness and slime of a couple of broken emu eggs were more than the horse could take. Off she went, bag banging against her flank with egg white and yolk going everywhere as she disappeared down the road, smashing all the eggs. Dennis managed to find another nest and until then, no cakes were to be had, thanks to Jack!

C.17

Happenings

The Pub, School Fete, Pregnant, A Wedding

Life was great. We worked hard all week and put one hundred and fifty percent into our job. During the weekend we played and we put two hundred percent in to that. I was getting more involved with Joan. She was my first girl I ever had. I am sure it was love, that's real love. We had a busy schedule; she played tennis, went to pony club and helped at home. Sometimes I went to the pub on Friday nights; Saturdays were rodeos, polocrosse, doing chores like washing and cleaning out the quarters and hunting. Joan and I always found time for Saturday night and usually one of the weekend days to go to some social event or I would go to her place.

Now Joan was brought up properly, like in the strict good old-fashioned way. So was I, but I pretended to be a bit rough round the edges just to annoy my mum, to show I was a manly man. It was the only thing I knew to do differently from the three women I lived with. But that was sixteen months ago and now I didn't have to act because Jack was Jack. Joan would not tolerate swearing at all and she spoke just a little bit posh. It must have been catching because all the men at Lota Plains teased me. When was I going to eat that 'plum' in my mouth?

George, the Aboriginal who worked with us quite a lot, would say when a question was asked of him, "Well, ac-tu-ally," in the poshest voice he could muster, with a grin as wide as the Great Australian Bight and a twinkle in his eye that would put Venus to shame. He just made everyone double up with laughter.

The day the boss was caught out by George, was when we had finished mustering 1400 sheep and had them all in the yard ready for drafting. We tied up our horses and gave the dogs a drink; we were all squatting down rolling a smoke, looking at all the sheep we had mustered, when the boss said to George, "What have you been up to?" pointing to the only black sheep in the middle of the 1399 white sheep.

There was a thirty second silence, and then George stood up, waving his arm from left to right, pointing to all the sheep and with his widest grin said, "Not as much as you have Boss!" We all laughed, except the boss. He didn't like being caught out.

The pub at Lota was the men's retreat of the town and it was only the locals who attended what really was a private men's club, except for the publican's wife. You couldn't have a woman in the public bar. Heaven forbid! The beer would turn flat and sour. And no man would stand for that. Dennis and I would sometimes walk the four kilometres to town and join the Friday night session. There was always something happening in the pub. The clientele was made up of workers, railway men, shearers, timber workers, stockmen, and two jackaroos. Sometimes there was a local grazier, who had decided the safest place to be was the pub, instead of his home.

"The wife is pretty upset tonight, I don't know why, but she will calm down in a while," was the usual excuse.

They seemed to have lots of bets at that pub. Dennis and I never joined in, as we were flat out affording the drinks. You've heard the one about Bill and the hackamore bridle. Well, another bet late in a session was who had the longest dick. Yep, you read it right. One bloke skited his was as long as a cat's tail, so bets were placed, and they caught the publican's cat and measured his tail: thirty centimetres long.

"Okay Ernie, whip yours out and let's measure it."

"Don't have to," said Ernie. "I can prove mine is longer than the cat's tail because you measured it from the cat's arse. So you got to do the same to me to prove that I am wrong."

The publican called the bet invalid and bets were off, but they were soon on again because a point had to be proved. The publican placed a piece of three by one length of timber on the bar, both ends exactly twenty-one centimetres from the bar's edge on the drinkers' side of the bar's top. The six contestants lined up, balancing on the foot rail with their flies undone, seeing if their penis would reach the timber line to collect the money. Quick as a flash, the publican's wife raced in, picked up the length of timber and brought it down with a crash on the extended organs with the words, "We won't have any of this sort of filth going on in this hotel thank you."

The howl of pain and rage, the holding of their bruised manhoods in their hands, jumping around the bar in pain. It was a sad and sorrowful scene to behold. Those of us that didn't participate still felt the pain in our groins. I must add that is the only time I have ever seen such a display in a pub or anywhere.

Another Friday night, the atmosphere was more sober as President Kennedy of the US and Premier Khruschev of Russia were having a debate about using Cuba as a missile base. Kennedy said war was imminent if the Russians tried to get missiles into Cuba. Some of the men had been returned soldiers and said war was a sure thing and blokes our age would be going to defend the country. That night the whole bar kept shouting us drinks as we were going to be the representatives of Lota to defend the country against the Russians. It was a grand night of war stories, mateship and free drinks. We were drunk. So drunk that we didn't get home that night. We both woke up in the table drain on the side of the road early the next morning, huddled together for warmth and soaking wet from a heavy dew. We only managed a kilometre from the pub. We still had another three miserable ones to stagger home as the sun was starting to rise. I am glad Joan's father didn't happen to drive by.

Mick, the schoolteacher, said to us one night that he thought half his grade six and seven students were pregnant and was unsure whether to mention it to his principal in case he made a fool of himself. We discussed the matter and we all thought the principal should be told about Mick's suspicion. It was about six weeks later when Mick informed us it was true. Half his class was found to be pregnant, after tests were done by a doctor and nurse sent from St George.

"And promise not to tell anyone. The police think it's seventy-year-old grazier, Mr Tiddlesbottom."

"Ah, come off it Mick, that old geyser is flat out putting his boots on, let alone getting half a dozen or so girls pregnant."

Sadly, it was true. Dennis and I never said anything to anyone, but the whole township knew.

The following Friday night at the pub, there were a lot of angry men getting steamed up over their daughters' misfortunes. Angry that it had happened, angrier that it was a wealthy grazier, having his pleasure with poor workers' children and just about out of control with the distress it caused and the alcohol they had consumed. Murder was talked about in hushed tones; one father pulled out a castrating knife and started to hone the edge on a sharpening stone. Others caught on to the idea and started to clean and sharpen their knives. The mood and talk got ugly as the session wore on. Just about the time the men were going to head out to Tiddlesbottom's property, the local constable, Tom, walked in. I suspect he had been rung up by the publican.

"I don't want to know what's going on, but you blokes put those knives away and get back to your families NOW, because they need you at this terrible time. The law will handle this in the proper manner and justice will be done. I am closing the bar as of now. If I have any trouble from anyone, I will lock them up for consorting."

There was a lot of mumbling from the upset fathers, but as rough and tough as they were, deep down they were law-abiding folk and shuffled off to their respective homes.

Turning to us, neither at the legal drinking age, Tom said, "You boys better get home too. I have my doubts whether you should be in the bar at all. But if you work like men, you have to be treated like men. My advice is take it steady and never push privileges, understand?"

We nodded and wished him a very good night and made the long walk home. Mr Tiddlesbottom was found to have been the guilty person but was given a stay from a prison sentence because of his age and frailty. It left a very distasteful message to the townsfolk, who felt the privileged always escaped true justice, and the poor copped it every time. A bit like Ned Kelly times, huh?

The big school fete was on and there was fun for everyone. Joan and I went and had a great time. There was a man sitting on the back of a tarp-covered truck, holding a very small piglet in his arms, applying grease on its skin and calling, "Who wants to catch the greasy pig? We have a greasy pig to catch. Only 50c to have a go and you can keep the pig. Hert, the greasy, greasy pig. Who's going to catch the greasy pig?"

The man called loud and often and drew a big crowd. I went up and paid my 50c like a lot of other blokes, 'cause it was going to be a cinch to catch the little fella and the other two dozen men thought the same. He had us all form a half circle about twenty-five metres from the truck.

"Well boys, you already?"

"Yes," we answered, "let her go!"

And then he flipped back the tarp on the truck to reveal a large cage structure. He opened the gate and the biggest wild razor-backed pig, with huge tusks, came bounding out of the cage. It went straight through the middle of us all, at least fifty kilometres a minute. Some stupid people tried to catch it, but it was a brave effort done in vain.

"Who wants to catch the greasy pig? The greasy pig. Only 10c and for children under twelve years. Yes, that's right folks, bring your young'uns to catch the greasy pig."

Then he let the piglet go. The kids had fun catching it and I am sure the pig was glad to help out with some fund raising. Yeah, but us adults were taken in. It was fun and for a good cause.

Joan frightened me at one stall. It was to see who could drive a ten centimetre nail into a block of hard wood. There were bent nails everywhere; you had to put four in to get a prize. I failed miserably, but Joan got a prize. I was so impressed, but slightly worried also. I was learning not to underestimate women.

There was throwing the broom; running with balloons between your legs; a greasy pole you had to sit on and try to knock your opponent off with a grain sack stuffed with wool. I nearly won that. There was Tom, the policeman and me as the finalist. Who knocked the other off would be the champion knocker-offer in Lota and I was hungry for the title. I had to impress Joan, but it was going to be great to unseat a copper and not be charged. Tom put up a good fight. I thought I did better. I looked at Joan for her admiring glance. That's when Tom knocked me flying with a huge double whammy. We shook hands and I congratulated him and said, "I hope I didn't hit you too hard with my blows."

He smiled and said, "I thought you were missing all the time. It was only the wind that I could feel." Believe me, I connected all right. He wasn't fooling me.

Sometimes, I would be invited to Joan's place for the day. Of course, she had to pick me up and drive me back that evening. This was sort of embarrassing to me. It was the early sixties. Who ever heard of a woman picking up her date and taking him home afterwards? It wasn't heard of. I suffered the indignity as a man because how else was I to romance this princess?

We would ride together side by side, cantering over the paddocks, sometimes holding hands as we rode. She was an excellent horsewoman and we enjoyed our rides together in the wide-open spaces. We also enjoyed our little wrestling in the long grass. Nothing untoward, mind you. Joan would help her mother make a delicious Sunday lunch and after the dishes were done, it was siesta time. The women went to their respective places while Mr Fisher laid down on the lounge floor, and soon was snoring quietly. I was young. I wasn't sleepy, but I had to pretend and lie down near the big man and wish the hour would soon pass.

After siesta, we would all go for a drive around the property in the big Humber. Mr and Mrs Fisher in the front, Joan and I in the back, taking turns to open and close gates and listening to a running commentary from Joan's father. He talked about the wool price, the cost of shearing, the feed in the paddocks, the work that had to be done next week. Mrs Fisher always answered with a murmur and a, 'yes, dear', and an, 'oh really?' or, 'do you think so?' I tried to ask intelligent questions but when I got the answers, I realised how stupid they were. Joan would have a dig at me silently with a look as if to say, "You really mean you didn't know?" During these drives, we also had to hold between us Mr Fisher's army point 303 rifle, loaded with a full magazine but with the safety on and nothing in the breach.

Seasons had been good for quite a few years and there was an abundance of wildlife, especially emus, red and grey kangaroos, and pigs. They were so prolific that once when we were driving to St George, we had to stop for five minutes for a large mob of 'roos to cross the road. Anyhow, as we were driving along one of the bush tracks, there was a mob of eight 'roos in single file starting to hop across the track about fifty metres to the left of us.

Stopping the car, Mr Fisher said, "Could you get those please Joan."

And to my utmost astonishment, this slim princess stepped out of the car with the 303 and worked the bolt. Bang, one down, worked the bolt again. Bang, another one. It was like a live shooting gallery. She shot every one of them, on the hop, clean kills, everyone. I challenge any shooter, man, or woman, to be so accurate and so quick with such a rifle. My princess had a lot of bush skills I wished I had.

We continued with our Sunday drive when another mob of 'roos were coming on the track. The Humber pulled up. Mr Fisher said, "Would you like to get those, Jack?"

I was getting to be a good shot with my Bruno .22 but hey, I wasn't going to make a fool of myself, no way. I was searching for an excuse when Mrs Fisher addressed her husband. "That's a bit unfair dear, you always said no one should touch another's gun."

A grunt was all the reply she got, but she saved my bacon because the 'roos had disappeared in to the scrub. I enjoyed my Sundays at Joan's place even though I had to watch my manners, and really think before I spoke.

There was a big wedding to be held at Lota Plains. It was the cook, Ethel, who was marrying some property owner to the east of us. The gardens were beautiful, the hibiscus, the roses, the white climbers on the archway, the bougainvillea, red and orange and an array of colour from the petunias, the red of the geraniums with a carpet of blue and white alyssum. Fruit trees flowering and even peach blossom. It was spring and everything was in full bloom and all was lovely. I knew it to be so, as the birds were happily chirping and whistling every day. The guests came from miles around, even from the city. You could tell the city ladies as they wore the pillbox hats with the netting in front or was it a fly veil? The country women had large, brimmed hats, decorated with a ribbon, fruit or flowers. Joan had a lovely blue hat, which matched her twinkling blue eyes. The wedding was held in the gardens with a pedal organ for the music, which Dennis and I had to carry out as well as all the chairs we could find, from cane chairs, kitchen chairs to lounge chairs, enough for seventy-eight bottoms.

We jackaroos weren't officially invited, but we were the waiters for drinks and savouries and directions to the toilets and anything else we were asked to do. I had never been to a wedding before, but if I was going to have one, it would be a garden wedding with the birds and flowers as my witness. What am I saying? Why would I be thinking such stupid things? I threw the thought to the wind as I listened to the father of the bride say his speech.

He said the usual stuff about what a great daughter he had and hoped the groom would look after her as well, or better, than he had done. Then he gave the groom the old advice about the horse and cart. You know the one where the horse trips and the groom says, "Once." The horse trips again and he says, "That's twice." The third time the horse trips, he pulls out his gun and shoots it. The bride says, "What did you shoot the horse for? It wasn't his fault it tripped." The new husband answers, "That's once!"

I didn't think it was very funny saying, more or less, shoot my daughter if she doesn't behave. What a great dad! But what I thought was funny, and so did everyone else, was when, as he was winding up from the long speech, he said, "Well, the newly married couple have got a lot to do tonight, so we better not waste any more of their time and let them get their things together."

I think he meant their suitcases. Everyone tittered and he went as red as a tomato as he realised what he had said. The couple got away. They were going to Brisbane, a four hundred kilometre drive. They would stop somewhere on the way, but that was a secret.

After the wedding, we, or should I say, Joan, every now and then, would slip little things into the conversation like, "How many children would you like to have?" and, "Would you like to live in this area all your life?" Worst of all, "Mum likes you a lot, she said it would have to be a lucky girl to marry a man like you." And, "Did you know Mum and Dad eloped and told their parents after!"

I used to get a tight feeling in my stomach when these little bits of information or questions were raised. Once in a night of mad passion, and that's all it was because, I was told, 'We are not interested in sex till after marriage or at least engagement, thank you'. This was very difficult for me, as my testicles would feel like bowling balls. The ache was incredible. But then it suited me, as I hated to imagine what my first bit of sex would be like. A disaster like my first kiss! I should buy more Reader's Digests!

Anyway, once in a night of wild passion, we did decide to elope. We got about fifty kilometres away and realised we had only half a tank of petrol and $8.00 between us. But we did love each other and what the future held was anyone's guess.

C.18

Men at Work

Fire, Wild Cattle, Timber Work, Mayhem

It was not all play and romance; we worked hard; dam hard. It was decided we would build a new set of sheep yards out in the plain paddock. The workers to do this job were Peter the overseer, the two jackaroos and Ernie the station hand. Our tools were axes, adze, an old green contrary Thames truck, brace and bits, pliers, chisels and a heap of wire plus the worst tools of all, post hole shovels and crowbars, then rope to tie the timber onto the truck. If I had forgotten anything, we would just have to come back and get it later, but I didn't forget the billy, tea and our lunches.

First, we had to get the timber. It was decided pine for the rails and iron bark for the posts. It was plentiful on the property and the theory was you use the timber that grows in the area, as it's the best timber to use. We found a good clump of iron bark that was suitable for posts. It was as tough as it sounds, with a very thick, rough bark. Peter gave us a choice of new axes as he pointed out that for the next few months, we will be doing a lot of axe work and we were responsible for our own tools. We were shown how to cut a holder for the axe, while we used a medium bastard file to get the shoulder off and get it ready for honing. Then, using an oiled round stone for the final sharpening, we had to have them razor sharp to be able to shave the hairs off our arms. The American hickory handles also had to be treated with a light oil and rubbed in to the wood so it wasn't slippery. I chose a Kelly axe; Dennis chose a Plum. We didn't know it then, but those two axes made us very fit axe men.

It wasn't long before we learnt our swing and accuracy of cuts with advice from Peter and Ernie. We worked hard cutting the tough trees down. Not only was the work hard, but we made it tougher for ourselves by competing. Ernie never joined in. He was a big strong bloke, done hard laboring all his forty years, and he took his time and wasn't much interested in our antics. We cut trees down, trimmed the branches off and barked them with the back of the axe, which, to my body, was harder than cutting them down.

An argument started up with Peter and Ernie. Ernie said it was stupid to bark them here, it was better to load them and bark them on site. He knew a man who lost his hand loading freshly barked slippery posts on to a truck and he wasn't going to help load if Peter insisted on continuing. Peter argued that it was much easier and quicker to bark them as soon as they were cut and that he could fit nearly a third more on the truck barked, against leaving them with their large bark on.

No one won the argument. We jackaroos didn't have a clue, but it did end up the three of us loading the very slippery logs onto the truck with near disasters on the cards. Ernie continued cutting trees down while we loaded. When we were barking the pine trees for the rails, they had hardly any branches until two thirds from the top. We barked them by cutting around the base, pulling the bark from the bottom and walking backwards, pulling it down. You could strip the bark off in three pieces before cutting the tree down.

We worked from 8.00 in the morning till 4.30 in the afternoon and the chores still had to be done. The killing, milking, running in horses etc. etc. by Dennis and myself before we started the day's work. We were exhausted and we both helped each other stagger to tea every night. The worst chore was mine. That was trying to stay awake to turn off the lighting engine at 9.30. I failed this chore a couple of times and Mick was kind enough to do it for me to save my skin. As one cannot fail to do his chores, whether dead or alive, they must be done.

We cut and barked, dug postholes, and filled them up with posts. We adzed rails and mortised posts with brace, bit, chisel and cob and coed the rails to the post. We all had a go at everything and became quite skilled with the adze, *use your elbow against the knee or you will cut your shin in half,* which saved Dennis and me from a severe injury. We worked, we sweated, we got lean and fit and we unconsciously were building our bodies up. Not that you would notice, but you could feel the muscles growing with a hardness yet suppleness within our frames.

The old truck gave us constant trouble, whether it was dirty fuel or fuel filter or carby, only Kevin the mechanic would know, but because we were using it all the time, he didn't have a chance to find the problem. One day we couldn't get the thing going. We were late finishing. We had wanted to finish the panelling in the forcing yard. Alas, the old girl wouldn't start. We ran the battery flat, then tried cranking it with the crank handle. Peter decided to drain some fuel into a can from the fuel tank and poured it in to the carburetor. On the third crank, the motor roared into life only to die again, so it was decided that I sit on the mudguard and dribble fuel into the carby with the bonnet tied up, so it wouldn't crash down and take my arm off. So, here was I, sitting on the mudguard with a ten litre tin full of petrol between my legs, dribbling fuel into the carby all the way back to the homestead.

The difficulty I had was, (a) keeping from sliding off the mudguard, (b) not falling into the engine compartment and getting ripped by the fan belt or burnt from the hot manifold when we hit bumps and (c) holding the drum still and the bit of garden hose from leaving my grasps. And finally, keeping the hose just above the carburettor without too much fuel going in, flooding it, or not enough, starving it. It was a job that required all the skills of a top jackaroo.

We made it home in the dark. Kevin spent a couple of days on the old girl, cleaning the fuel system. When we finally went out to finish the yards, we only had the one panel to go plus the cleaning up to do. We got a shock when we came across some burnt country.

"There's been a fire," said Dennis.

We wondered if the fire had reached the new yards. Did it burn them down? Who was responsible for the fire? And who was going to tell the boss? All very difficult questions to be answered shortly.

The biggest dread was, we would have to rebuild another set of yards that only two days before, we were very proud of. Not to mention the blood, sweat and tears that went into building them. As we approached, we all gave a huge sigh of relief. We could see the yards standing, but the fire had burnt all around them. We pulled the truck up quickly and Dennis and I jumped off the back while Peter and Ernie exited the cab to investigate. Our tracks walking around the yard had worked as a firebreak and the grass fire hadn't crossed over. Also, the posts and rails were green, so we were lucky not one piece of our labour was damaged.

The next thing to ask was, how did the fire start? Well, we were late trying to get the truck started the other day. Petrol spilt as we siphoned some out of the truck. There was a discarded cigarette and maybe we didn't notice a smouldering fire as we were driving home. I certainly did not, sitting on the mudguard.

Our investigation acquitted the four of us. There was no proof any one person started the fire. Dennis and I reckoned it was Peter and Ernie as the culprits, but what would jackaroos know?

It was raining, day after day, wet and muddy everywhere. We did all the wet weather jobs. Oiling saddles, repairing leatherwork, sharpening our axes, helping Kevin servicing the vehicles and cleaning the homestead's silver. The rain continued and the boss was running out of ideas to keep us occupied. Shearing was coming up and there was a new rule that the shearer's mattress had to be ten centimetres thick. So, we had to get all the mattresses out of the shearers' quarters into the shearing shed. That's the whole thirty-five of them. With two big tin tubs filled with water, we had to slit the ends open, pull out all the coconut fiber, at least, I think that's what it was, then tease it out into the tubs, washing it, then letting it dry. The dust and the smell of the stuff crept up our noses and down into our throats. It also attacked our eyes. It was a rotten job and took the best part of a week by the time we washed and dried the fiber, stuffed it back into the mattress and sewed the ends up. And stuff we did. We could not put the entire fiber back that had come out of the mattress. We would sit on the floor hanging on to both sides of it, using our feet as rams to punch all the fiber we could into it and we still couldn't manage to get it all in. We tried so hard. When the boss came up, he tried. So did Peter. We even got Ernie, but no one could get the entire fibre back where it belonged. They looked fine and were more than ten centimetres thick until the shearers slept on them. After the first night they were flat out being three centimetres. The whole exercise had been a waste of time and the boss had to run out and buy more mattresses before the shearers went on strike.

Stock work was my forte and the animals knew it. There was some silent communication between us I could never really figure out. Skipper, my beloved kelpie sheep dog, always seemed to know what I was going to do and when I would do it. I am sure some mental telepathy goes on between animals and humans, but too often messages get mixed up. As an example, human thinks, "I love you so much I want to cuddle you." The message the dog receives is, "I am going to squeeze the guts out of you. Yelp, I'm out of here!" Anyway, it's a thought, because Skip and I always seemed to be on the same wavelength. And even though he had a tough life, like all working dogs, he was as loyal as anything could be.

Working sheep in the paddock was just about all automatic for us. An occasional whistle or pointed direction is all Skip needed, and the sheep would do our bidding. Now it was altogether different with Dennis. Peter had given him a new dog because his other one, remember, wouldn't follow him on a horse. Dennis thought, seeing we had a nice boss, he would call him by the boss's first name, which was Dan. But Dan the dog wasn't a good communicator with Dennis. He'd run through the middle of the sheep or hold the lead up and Dennis would start yelling orders at the dog.

"Here Dan, get behind, you bloody bastard. Dan, you mongrel, get away there. Dan, I'll whip your arse off if you don't come behind."

The boss rode up to Dennis quietly and said, "It might be in your interest to change the name of your dog. Perhaps Dennis might be a good alternative, but I suggest you do it now!"

He then rode away to concentrate on working his dogs, which also was quite remarkable. He had two little black dogs; I don't know what breed they were, but they were much smaller than a kelpie. They could be around the lead of the sheep, a good two hundred metres away, and yet they could hear the boss when he hissed, which was his way of whistling at them. How they heard him I am blowed if I know. It just must be that telepathy thing.

"There are 150 head of Aberdeen Angus we have to get in and brand the calves," said Peter. "They haven't been mustered for a year, so we will have to take care."

Dennis and I were excited. This should be fun, and it was. An early morning start, which meant all chores had to be done before we left, and a ride out to the back paddock, which had a fair bit of timber in it and abundant feed from the good seasons that the animals enjoyed for a few years. The cattle were toey; life was good and they didn't want to be herded together by humans. We had to get them out of the scrub and onto the open plain. That's where we wanted them, but they had different ideas. All our riding skills came to play. Dodging trees, dodging charging cattle, getting them together, watching for breakaways, getting rogues back into the mob, it was a good half day's work before we had them circling on the plain to quieten them down and take a bit of sting out of them. Around and around, we milled them until they stopped, ready to take the lead. The boss put on a magnificent show. As I said, he was a light horseman in the First World War and had to be in his mid-sixties. But there he was on this sixteen-hand chestnut horse, which was bucking profusely, while he was cracking his stock whip. One hand on the reins, one hand wheeling the whip and bum not moving an inch from the saddle, he rode that horse cracking the whip until the horse resigned itself to its sound and ignored it forevermore. I have been to a lot of rodeos but have never seen such a fine display of horsemanship and control.

We eventually got the stock to the yard, with tired cattle, tired horses, and tired men; the cattle tested us the whole twelve kilometres back to the yards. But try as we might, they just wouldn't go into the yard gate way. We tried milling them around, cutting a few off, and trying to force them in, hoping the others would follow, but they wouldn't budge. Peter had a great idea; I don't know why, but it always seemed when someone had a great idea, it meant involving me. How Dennis missed out on great ideas was a mystery to me.

"Jack, get off your horse and tie it over there" He pointed to a small pine tree. This I did and waited for good idea instructions.

"Now, walk around to the other side of the yards, get into the yard and see if you can provoke one of the beasts to charge you, but don't get yourself caught."

"Yea fine," I replied, "don't forget to write to my mother and tell her how I was killed."

With the three men pushing the cattle again, trying to get them into the yards, here I was in the front of the gate, well about three metres back, yelling and jumping around to get some mad beast's attention. I always had a fascination for the bullfighters in Spain, as a matter of fact, I had a bull fighting poster in my room with a toreador flashing his pink and yellow cape at an outraged bull. I took my shirt off to use as a cape and tried to entice the cattle into the yard, using the steps as I had seen the toreadors use.

I was too busy putting on a bit of an act to notice I had caught the bloodshot eye of a very angry overheated cow. She charged me. The onslaught was so sudden, my feet were running but I wasn't getting anywhere, but the bloody cow was and so were the other 149 behind her. I think it was the wind from her nostrils that finally got my feet scrambling gravel as I took off for the other side of the yard and up on to the top rail I went. I turned round to see the gap I had created; I didn't see a gap. I saw a very enraged head spraying slobber over me. The bitch was trying to climb the rail to get at me. It may be of interest to know that a mad cow is twice more dangerous than a mad bull and I think it's the same with all animals.

It was a success. The cattle were in and the gate bolted. We decided to leave them the rest of the day to calm and cool themselves off before drafting and branding, which we decided to do early the next morning. After rubbing our horses down and washing our sweat sodden saddle blankets, we got all the gear for branding the next day.

We drafted the calves off their mothers; some of them were eleven months old and a fair size. Some of the bull calves were at least half the size of a full-grown bull. Now these cattle were pretty wild, but because the Aberdeen Angus don't have horns, you would think they wouldn't be dangerous. Well, you'd be mistaken. What they do is charge and knock you over with their big black heads and when you are down, they will kneel and try and crush you with their knees. We had to use the same tactics as yesterday to get them into the smaller yard. Dennis helped this time, thank goodness. With rushes of adrenaline and slight heart attacks, we managed to draft all the calves successfully.

The operators of the branding are listed here in order of importance. Two jackaroos as catchers, the boss in charge of the branding irons, three for the station brand and two for the year of branding, Peter in charge of the knife and pliers for castrating and ear-marking and George and Ernie as the relief catchers.

The scene was a small round yard with a good fire going in an upright hollow log, cut and made specifically for the job. This was in an adjoining empty yard with the handles of the irons just poking into the round yard where we had drafted ten calves of various sizes. Another adjoining yard held all the drafted calves, ninety-two to be exact. The boss, Peter, George and Ernie were sitting on the top rail, and so were the two jackaroos. Why were we all on the top rail? Because the bigger calves were charging us and being very aggressive.

"See that one," said Dennis, pointing to one of the smaller ones, "I will get his head and you back me up on the tail."

In other words, we were scruffing the calves. We got down off the rails, Dennis grabbed the head, I the flank, and we threw the calf on its side. We were pummeled, trodden on and butted, but we held on. Peter jumped off the rail, and in a second or so, had two balls cut out and an earmark on, then got knocked arse over head before regaining the safety of the yards. The boss had the irons on the calf, branding it and then, when given the all clear, Dennis and I let go of the squirming animal together and made for the safety of the rails.

"Right, don't waste time. George and Ernie, it's your turn," said Peter, and they jumped down off the rail and scruffed the next calf, while Dennis and I caught our breath and started to pick our next victim out. The first few times were scary, but then we became immune to the charging and the kneeling and the pummelling we were getting, like footballers or boxers do in the heat of a match or fight. But it was awful to see the boss get knocked over and his large straw hat squashed into an unrecognisable piece of mash. In the first two hours, we got twenty-four done, then we had smoko. Boy, we needed that. Then the two hours before lunch we did twenty-one, and again, we needed every minute of our lunch break. We even had to shower and change our clothes for lunch, because we were covered in dust, dirt, blood, and shit.

After lunch, we changed back into our torn and blood-soaked clothes. Not all the blood was from the calves we discovered when we had our showers. Those pointy, cloven hoofs of the calves were sharp as knives and we had weals and cuts all over us. The big yellow and grey bruises came out later.

After lunch, we got another eighteen done and a very hard fifteen late that afternoon. Thank God it wasn't a Tuesday or Thursday when I had to kill. We had another fourteen to do tomorrow, but they were much too big for us to handle, so they were done in the crush. We were so stiff, sore and bruised the next morning and so slow doing our chores that we were late for breakfast, but nothing was said.

We got the other lot branded and after lunch, the boss trusted us to take the cattle back to their paddock. Whether he thought we were better than we were, or that everyone else was so buggered, we were the only choice, but I am sorry to say the trust was gone when we lost all the cattle. They just bolted on us halfway to their paddock and went in all different directions, smashing through fences just in a mad rush. We went home and told Peter what had happened and he admonished us for not taking a lead but said, "Don't worry, I will tell the boss and Ernie can check the fences tomorrow. The cattle will find their way eventually to their own paddock."

Stock work was good. Timberwork was hard. We used to follow Kevin as he drove the old D8 Caterpillar bulldozer over the mass of coolibah suckers. With our five litre tins with wire handles and a stick, one end wrapped in cloth, we would dab poison on to the small stumps that were left behind. It was a rotten job, walking over the pulled trees, and not tripping over, and while looking for the torn ends to poison, as they were covered with the leaves of the fallen suckers. But the worst of the job was the poison we used. It was pure arsenic boiled in a two 220-litre drum. The missus was worried about this, as the milking cows would hang around the drum for warmth; she thought the milk might be tainted with arsenic. Anyway, we ended up with sores on our legs from the small splashes that landed there when we pulled the stick out to dab on the sucker stems. We called it arsenic pox and didn't worry about it much. Until the day we were lifting a half empty drum onto the back of the ute and the bung came out. The arsenic liquid poured all over Dennis's feet. By the time I got him home, the stitches in his work boots were eaten and they fell apart. The boss rushed him to the St George hospital where Dennis had a restful couple of days, but he lost all his toenails. That was the end of the arsenic.

So the next job was grubbing the suckers out. This was tough work. You had to swing the mattock hard to get it under the tap root and then pull up to unlever the whole sucker from the ground. This jerking movement of hitting the ground and pulling up was tough on the body. One also had to have the dexterity of a gymnast and the sprightliness of a quick-change artist. When one hit a sucker with the mattock, a horde of very nasty green-headed ants would end up under one's shirt or in one's pants or, worse still, in one's underpants. Whoever this happened to, the person would drop his tool and do the dance of the seven veils in tenths of a second, to strip the clothes off and get to the offending, painfully biting ants. It was nothing to see trousers down around the ankles, bare hairy bums shining in the sun and a dance that Fred Astaire would be proud of.

It was a dangerous job too, not only because of the wrenching of our bodies that caused problems. Dennis had another trip to the doctor's as he'd pulled his shoulder out and damaged tendons. Me, I was just damaged. But it was the snakes that nearly got us. Ernie got one wrapped around his ankle and he screamed and panicked and tried bashing the snake and his leg with the mattock. We saw it was a non-poisonous grass snake and laughed at his antics. After a short while, he calmed down and got the snake off. He got rather emotional as he took his boot and sock off to show us his foot. To our amazement, there was no big toe. He told us he had been bitten by a death adder a few years ago and to save himself; he tied a bit of string around the butt of his big toe and then chopped it off with his axe, as he had no means of help.

My day of reckoning was the day after Ernie had the fright with the grass snake. I had pulled out a sucker and curled under it was a rather large western taipan. We both got a fright. He uncurled his two and a bit metres and started to get away. I did a very silly thing. I was off to the side of the reptile, about halfway between its head and tail, when I had a go at it with my mattock. It had a go at me. It was so fast that I didn't see the movement; it whipped back then to the side and struck. I stumbled back and fell flat on my back with legs apart and knees up. The snake was in between my legs, curled up tight with his head back, mouth open, ready to strike my torso. To me, the open mouth of the serpent was like looking down into the open jaws of a hippopotamus. I was paralysed with fear. My brain was numb. I was going to die. Then whoosh! Someone had thrown their mattock at the snake. It diverted its attention, and someone else got me under the arms and dragged me away from eternity. No one laughed. It was a very close call and I was badly shaken. It was decided to have an early lunch and boil the billy. Dennis killed the snake, but it was entirely my fault. I should have left well enough alone. The snake was right to defend his home and his life. Jack learnt a valuable lesson that day.

Dennis and I found out why Peter gave us a couple of new axes and said we would be using them a lot. We sure did. We ended up on the ring-barking team with Bill Dobson. Besides Dennis and myself, there was Ernie, George and two of his fellow Aborigines, and the man in charge was Bill. Now, Bill was in his late fifties, hunched back, shifty-eyed, always half shaven and very slightly mentally unstable, or so Dennis and I thought. He ran a mean work schedule. We were each given a line of trees to ring-bark and we had to work to the other end of the paddock. Your line was yours and old Bill would check to see everyone was doing his share and keeping up with the others. We jackaroos got blisters on our hands, we got blisters on our blisters; the blisters giving away to blood. We tried bandaging our hands, but it was no good. We couldn't hold our axes properly.

"Piss on 'em," said Bill.

"Soak them in condy's crystals," said the missus.

"Spit of 'em," said George.

We tried all suggestions. I don't know which worked, but after a couple of agonising weeks, our palms were covered with calluses. We could stub out lighted cigarettes anywhere on the palms of our hands and wouldn't feel them.

We mustered at the saddle shed at 8.15, after breakfast and when all the chores were done. We would pile into the back of the battered Customline with our axes, round stones, file and lunch. Four in the back and three in the front. We jackaroos stayed in the back with George and one of his mates. Someone in the front had an odor problem and we thought it was Bill. We would arrive at the paddock, light a fire, then spend time honing our axes and listening to Bill as he rambled on about everything and nothing.

Then, without warning, Bill would say, "Jig-e-Jig."

That meant, get to work ring- barking immediately, no matter what. One day, I was relieving myself and halfway through the act, the words "Jig-e-Jig" were heard. I continued to finish what I was doing. Bill came over, blew hell out of me and pushed me with force to my line of trees and said, "When I say Jig-Jig, you Jig e Jig, or else." It was frightening. He frothed at the mouth and his face had murder written all over it. Everyone was frightened of Bill, some terrified, but he did have a soft spot for George and his two men. When one was Jig e Jigging, one could not stop for any reason: toilet; drink; smoke; talk or injury, it didn't matter. The wrath of Bill wasn't worth your life.

Then at any time, there would be a call of, "Axes down." That meant stop immediately, even if you were halfway through doing a tree. You would have to go directly to where Bill had just sat down, sit down with him, then you could have a smoke or a drink or even talk. But it was hard to get a word in. Bill liked to tell stories about his illustrious life, the high society women he'd had. He told us he was a very rich man once, but his wife left him, taking his mansion, his rolls and all his money for someone ten years younger than herself. We often discussed between ourselves at night if what Bill said was true, half true, or a pack of lies. It's something we will never know.

Once, when Bill was talking about his conquests with women, which embarrassed George and his mates, Aborigines don't like talking or hearing about sex, I think that it was a taboo subject, Dennis asked of Bill, "Seeing you have a lot of experience, Jack and I want to know if women like big ones or small ones?"

Bill thought for a while and then said in his slow country drawl, "I think it might be like this, if ya stick a straw up yer nostril it tickles, if yer stick yer thumb up it hurts, Jig-e-Jig," and off we went lickety split to work again.

Now, Dennis and I were accused of pinching lots of fruit off the fruit trees. We were told, if you need more fruit, just ask. We knew it wasn't us; it was Bill. He was giving bags of the fruit to George and his mates and Dennis was very upset about being accused of something he did not do. So next time it was 'axes down' and we were sitting listening to Bill and his wild yarns, Dennis said, "Bill, you have been thieving bags of fruit from the homestead and Jack and I have been accused of it."

Bill's face went purple, his eyes glazed over and he yelled, "WHAT?"

Dennis didn't see the signs, so he repeated the accusation, "Bill, you're a thief."

Bill jumped up, grabbed his axe and, frothing at the mouth, said, "I am going to knock you block off, you bloody little rouser."

He swung the back of the axe at Dennis' head. Dennis ducked, then got to his feet and took off. Bill went after him, axe swinging, shouting murder, and he meant it.

The five of us waited for about fifteen minutes in shock. I knew Bill would never be able to catch Dennis unless he tripped or took a wrong turn. George said, "Jack, you better take us all back to the homestead and tell the boss what's happened."

And so we did. I went with the boss in his ute looking for my mate and Bill, but we couldn't find them. We drove along the roads and paddocks that Dennis might have taken, but not a sign. We went to Bill's quarters, but he wasn't there. The boss said he was going to ring the police when we got back to the homestead. And that's where we found Bill, squatting down calmly rolling a cigarette with his back leaning against the homestead fence.

"Where's young Dennis?" said the boss sternly.

"Mr Williams, I don't care where your cheeky jackaroo is. He could be dead for all I care, and you can write my cheque out as I'm finished."

The boss turned to me and whispered, "Search the quarters and anywhere you would hide, if you thought your life was in danger, for Dennis. I will keep Bill here till you find him."

I found him. It took quite a while, as he was hidden in the corner of the butcher's shop with a meat cleaver in his hand.

"It's alright mate, the prick didn't get you and I think he is leaving."

"Well, I'm not leaving until that lunatic is off the place. He is as mad as a cut snake."

I went to the boss, who was still talking to Bill, and indicated that I had found Dennis without raising any suspicion. I heard the boss say, "Bill, you can go up to your quarters and pack your things. Peter will come up and give you your cheque and drive you to town. Now, have you any problems?"

"Nah, she'll be jake. I might get a job off you some other time." Bill stood up and slowly walked towards his quarters. As he passed me, he said under his breath, "I would have killed that little squirt if I had caught him."

He had a horrible gleam in those shifty eyes as he said it. It gave me the heebees.

After he had gone, I went back to Dennis and said, "He's gone. What happened?"

Dennis put the cleaver down on the chopping block, looked around to make sure Bill was nowhere in sight and said, "The bastard nearly got me twice. Yea, I thought I would do a big circle and get back to you blokes and the ute, then I thought we could all hightail it back to the homestead. But he outguessed me and cut me off. I thought I was well clear of him, but he was like a charging bull. He just flew over the ground. He got within a couple of metres of me, threw his axe like a boomerang. It just missed my legs, but I felt the spray of earth it made."

"Geez, that was close. What happened then?"

I was now caught up in the excitement of the chase as Dennis relayed it.

"You know it nearly tripped me up, then I would have been a goner. The fright of almost being caught really got me going, so I headed for the road and home, thinking I might see someone on the way. I don't know where Bill got to. I was expecting him to jump out from behind every tree I passed."

"Crikey, you must have moved because we were about seven k's away and we never saw you when we drove home," I exclaimed.

"Yeah, but I saw you blokes in the ute pass me. I was hidden in some scrub. I didn't know if Bill was with you or not. Then I skirted around to the butcher shop the long way so I wouldn't be caught. Jack, I had the shit frightened out of me. He was going to kill me, that's fair dinkum."

"You bet he was going to knock you off, and I am sorry I didn't help, but I just didn't know what to do, but you said he nearly got you twice?"

"The first time was when he swung the axe at my head."

"Fair enough, look it's early, so I will give you a hand with your chores."

That night after tea, Dennis was called in to the boss's office to make a statement.

C.19

Not All Beer and Skittles

Sheep Killers, An Intruder, The Fight, Death

I haven't talked about the station's kids; well, the boss's kids were away at boarding school in Toowoomba. When they came home for school holidays, they naturally spent their time with their parents, so we only saw them at mealtimes or every now and then when they would go mustering with us. Kevin's kids were at primary school at Lota and we didn't see much of them, as Kevin's house was a kilometre away from the main buildings of the station. Anyway, kids are a nuisance at our age. But an extraordinary thing happened that Dennis and I saw a few times and it was with Peter the overseer's kids, being worked by the sheep dogs. Let me explain.

Peter had well-trained dogs that were excellent workers. They were large for sheep dogs with a light tanned coat and yellow eyes and were a breed of kelpie. The kids would be playing outside when the dogs would start working them like sheep, crouching down and running around then diving in a bit to pretend to bite and out again working them to the kitchen door, the kids would run inside and the dogs would follow. Then they worked them to the kitchen cupboard till the kids gave the dog's cookies or whatever feed they could lay their hands on. It sounds bizarre, but that's what happened.

When we told Peter what was going on, he didn't believe us. One day, he ended up seeing it for himself. How, you ask, did we know what went inside the house? We kept our distance, but followed the dogs and could see through the screen door what was happening in the kitchen.

After that, Peter kept his dogs tied up every day, except when they were working or with him. Sadly, one day he forgot and my beloved dog Skipper and one of Peter's dogs went missing. This is not uncommon for good sheep dogs to pair up and go missing when there is not much sheep work going on. The problem is they can go and round up sheep and kill them through idleness and frustration and become sheep killers. The answer to the problem is to find the dogs and then shoot them; it's the owner's responsibility. The dogs came home the next day exhausted, but looking pleased with themselves, tongues out, panting and tail wagging.

Peter said, "You know what you have to do."

I answered with a very heavy heart, "I will when you shoot your dog."

Peter, with a tear in his eye, caught his dog, put a chain around its neck and led him away. A rifle shot echoed through the sand hills a few minutes later.

I had a dog called Sandy for a little while when I was a kid. It was a white and tan fox terrier and was the only mate I had. It would wait for me at the end of the road when I came home from school and we would walk home together. But it was only for a little while. My grandmother didn't like him and had him sent away without telling me. I grieved for Sandy, my mate, for a long time and now it was happening again.

I went and tied Skipper up, got my gun and stopped off at the butcher shop and cut off a shank from one of the sheep I had killed last night. With dog, shank, shovel and gun, I walked down to a beautiful old gum tree with branches reaching to heaven. There I gave my mate his bone, as he ate blissfully unaware, I sent him to kingdom come. The tears were coming from my eyes like miniature waterfalls as I dug a deep hole under the shade of that lovely big tree and there I laid my mate to rest. I put the shovel and gun back in their rightful places and told Dennis I would not be at lunch and could I be excused. I took a long walk beside the river, wondering about me, the world and life. May God be with all good working dogs.

I've mentioned Ernie's wife, Beatrice, was very large. She once applied at the homestead for a cleaner's job. She didn't get the job, as one of the requirements was to get into the homestead to clean it. She tried but couldn't fit through the doors. Maybe it was the consumption of thirty-three kilos of sugar between the two of them every month. We knew this because the Williams had a fortnight's break and asked Beatrice to cook for us while they were away. Besides annoying me at the killing block, she was a jovial person and quite a bit of fun, except when she and Ernie came home on a Saturday afternoon after a heavy drinking session. Then they were a couple to keep away from.

The meals were awful and the pudding was pure sugar. We tried our best, but we had trouble getting it down. Mick decided he would have his meals in town and, suddenly, both Dennis and I lost our appetites. Beatrice, who we called Mrs Small to her face, couldn't understand, "Hardworking boys like yourselves, how you survive without eating, I just don't know."

We survived alright, helping ourselves and cooking in the main kitchen. We had been given that choice, but we still called up for small meals so her feelings wouldn't be hurt and she would be paid for feeding us.

Mick woke both of us up in the middle of the night and asked us to listen.

"Did you hear that?" he said in hushed tones.

"Hear what"? We were annoyed at being woken up from a sound sleep.

"That," said Mick.

"I hear it now," said Dennis, "it's someone up at the homestead walking around."

"That's what I think too," answered Mick, "can't you hear it, Jack?"

I thought I could hear footsteps, but I wasn't sure until I heard the door bang.

"Let's check it out," said brave Dennis. "I'll get my gun. You get yours Jack. We will be right behind you, Mick."

And Mick did lead our little posse to the homestead. We crept with our guns ready; all three brave souls could hear footsteps and doors being open and closed. There were only two staircases leading to the upper floor of the building. I manned the bottom of one with cocked gun and Dennis manned the other one on the opposite side of the homestead. We sent Mick up to investigate. He came down my stairs warning me beforehand in case he got shot and said, "Jack there is nothing up here, come and have a search for yourself."

We went through the rooms, opened wardrobes, looked behind doors and curtains, but not a soul to be seen. We wandered back to our quarters and to bed, mystified as to what, or who it was, that was visiting the upstairs of the homestead.

When the Williams came back from their holidays, we told them of the weird experience we had had. The boss just smiled and the missus explained, very matter-of-factly, that it was her dad seeing if everything was all right.

"He does it quite often you know."

Dennis and I looked at each other. Mrs Williams' father had been dead for six years. We knew that, as he was buried not far from the homestead gardens.

We had an agreement between ourselves, that's Mick, Dennis and I, that we could borrow or use anything in each other's room as long as we returned it or replaced it as soon as possible. This agreement worked very well and it benefited us all. If we were out of smokes, writing paper, stamps or what have you, we could check out our neighbor's rooms and usually find what was needed. Twice it didn't work out.

Once, on an extremely hot day, I had been hard at work digging post holes for a new fence near the back of our quarters. Mick was at school and Dennis was helping Peter do some straggler mustering. I was hot, sweaty and thirsty. The hot water in the taps didn't 'satisfy my thirst. If only there was some lemonade about. I went to our quarters, searched Dennis' room, nothing. Looked in Mick's room and voila! There on his desk was a Cottee's bottle, which I was sure the contents were lemonade. Flat, I expect, as the bottle had been opened with a cork jammed in the top. It was nearly full and the bottle felt cool compared to everything else out in the blazing sun. I pulled the cork out and thirstily drank so quickly I didn't taste much until after I had finished. And the taste wasn't lemonade, it was warm and thick, but I didn't care. That night when Mick came home, he was distraught.

"Who has touched my holy water?"

He was a very strong Catholic and he had been given the holy water from the local priest. We both denied it, but I had a funny feeling in the pit of my stomach. I said, rather hesitantly, "Mick, what was the holy water in?"

"In a lemonade bottle on my desk."

I confessed that it was me and I thought it had been lemonade. Mick was cross but Dennis doubled up with laughter, saying, "Bless Jack's guts."

We all got on well, but with the hard work and the frustrations young virile men have, sometimes there were tensions. Once, I am sad to say, there was a fight. Dennis borrowed my chair, which was fine, but he wouldn't give it back. We struggled. I tried to get it off him but he hung on, then it turned in to a punch up. We were going hammer and tongs at each other, blow for blow. We were evenly matched and even though we were angry, we could feel the physical tensions in our bodies being relieved.

Then Kevin, who was walking past, decided to try and break the fight up. He pushed his way in between us and grabbed my arms, saying, "That's enough, boys. C'mon break it up now."

Ever since those men at Tee Tree stud held me and pretended to castrate me, and the queer at the Y in Sydney had attacked me, anyone who held me would make me go crazy. *Except Joan, of course*. I really don't know what happened. I got out of Kevin's hold, picked him up bodily and, with adrenaline strength, threw him down the three steps leading to the veranda of the quarters. He landed on his back, he started to twitch, and his face went purple. His eyes started to roll to the back of his head.

Dennis yelled, "You've killed him. I'm getting the boss. Fight forgotten; I knelt down beside Kevin. I could just make out he was breathing, but his chest was rising and falling like it was fighting for life. The boss and Dennis came rushing up.

The boss took one look at Kevin and said, "Get my car and make sure it's full of benzene."

He turned to me and said, "I think we have a problem here, and I think you could be in a lot of trouble, Jack."

Dennis brought the car round and we lifted Kevin gently into the back of the Zephyr.

"Tell Mrs Williams what happened and get her to let Kevin's wife know. I am taking him straight to St George Hospital."

We didn't know it then, but Kevin had lost one lung and most of the other one and had to live on pills to keep him going. Now we knew why Kevin never helped in the hard physical work. It seems when he landed on his back, it bruised what little lung he had left and it couldn't provide oxygen to his heart.

When the boss came back after tea, Dennis and I were called into the office where we had to write statements about what had happened. The boss said Kevin was a very sick man and his condition was very serious and the police could be involved. I felt sick. I felt really frightened. As we walked back to the quarters, Dennis said, "And if he dies, you could be up for murder, and they hang people for murder."

I thought about jail and hanging and couldn't get to sleep all night. I was worried that I'd hurt Kevin and I would need to apologise to Kevin's wife, Sally. Just a second and my life was turned from a happy jackaroo to a potential murderer, a criminal. What would Joan think? The boss told me at breakfast that Kevin had had a comfortable night and he was stable, but they were keeping him there for a week on oxygen. I was relieved and surprisingly not so much for myself, but for Kevin's wife and young family. I asked the missus if I could pick some flowers and take them up to Kevin's place so I could apologies. She thought it was a good idea. I did this and they were graciously accepted. She thanked me for the flowers and the apology. As I was leaving, Sally said, "Don't be too hard on yourself Jack, Kevin knows his condition and should not have interfered with you two boys."

I answered, "He was only trying to help, and if there is anything I can do for you, I would love to do it as it would help me not feel so bad."

"Alright Jack, seeing you have put it that way, you can come up Saturday and weed the garden and mow the lawn, so the yard will be tidy when I bring my man home."

"That's a deal," I said as I went back to the horse yards, where I had another horse to handle.

I spent all day Saturday in the garden and had it looking really good. Sally took the kids up to see their dad and hopefully bring him back home. I missed out on a date with Joan that day, but when I explained why the date was cancelled, she told me she would have expected me to do what I had done for Sally and that she would make it up to me next Saturday. Kevin did come home on that day. I apologised to him, we shook hands and Kevin said, "No hard feelings, mate."

On the Monday they left for a fortnight's holiday.

We liked to go hunting. Mick used to come too. We would borrow the Customline and Bouncer, the boss's pig dog. We were mostly after pigs as they were good sport but also because they were feral and caused a lot of damage and killed a lot of lambs. We shot kangaroos mainly for dog food, and the occasional emu. We got rid of quite a few pigs, and the boss was happy we always brought enough meat to feed all the station dogs, which tallied fourteen, for a week or more. Sometimes in the summer we would put all our game in a huge old scourer that was once used for the wool and boil it all up, 'roo, pigs and emu and make a huge stinking stew for the dogs. They loved it.

We caught quite a few sucker piglets and put them in the sty. It was Dennis's job to feed them, but as I was the station butcher, I was the one to slaughter them. My first one was something of a disaster. First, I had to light the copper, that was after chopping the wood, and while waiting for it to boil, I collected all the killing gear and put twenty litres of cold water into an old tin bath which was used for this specific job. Then I would pick out my victim and catch it. It did plenty of squealing and running around the sty until I caught it. I then tied its two back legs and one front together and carried it to the tin bath, where I set it down alongside.

By this time, the water was boiling in the copper. I put forty litres of boiling water from the copper on top of the twenty litres of cold in the tin bath. Then, before the pig could get another grunt out, I cut his tail off and held it in the water as a tester. If the hair didn't scrape off, the water was too cold. If the hair fell out and the skin turned red, it was too hot. If the hair was rubbed and came away cleanly and the flesh was white, it was just right. I did the test and had to add more hot water to get it right. To kill the pig, I had to push the knife straight down the side of its gullet into its heart to execute a quick death and to bleed it. The pig, when I did this, always screamed blue murder.

I did all this with my first pig and put him in the hot water, but he was still alive! The hot water must have revived him somewhat and it was clear my heart shot wasn't accurate. The tie on his feet came off and he went to jump out of the tub. Without thinking, I put my foot on top of the pig to stop it. I lifted my foot out of the hot water, badly scalded. The pig jumped out of the tub with his terrible wound and blood gushing everywhere. It took off down the paddock and me after it, knife in one hand, hopping and running at the same time. It all ended well, with the pig quite unaware it was hanging upside down in the butcher's shop, minus quite a few important parts but nevertheless comfortable, while I had a restless night with my scalded leg. I did get much better at preparing pigs for the table.

We often talked at dinnertime about eating kangaroo or emu. The missus said we wouldn't know what we ate if it was cooked properly. Mick and we two jackaroos said we would pick the gamey taste, no matter how it was cooked and anyway, we wouldn't eat it, especially the 'roo meat as we had seen all the worms in them when we cut them up for the dogs. The fricassee was terrific and we all had second helpings. When we had finished, the missus said, "I see you boys ate up all your emu."

We were not impressed. A few nights later, we had a stew with mushrooms and again we fell for it. We were gleefully told how we relished the 'roo. Thanks, Mrs Williams.

Sunday, we decided to go hunting and were disappointed that we didn't see any pigs. So was Bouncer, the boss's favourite pet and a superb pig dog. Game as anything, he would grab the nose or ear of the biggest pig helping us to catch it. This day there were no pigs, so we were on our way home disappointed that we'd had no success. A huge red buck kangaroo suddenly stood up out of the grass about fifteen metres from us and started to rock back on his legs, scratching his belly.

"What a shot," cried Dennis as Mick put on the brakes. Before we could say 'dog gone', he was. Bouncer jumped out of the back and went straight for the 'roo. The three of us got out and lined the big fella in the sights of our guns, but we couldn't shoot as we might hit the dog. Bouncer did a mighty leap at the 'roo, hoping to get hold of his nose. We tried in vain to call him off, but he wouldn't listen. The 'roo caught this magnificent dog, held him tight in his front paws and disemboweled him with one good kick from his hind leg. He was dead before the 'roo let him go and hit the ground. The 'roo looked at us, turned his back and slowly hopped away.

We were dumbfounded. Poor Bouncer. We didn't even worry about trying to shoot the 'roo or, for that matter, go and see the body of the boss's favourite dog. We just got back in the ute, remorseful for what had just happened, and started to drive slowly home, discussing who was going to tell the boss and how. We decided to lie and Dennis was given the draw of telling it. The lie was that Bouncer jumped out of the back of the ute and chased this 'roo. We had no success calling him back and we hoped he would find his own way home. I think the boss knew what really happened or Mick told him later. But nothing was said, and us boys carried the guilt for quite a while, even though we were powerless to stop what happened.

Everyone was away this Saturday, and so would I have been, except I had a nasty cold and just felt like staying at home. It was about two o'clock when I heard a noisy car pull up. I got off my bed to investigate. It was George in an old, battered Holden ute with about eight of his Aboriginal mates. They were full of booze and egging George on.

"Go on, ask him. Here George, you go ask him."

George approached me, slightly embarrassed, slightly drunk and still being cheered on to ask me something.

"Hey Jack, give us some money and petrol," he pleaded.

"I don't have any money on me." Which was the truth. "And the boss has the key to the bowser and I don't know where it is." Another truth.

"George, I don't think you are allowed on the property with your mates on a Saturday."

He turned back to the car with rebukes from his fellow tribesmen and drove off to a howl of 'gutless' and 'chicken'. I knew they would be back, and they were.

This time when the battered ute pulled up, it wasn't George that got out. It was five very drunken, menacing fellows, two with fair sized sticks.

"You, boy, give us money and petrol or we will deal with you blackfella way."

I walked toward them and said very forcefully, as I was a bit scared now, "You better clear out. I have no money and I can't get you petrol. You can't talk blackfella way to me cause real blackfella way is kindness."

That got 'em. They walked back to the ute being chided by the others. One turned around and waved his stick and said, "We'll be back," and they drove off again with loud cries and yells. I was really frightened. I knew they would be back, more drunk, more aggressive and more dangerous.

I got ready for them. I got a good two metres of heavy chain that was for me to swing if they came at a rush and placed it near the petrol bowser. Then I got my rifle and checked it twice to make sure it was unloaded and no bullets in the magazine. It was only a week ago that I thought I was up for murder and I didn't want to go through the mental torture of that. The gun was for bluff only.

They did come back, they all got out of the old bomb, some still carrying large heavy sticks. George stayed behind near the ute, but the others approached very menacingly and very drunk.

"You boy, we want money now! And we are going to get it, and petrol. We need petrol."

They were walking towards the petrol bowser, encouraging each other and building up their confidence that to my mind, they didn't need. I walked quickly to the bowser. I had to get there first, and I wanted to get the piece of chain before they did.

"You blokes are causing yourselves a lot of trouble. Boss will give you no work, then you will have no money or petrol," I said slowly so the message might sink into their fuzzled brains. But no, they still came, still threatening. We were about three metres from each other and I was just about to grab the chain to swing around my head, hoping to force them back to their ute, when mercy of mercies arrived. It was Peter coming back from a grazier's meeting. His Ford pulled up to a sudden stop and he quickly took in the situation, stepped out of the car and with four quick strides, was standing by my side.

"What's going on?"

I told him what was happening. As I was explaining, the mob lowered their heads as well as their weapons.

"You lot, back in that car this minute or the police will be here and not one of you will be ever working here again. That includes you too George, if you do not leave this property immediately," said Peter in the most forceful way that was, until now, very unbecoming of his nature.

They shuffled back to the ute, squeezed in to the front and the back. George turned the key and cranked the motor. The starter engine worked well, but nothing else did in the old car. George got out and walked toward Peter in a very subservient way and said, "Excuse me Boss, but I think we are out of petrol. Could we have some petrol please, Boss?"

"I will tell you what I am prepared to do. I am towing you back to town. Jack, you get the tow chain and I will get the Thames Truck and you, George, get back to your ute." I got the chain; George was back in the driver's seat and Peter was backing the truck up to the front of the old bomb ute. I hitched the chain around the wishbone on the ute and the other end to the tow bar on the truck. I waited to give the signal for when the slack was taken up in the tow chain. But Peter said, "Don't worry about that, just get in." Then he put his head out the window and yelled to George and his mob, "Are you all in then? Hang on tight." He slipped the clutch and flattened the accelerator.

The old green truck leapt forward, then gave a terrific jerk as the slack took up in the towline. I said, "That was a bit unfair."

Peter, with lips pursed tight and a very angry look on his face, said nothing. This surprised me, as Peter was one of those calm sorts of chaps that never got worked up, but he was today. We towed that car in top gear along the dirt road. I tried to see if the car was following, but the cloud of dust from the truck stopped any visual contact. We did a racing change with a double clutch down to second as we did a right-hand turn onto the main road, then to third and fourth with a jerk at each mesh of the gearbox. It was the roughest ride I ever had; goodness knows what it was like in George's car.

We came to a stop with much braking and changing of gears in sight of Lota.

"Jump out Jack and take the towline off quickly and get back in."

I had hardly unhooked the chain from both ends when Peter put the truck into first and did a U-turn to head back to the station. I had to run and jump on the running board, then into the cab while it was still moving. As we headed back, Peter said, "Hey, there's a mudguard on the road."

He swerved around it, still mad. Then I spied a headlight on the side of the road, and then a tailgate, and further along a door. I said, "Peter, it all belongs to George's ute. I think you pulled the bomb to bits."

"I don't care. I don't like drunks and I don't like hooliganism, especially from casual town workers."

And then, as we turned left into the Lota Plains turn off, who should we see walking along the road, but George himself. How did George fall out? Who steered the car the three kilometres into town? How many were left in the ute when it stopped? And was anyone injured? I don't know the answers to these questions, but my imagination has had a good time trying to answer them.

C.20

The End of a New Beginning

A Mate Gone, Christmas, Heart Break, Success

I got a promotion. I was put in charge of the ringbarkers, but still had my chores. Ernie, the station hand, George and four of his Aboriginal mates from town, Ruben, Cliff, Wiley and Trudy, were the team. Mondays, they were half drunk and had hangovers, Tuesdays we got a bit of work done, Wednesdays and Thursdays we got a lot of ringbarking done but alas, Fridays, hardly anything was done as all were anxious to get back to town. Now the boss gave me a time to do each section of a paddock. I informed 'my' men, if we didn't get the work assigned to us done, we would all get the sack. It didn't work. So Monday became equipment day, Tuesday, Wednesday, Thursday became hard workdays and Friday was cleaning up day.

For this to work, I decided on a reward for best axe man of the week. Because I was the butcher on the property and each worker got half a sheep, I had some say at who got the offal. The deal was the best axe man of the week got four kidneys, two livers, two brains and one tripe, as well as their normal ration. It worked. We got five days' work done in three. The boss was impressed and all the ringbarkers were my best mate.

It became hard to pick the best axe man of the week, as they all worked hard, even Ernie, to get their reward. On Friday, I had to put on a big act saying how all were so good that I couldn't pick a winner. I would walk around, tip my hat back and scratch my head in deep thought while mumbling. At last, I would nominate a winner, delight from one and groans from the rest. The same game was played every Friday and all had a turn as the winner. I think it was only once they all missed out, because of one bludging week.

Things were slowing down. The sheep were shorn, the cattle branded, the horses broken in and ridden. The yards were built, the paddocks cleaned and the chores were done; it was December. The kids were soon home for Christmas holidays, annual leave taken, and all that was left was getting ready for Christmas. The days were hot; the nights were restless; I had things on my mind. My mate Dennis had left a fortnight before. I did miss him; we were good competing mates. And it was him that put some thoughts into my head.

"I'm giving a week's notice," said Dennis out of the blue, one night. "I'm not working my guts out for $15.00 a week. Dad got me a job as a truck driver in the New Year at $35.00 a week back home in Gatton and I'm taking it."

A fortnight later, he was gone. Just a 'see ya' and he left.

I was thinking, did I love Joan enough to marry her? How can I on my lowly wage? What is my future here? I decided to ask the boss the last two questions, but the first I had to answer myself. I did love her like I never loved a girl before. I always looked forward to seeing her and felt sad when she left me to drive home. But I felt constricted, tied down. It was only eighteen months previously since I got away from living with three women. Was I ready to sign up to live with one?

I picked up my courage after tea one night and asked to see the boss in his office. He sat at his desk as I stood in the doorway. In his normal friendly tone, he asked, "Well Jack, what is it?"

What had to be said had to be said. I replied rather nervously, "Mr Williams, I really like it here at Lota Plains and you have taught me so much about horses. I also appreciate your trust in putting me in charge of the ringbarkers. But I feel it's unfair that the blackfellas are getting $30.00 a week and I only get half their wage doing the same work, plus all the chores on top of taking them out each day and working with them."

I continued, "I think in the New Year I should be worth as much as them!"

The boss leaned back in his chair and smiled.

"Jack, there are plenty of jackaroos around that will work for $15.00 a week."

"Mr Williams," I asked, "what are my future prospects on Lota Plains?"

"Jack, you have three years to go as a jackaroo and then you might find yourself as an overseer, but I can't promise you anything."

Taking a deep breath, I replied, "Well, in that case, you better find yourself another jackaroo. I regretfully give my notice till the end of the month."

"I am sorry you feel that way Jack, you're a good chap but $15.00 a week is the wage."

"I will do my best by you till I leave, but if you change your mind, I would love to stay." I turned and left, feeling doubtful about whether I had done the right thing.

It was Saturday night as Joan and I cuddled that I broke the news.

"Darling, I have had to make some big decisions. I want to ask you something special."

She started to interrupt, but I put my finger on her lips.

"Wait till I finish," I whispered.

"I want to ask you something special," I repeated, "but I can't, I don't feel like I am in the position to ask a special question and think we need a bit of time on our own to make a sensible decision."

"What are you trying to say, Jack? You're getting me worried."

"I'm leaving Lota Plains at the end of the month to go shearing for a year, so I can make some money. Then I can ask you a special question that I hope you will answer with a 'yes'."

I could feel a wet tear sliding down the princess's cheek.

"I do not want you to go. You don't need money. I have a property we could manage. Oh Jack, do not leave me."

She clung to me and I loved her with my touch.

"Joan, my one and only, I am a man. I must provide and be able to prove myself. My darling, please give me that chance. What is a year in fifty years if our love is strong? Surely twelve months is nothing." I kissed her salty cheeks, her wet mouth and felt her warm body against mine. But I knew I needed breathing space, not here in the car, but in the wild blue yonder.

The last couple of weeks at Lota Plains were like holidays. I helped the kids with their horses. We rode everywhere, chasing suckers (piglets) jumping logs and doing some straggler mustering. Joan drove me to St George for Christmas shopping. I got Mum a small genuine aboriginal carving, my sister a book and Gran. a nice brooch with a wattle flower in it. We wrapped them up there and then so they would get to Melbourne by Christmas. Joan helped me pick out the gifts, then we separated to each do some special shopping on our own. I went to the jewelers and ummed and ahhed over rings, necklaces, bangles and beads. I settled on a nice fine silver chain bracelet with miniature blue birds on it that matched the blue of Joan's eyes. It was nice and expensive and I knew it was right for her. I didn't think a ring would be right at this time.

As we were driving back, Joan handed me a little note from her mum, inviting me to their place for Christmas. I wanted to know if a simple verbal 'yes' would do, or should I write an acceptance note. Joan thought acceptance note was the proper thing, and bless her, she had pen, paper, and envelope ready for a written reply. I wrote on it a 'thank you' for the invitation and I gratefully accepted and looked forward to spending Christmas with the Fisher family.

I told Mrs Williams I had been asked to the Fishers' property for Christmas and what should I give them, as I had already done my Christmas shopping. She smiled at me and said, "Don't worry Jack, the Lord will provide." Well, he might and he mightn't, but I would have liked something more positive.

Christmas arrived, hot with clear blue skies, a heat haze already shimmering over the paddocks. Chores done; we had an exciting breakfast with the kids showing their gifts from Father Christmas. A dressage saddle for one, a handsome bridle, crop and saddle-blanket for the other, the boy got a fine 22 repeater rifle. Cripes, I didn't think Father Christmas had them sort of toys in his sack. I gave the kids a novelty biro each and to the Williams: two books, one written by Wilbur Smith and a book on birds. I was given a great book on horsemanship, a leather belt, and a large tin of shortbread biscuits with an empty card on it. I looked puzzled at Mrs Williams. She smiled, saying, "The Lord has provided."

I clicked. Thanked them all and wished them a happy day and got ready for Joan, who was picking me up.

She was beautiful, in a simple light blue frock, with a lace edged collar and pearl buttons on the bodice. Her hair shone, her cheeks glowed and those blue eyes sparkled. I gasped for breath. I thought, *Jack, grab her son and never let her go.*

"Merry Christmas, my handsome man," she said with a light but delicious kiss on my lips.

"And a Merry Christmas to you, my beautiful one," and I hugged her so.

It was a lovely Christmas dinner, a sparkling tree, balloons and streamers. Crackers on a lace tablecloth with holly leaves spread on top, the finest of silverware and the sparkliest of crystal glasses. A traditional Christmas lunch with roast turkey, plum pudding and the works. There was only one thing slightly wrong, the meal was hot and so was the day, a good forty degrees, but it was Christmas and as I said, it was lovely and I was one of the Fisher family. Life was good.

I thought back to Lostmans Motel and wondered how Bill, Don, Norm, Eric and Ralph were spending Christmas.

"Wake up, Jack," said Mrs Fisher. "Has the wine got to you? You look so sad."

I must have been daydreaming. I shook myself and said, "I'm sorry. I was just daydreaming about something in my past and how lucky I was to be sharing such a day with a wonderful family."

The girls cleaned up after lunch. I offered to help but Mr Fisher said it was time for a nap and lay down on the carpet and bade me to do the same. We had salad and cold turkey for tea. Mr Fisher said he was disappointed about me leaving Lota Plains and that Joan had told him why. He said he thought Mr Williams could have given me a few more dollars and he admired me for my stance. The Fishers gave me a fine pair of plaited reins and I, their tin of biscuits. Joan and I saved our presents for later. After tea, I thanked the Fishers for a great day, my present and how much I appreciated their hospitality.

Joan drove me home for the last time. We parked at our favourite spot on the banks of the river beside the willow tree. The hot day was cooling off slowly as the sun had gone to bed a few hours ago; the moon was late in rising. We got out the tartan travel rug and sat on the banks of the Moonie River, arms around each other. As the night creatures were saying their nightly hellos, she rested her head on my shoulder. We were deep in our own thoughts and love.

Joan spoke softly, still facing the river, "Jack, I do love you and want you, but as you say, 'what is twelve months in a love as strong as ours?'"

She turned to me and we gently kissed. She produced from somewhere a little package wrapped up in gold Christmas paper.

"Merry Christmas, Jack." And she kissed me again. I opened the present; it was a thin wallet made from the best of English leather.

"It's beautiful, thank you, and when I see you next Christmas, I will have it bulging full of $100 notes."

"I don't care about the money, Jack, but I want you to keep it in your left shirt pocket so I can always be near your heart."

I produced my gift with a Merry Christmas, a kiss and a hug. She opened the jewelry box and showed a hint of disappointment, then she smiled and said, "It's beautiful Jack, please put it on my wrist."

As I did, I told her, "There are twelve little bluebirds and each one is a month my heart will ache for you until we meet again. But for you, my love, it is for twelve months of happiness, as they are the bluebirds of happiness."

We kissed and cuddled.

It was getting late. We shook out the rug and put it back in the car. The moon had risen and we stood hand in hand, as we watched the reflection of the moon rippling in the waters of the river. We were silent; we were empty; we were not game to utter the words we had to so we stood and procrastinated.

After some time, I said, "My princess, do you mind if I just walk back to my quarters?" as I escorted her to the car.

She had tears tumbling down her sweet cheeks. I wiped them gently and said, "Darling, I will think of you every day and I shall write, and I do love you so."

I kissed her on her forehead, turned and walked away so she couldn't see my trembling chin and tears, I forgot I had. It was sometime before I heard the car start and my beloved returned to her home.

Four days later, Mrs Williams was going to drive me to the railway station. But Joan had rung up and said she would like to. I didn't want to go through the heart wrenching again, but I still wanted to see her just one more time. She arrived on that final day, looking as lovely as ever, with a smile as big and bright as the morning sun. I put my belongings in the back of the little Ford Angler. I went and thanked Mrs Williams for the great cooking and Mr Williams for passing on his horsemanship. We shook hands and the boss said, "We will always have a job here for you Jack." I thanked him as I got into the car and waved a cheery goodbye. A much better leaving than I'd had with the Shorts.

Joan let me drive, but we were both stuck for words. We talked about the weather, horses and where was I going shearing. I said I didn't know, but I was going to Goondiwindi to find a shed. It was no time before we reached the railway station. As I got my luggage out, I asked Joan if she would mind my radio, and Bruno rifle as I had too much to cart around, and anyway I wanted to leave something for Joan so she would know her man would return.

The train arrived as did the tears, the hugs, the untold love to each other and a long and loving kiss.

"All aboard." The rail guard blew his whistle and waved his green flag. We broke our embrace and I hurriedly got on the train as it started to move. I turned in the doorway for a final wave to my beloved. She waved back. She looked so lovely, so lonely, so beautiful, so vulnerable. That was my last sight of that lovely princess, my first love.

Thank God I had the carriage to myself. I felt sad and lost as I gazed out at the passing countryside. I was having a hard time controlling my emotions. I reflected on the last eighteen months. A boy, rather small and slightly effeminate, who wanted to be a man, who wanted to ride a horse, swing an axe and crack a whip, a boy who desperately wanted to be a man's man. I was starting to feel better. I knew I had passed the initiation test from boyhood to manhood very well.

Clickety clack went the wheels over the track. Yes, I could look any man in the eye now, for I was one. Tan, tall *except for my short legs*, fit and well-muscled, I could hold my own with anyone. I was confident and I knew I could do anything I wanted to do. Clickety clack, the wheels moved faster as the train built up speed, clickety clickety clack. Not only could I milk, ride and kill, I was a Queensland country jackaroo. I had filled my ambition.

Clickety, clickety clack, clickety, clickety, clack, over the rails. I imagined the sound of a whirling airplane propeller, the jerking of the carriage. We were lifting off. Reaching, reaching for the boundless sky, where new horizons are found I am free, free as a bird, I am flying:

Flying to new horizons, I'm free,

From boy to manhood now I'll be,

I have loved, but loved not divine,

My world is thine, to make as mine.

A Lie in the Tale

Searching and finding a new beginning,

This time surely, I must be winning,

So come with me, for I'll be back,

The future is mine, for I is Jack.

Shawline Publishing Group Pty Ltd
www.shawlinepublishing.com.au

SHAWLINE PUBLISHING GROUP

More great Shawline titles can be found by scanning the QR code below.
New titles also available through Books@Home Pty Ltd.
Subscribe today at www.booksathome.com.au or scan the QR code below.